Sources in Greek Political Thought
From Homer to Polybius

HISTORY OF WESTERN POLITICAL THOUGHT
and SOURCES IN WESTERN POLITICAL THOUGHT

GENERAL EDITOR: *Andrew Hacker,* Cornell University

In Search of Authority: HISTORY OF TWENTIETH-CENTURY POLITICAL THOUGHT
By *Henry S. Kariel,* Bennington College
Sources in Twentieth-Century Political Thought
Edited by *Henry S. Kariel*

The Great Dialogue: HISTORY OF GREEK POLITICAL THOUGHT FROM HOMER TO
POLYBIUS
By *Donald Kagan,* Cornell University
Sources in Greek Political Thought from Homer to Polybius
Edited by *Donald Kagan*

Conflict and Compromise: HISTORY OF BRITISH POLITICAL THOUGHT, 1593–1900
By *Wilfrid Harrison,* Warwick University
Sources in British Political Thought, 1593–1900
Edited by *Wilfrid Harrison*

History of American Political Doctrines
By *Thomas P. Jenkin,* University of California, Riverside
Sources in American Political Doctrines
Edited by *Thomas P. Jenkin*

History of Medieval Political Theory
By *Ewart Lewis*
Sources in Medieval Political Theory
Edited by *Ewart Lewis*

History of Continental Political Theory
By *Michael Walzer,* Princeton University
Sources in Continental Political Theory
Edited by *Michael Walzer*

SOURCES IN GREEK POLITICAL THOUGHT

From Homer to Polybius

Edited by

DONALD KAGAN

Cornell University

The Free Press, *New York*

Collier-Macmillan Limited, *London*

Copyright © 1965 by The Free Press

A DIVISION OF THE MACMILLAN COMPANY

Printed in the United States of America

For information, address:

THE FREE PRESS

A DIVISION OF THE MACMILLAN COMPANY

60 Fifth Avenue, New York, N.Y. 10011

Collier-Macmillan Canada, Ltd., Toronto, Ontario

Library of Congress Catalog Card Number: 65-12728

For Myrna

Preface

This volume of readings is intended to illustrate the development of Greek political thought from its rudimentary stage in the Homeric epics to the point of its application to an alien world, the Roman Empire. The selections have been chosen and arranged in accordance with my interpretation of the development of Greek thinking about politics as presented in my book *The Great Dialogue: A History of Greek Political Thought from Homer to Polybius.* The chapter headings correspond with those in *The Great Dialogue* but the remarks introducing the chapters and individual selections have been kept brief and, hopefully, objective so that this collection may be of use to a wider circle of readers than those persuaded by my own opinions.

The reader will be struck immediately by an important factor, almost amounting to an omission: only brief selections from the major political works of Plato and Aristotle—titans of Greek political thought—are to be found in this volume. To have included more of them would have required several books of this size, and their presentation here would be needless duplication. They are readily available in many editions and are, of course, vitally necessary for the study of Greek political thought. Perhaps their omission here may prove a blessing, for all too often the study of our subject both begins and ends with Plato and Aristotle. It is my hope that this volume will help to call attention to works less frequently considered and thus correct the distortion caused by this approach, giving us a clearer and truer picture of what the Greeks thought. Nevertheless, any understanding of the subject requires a familiarity with the work of Plato and Aristotle. In a sense everything each man wrote had political significance, but their essentially political ideas are contained in the following works:

Plato: *The Republic, The Statesman, The Laws*
Aristotle: *Politics, Nicomachean Ethics, Rhetoric*

The student of political thought should not be content with the excerpts presented in this volume but should read the works of the included authors entire so that the pertinent passages may be understood in their proper context. The poems of Homer, the histories of Herodotus and Thucydides, the Dialogues of Plato, the speeches of Isocrates, all should be read in their entirety. Besides these, I offer a short list of authors and works not treated or treated too briefly in this collection:

Aristophanes, *Comedies*

Euripides, *Plays*, especially *Phoenissae, Heraclidae* and *Supplices*

Sophocles, *Plays*, especially *Antigone* and *Philoctetes*

Finally, Greek political thought can best be studied as part of the total Greek experience and must not be separated from the events of Greek History.

DONALD KAGAN

Cornell University

Contents

Sources in Greek Political Thought
From Homer to Polybius

1.   The World of Homer

The Homeric poems were the fountain of wisdom for the Greeks, almost their bible. They sought in Homer light on every aspect of life and not least on the political. The world of Homer was pre-political, in the sense that it was a world in which the polis *did not yet exist. It is clear, nevertheless, that the poems of Homer represent a sharp break with the Oriental view of human government, despotic and theocratic. It is further true that they foreshadow many political concepts which were to be developed and elaborated in subsequent centuries.*

1. The Code of Hammurabi*

Hammurabi ruled Babylon from 1728 to 1686 B.C., the sixth ruler of the Amorite dynasty. His law code is the most complete example of ancient legal compilations. This selection from its Prologue and Epilogue gives evidence of the theocratic and despotic view of government typical of pre-Greek thought.

The Prologue]

When lofty Anum, king of the Anunnaki,
(and) Enlil, lord of heaven and earth,
the determiner of the destinies of the land,
determined for Marduk, the first-born of Enki,
the Enlil functions over all mankind,
made him great among the Igigi,
called Babylon by its exalted name,
made it supreme in the world,
established for him in its midst an enduring kingship,
whose foundations are as firm as heaven and earth—
at that time Anum and Enlil named me
to promote the welfare of the people,
me, Hammurabi, the devout, god-fearing prince,
to cause justice to prevail in the land,
to destroy the wicked and the evil,
that the strong might not oppress the weak,
to rise like the sun over the black-headed (people),
and to light up the land.
Hammurabi, the shepherd, called by Enlil, am I;
the one who makes affluence and plenty abound;
who provides in abundance all sorts of things for
    Nippur-Duranki;
the devout patron of Ekur;
the efficient king, who restored Eridu to its place;
The laws of justice, which Hammurabi, the efficient king, set up,

* Translated by Theophile J. Meek in *Ancient Near Eastern Texts Relating to the Old Testament*, 2nd ed. (Princeton, 1955). By permission of the Princeton University Press.

The Epilogue]

and by which he caused the land to take the right way and have
   good government.

I, Hammurabi, the perfect king,
was not careless (or) neglectful of the black-headed (people),
whom Enlil had presented to me,
(and) whose shepherding Marduk had committed to me;
I sought out peaceful regions for them;
I overcame grievous difficulties;
I caused light to rise on them.
With the mighty weapon which Zababa and Inanna entrusted
   to me,
with the insight that Enki allotted to me,
with the ability that Marduk gave me,
I rooted out the enemy above and below;
I made an end of war;
I promoted the welfare of the land;
I made the peoples rest in friendly habitations;
I did not let them have anyone to terrorize them.
The great gods called me,
so I became the beneficent shepherd whose scepter is righteous;
my benign shadow is spread over my city.
In my bosom I carried the peoples of the land of Sumer and
   Akkad;
they prospered under my protection;
I always governed them in peace;
I sheltered them in my wisdom.
In order that the strong might not oppress the weak,
that justice might be dealt the orphan (and) the widow,
in Babylon, the city whose head Anum and Enlil raised aloft,
in Esagila, the temple whose foundations stand firm like heaven
   and earth,
I wrote my precious words on my stela,
and in the presence of the statue of me, the king of justice,
I set (it) up in order to administer the law of the land,
to prescribe the ordinances of the land,
to give justice to the oppressed.
I am the king who is preeminent among kings;

3

my words are choice; my ability has no equal.
By the order of Shamash, the great judge of heaven and earth,
may my justice prevail in the land;
by the word of Marduk, my lord,
may my statutes have no one to rescind them;

in Esagila, which I love, may my name be spoken in reverence
    forever!

Let any oppressed man who has a cause
come into the presence of the statue of me, the king of justice,
and then read carefully my inscribed stela,
and give heed to my precious words,
and may my stela make the case clear to him;
may he understand his cause;
may he set his mind at ease!
"Hammurabi, the lord,
who is like a real father to the people,
bestirred himself for the word of Marduk, his lord,
and secured the triumph of Marduk above and below,
thus making glad the heart of Marduk, his lord,
and he also ensured prosperity for the people forever,
and led the land aright"—
let him proclaim this,
and let him pray with his whole heart for me
in the presence of Marduk, my lord, and Sarpanit, my lady!
May the guardian spirit, the protecting genius,
the gods who enter Esagila, (and) Lebettum of Esagila,
prosper the wishes (made) daily
in the presence of Marduk, my lord, (and) Sarpanit, my lady!

In the days to come, for all time,
let the king who appears in the land observe
the words of justice which I wrote on my stela;
let him not alter the law of the land which I enacted,
the ordinances of the land which I prescribed;
let him not rescind my statutes!
If that man has intelligence
and is able to guide his land aright,
let him heed the words which I wrote on my stela,
and may this stela show him the road (and) the way,

the law of the land which I enacted,
the ordinances of the land which I prescribed;
and let him guide aright his black-headed (people)!
Let him enact the law for them;
let him prescribe the ordinances for them!
Let him root out the wicked and the evil from his land;
let him promote the welfare of his people!

I, Hammurabi, am the king of justice,
to whom Shamash committed law.
My words are choice; my deeds have no equal;
it is only to the fool that they are empty . . .

2.   The Quarrel of Agamemnon and Achilles*

Book I of the Iliad *describes a quarrel between Agamemnon, the leader of the Greek expedition to Troy, and Achilles, the greatest of the Greek warrior-chieftains. The episode reveals a sharp contrast between the society and attitude of the Homeric Greeks and their Oriental predecessors.*

Sing, goddess, the wrath of Achilles Peleus' son, the ruinous wrath that brought on the Achaians woes innumerable, and hurled down into Hades many strong souls of heroes, and gave their bodies to be a prey to dogs and all winged fowls; and so the counsel of Zeus wrought out its accomplishment from the day when first strife parted Atreides king of men and noble Achilles.

Who then among the gods set the twain at strife and variance? Even the son of Leto and of Zeus; for he in anger at the king sent a sore plague upon the host, that the folk began to

* The *Iliad*, translated by Andrew Lang, Walter Leaf, and Ernest Myers, rev. ed. (London, 1900), pp. 1–10. By permission of Macmillan & Co., Ltd., St. Martin's Press, Inc., and the Macmillan Company of Canada, Ltd.

perish, because Atreides had done dishonour to Chryses the priest.
For he had come to the Achaians' fleet ships to win his daughter's
freedom, and brought a ransom beyond telling; and bare in his
hands the fillet of Apollo the Far-darter upon a golden staff; and
made his prayer unto all the Achaians, and most of all to the two
sons of Atreus, orderers of the host: "Ye sons of Atreus and all ye
well-greaved Achaians, now may the gods that dwell in the
mansions of Olympus grant you to lay waste the city of Priam,
and to fare happily homeward; only set ye my dear child free,
and accept the ransom in reverence to the son of Zeus, far-
darting Apollo."

Then all the other Achaians cried assent, to reverence the
priest and accept his goodly ransom; yet the thing pleased not
the heart of Agamemnon son of Atreus, but he roughly sent him
away, and laid stern charge upon him, saying: "Let me not find
thee, old man, amid the hollow ships, whether tarrying now or
returning again hereafter, lest the staff and fillet of the god avail
thee naught. And her will I not set free; nay, ere that shall old
age come on her in our house, in Argos, far from her native
land, where she shall ply the loom and serve my couch. But
depart, provoke me not, that thou mayest the rather go in peace."

So said he, and the old man was afraid and obeyed his word,
and fared silently along the shore of the loud-sounding sea. Then
went that aged man apart and prayed aloud to king Apollo,
whom Leto of the fair locks bare: "Hear me, god of the silver
bow, that standest over Chryse and holy Killa, and rulest Ten-
edos with might, O Smintheus! If ever I built a temple gracious
in thine eyes, or if ever I burnt to thee fat flesh of thighs of bulls
or goats, fulfil thou this my desire; let the Danaans pay by thine
arrows for my tears."

So spake he in prayer, and Phoebus Apollo heard him, and
came down from the peaks of Olympus wroth at heart, bearing
on his shoulders his bow and covered quiver. And the arrows
clanged upon his shoulders in his wrath, as the god moved; and
he descended like to night. Then he sate him aloof from the
ships, and let an arrow fly; and there was heard a dread clanging
of the silver bow. First did he assail the mules and fleet dogs,
but afterward, aiming at the men his piercing dart, he smote;
and the pyres of the dead burnt continually in multitude.

Now for nine days ranged the god's shafts through the host;
but on the tenth Achilles summoned the folk to assembly, for

in his mind did goddess Hera of the white arms put the thought, because she had pity on the Danaans when she beheld them perishing. Now when they had gathered and were met in assembly, then Achilles fleet of foot stood up and spake among them: "Son of Atreus, now deem I that we shall return wandering home again—if verily we might escape death—if war at once and pestilence must indeed ravage the Achaians. But come, let us now inquire of some soothsayer or priest, yea, or an interpreter of dreams—seeing that a dream too is of Zeus—who shall say wherefore Phoebus Apollo is so wroth, whether he blame us by reason of vow or hetacomb; if perchance he would accept the savour of lambs or unblemished goats, and so would take away the pestilence from us."

So spake he and sate him down; and there stood up before them Kalchas son of Thestor, most excellent far of augurs, who knew both things that were and that should be and that had been before, and guided the ships of the Achaians to Ilios by his soothsaying that Phoebus Apollo bestowed on him. He of good intent made harangue and spake amid them: "Achilles, dear to Zeus, thou biddest me tell the wrath of Apollo, the king that smiteth afar. Therefore will I speak; but do thou make covenant with me, and swear that verily with all thy heart thou wilt aid me both by word and deed. For of a truth I deem that I shall provoke one that ruleth all the Argives with might, and whom the Achaians obey. For a king is more of might when he is wroth with a meaner man; even though for the one day he swallow his anger, yet doth he still keep his displeasure thereafter in his breast till he accomplish it. Consider thou, then, if thou wilt hold me safe."

And Achilles fleet of foot made answer and spake to him: "Yea, be of good courage, speak whatever soothsaying thou knowest; for by Apollo dear to Zeus, him by whose worship thou, O Kalchas, declarest thy soothsaying to the Danaans, no man while I live and behold light on earth shall lay violent hands upon thee amid the hollow ships; no man of all the Danaans, not even if thou mean Agamemnon, that now avoweth him to be greatest far of the Achaians."

Then was the noble seer of good courage, and spake: "Neither by reason of a vow is he displeased, nor for any hecatomb, but for his priest's sake to whom Agamemnon did despite, and set not his daughter free and accepted not the ransom;

therefore hath the Far-darter brought woes upon us, yea, and will bring. Nor will he ever remove the loathly pestilence from the Danaans till we have given the bright-eyed damsel to her father, unbought, unransomed, and carried a holy hecatomb to Chryse; then might we propitiate him to our prayer."

So said he and sate him down, and there stood up before them the hero son of Atreus, wide-ruling Agamemnon, sore displeased; and his dark heart within him was greatly filled with anger, and his eyes were like flashing fire. To Kalchas first spake he with look of ill: "Thou seer of evil, never yet hast thou told me the thing that is pleasant. Evil is ever the joy of thy heart to prophesy, but never yet didst thou tell any good matter nor bring it to pass. And now with soothsaying thou makest harangue among the Danaans, how that the Far-darter bringeth woes upon them because, forsooth, I would not take the goodly ransom of the damsel Chryseis, seeing I am the rather fain to keep her own self within mine house. Yea, I prefer her before Klytaimnestra my wedded wife; in no wise is she lacking beside her, neither in favour nor stature, nor wit nor skill. Yet for all this will I give her back, if that is better; rather would I see my folk whole than perishing. Only make ye me ready a prize of honour forthwith, lest I alone of all the Argives be disprized, which thing beseemeth not; for ye all behold how my prize is departing from me."

To him then made answer fleet-footed goodly Achilles: "Most noble son of Atreus, of all men most covetous, how shall the greathearted Achaians give thee a meed of honour? We know naught of any wealth of common store, but what spoil soe'er we took from captured cities hath been apportioned, and it beseemeth not to beg all this back from the folk. Nay, yield thou the damsel to the god, and we Achaians will pay thee back threefold and fourfold, if ever Zeus grant us to sack some well-walled town of Troyland."

To him lord Agamemnon made answer and said: "Not in this wise, strong as thou art, O godlike Achilles, beguile thou me by craft; thou shalt not outwit me nor persuade me. Dost thou wish, that thou mayest keep thy meed of honour, for me to sit idle in bereavement, and biddest me give her back? Nay, if the great-hearted Achaians will give me a meed suited to my mind, that the recompense be equal—but if they give it not, then I myself will go and take a meed of honour, thine be it or Aias', or Odysseus' that I will take unto me; wroth shall he be to whomsoever I come. But for this we will take counsel hereafter; now let us launch a black ship on the great sea, and gather picked oarsmen, and set therein a hecatomb, and embark Chryseis of the fair cheeks herself, and let one of our counsellors be captain, Aias or Idomeneus or goodly Odysseus, or thou, Peleides, most redoubtable of men, to do sacrifice for us and propitiate the Fardarter."

Then Achilles fleet of foot looked at him scowling and said: "Ah me, thou clothed in shamelessness, thou of crafty mind, how shall any Achaian hearken to thy bidding with all his heart, be it to go a journey or to fight the foe amain? Not by reason of the Trojan spearmen came I hither to fight, for they have not wronged me; never did they harry mine oxen nor my horses, nor ever waste my harvest in deep-soiled Phthia, the nurse of men; seeing there lieth between us long space of shadowy mountains and sounding sea; but thee, thou shameless one, followed we hither to make thee glad, by earning recompense at the Trojans' hands for Menelaos and for thee, thou dog-face! All this thou reckonest not nor takest thought thereof; and now thou threatenest thyself to take my meed of honour, wherefor I travailed much, and the sons of the Achaians gave it me. Never win I meed like unto thine, when the Achaians sack any populous citadel of Trojan men; my hands bear the brunt of furious war, but when the apportioning cometh then is thy meed far ampler, and I betake me to the ships with some small thing, yet mine own, when I have fought to weariness. Now will I depart to Phthia, seeing it is far better to return home on my beaked ships; nor am I minded here in dishonour to draw thee thy fill of riches and wealth."

Then Agamemnon king of men made answer to him: "Yea, flee, if thy soul be set thereon. It is not I that beseech thee to tarry for my sake; I have others by my side that shall do me honour, and above all Zeus, lord of counsel. Most hateful art thou to me of all kings, fosterlings of Zeus; thou ever lovest strife and wars and fightings. Though thou be very strong, yet that I ween is a gift to thee of God. Go home with thy ships and company and lord it among thy Myrmidons; I reck not aught of thee nor care I for thine indignation; and this shall be my threat to thee: seeing Phoebus Apollo bereaveth me of Chryseis, her with my ship and my company will I send back; and mine own self will I go to thy hut and take Briseis of the fair cheeks, even that thy meed of honour, that thou mayest well know how far greater I am than thou, and so shall another hereafter abhor to match his words with mine and rival me to my face."

So said he, and grief came upon Peleus' son, and his heart within his shaggy breast was divided in counsel, whether to draw his keen blade from his thigh and set the company aside and so slay Atreides, or to assuage his anger and curb his soul. While yet he doubted thereof in heart and soul, and was drawing his great sword from his sheath, Athene came to him from heaven, sent forth of the white-armed goddess Hera, whose heart loved both alike and had care for them. She stood behind Peleus' son and caught him by his golden hair, to him only visible, and of the rest no man beheld her. Then Achilles marvelled, and turned him about, and straightway knew Pallas Athene; and terribly shone her eyes. He spake to her winged words, and said: "Why now art thou come hither, thou daughter of aegis-bearing Zeus? Is it to behold the insolence of Agamemnon son of Atreus? Yea, I will tell thee that I deem shall even be brought to pass: by his own haughtinessess shall he soon lose his life."

Then the bright-eyed goddess Athene spake to him again: "I came from heaven to stay thine anger, if perchance thou wilt hearken to me, being sent forth of the white-armed goddess Hera, that loveth you twain alike and careth for you. Go to now, cease from strife, and let not thine hand draw the sword; yet with words indeed revile him, even as it shall come to pass. For thus will I say to thee, and so it shall be fulfilled; hereafter shall goodly gifts come to thee, yea in threefold measure, by reason of this despite; hold thou thine hand, and hearken to us."

And Achilles fleet of foot made answer and said to her: "Goddess, needs must a man observe the saying of you twain, even though he be very wroth at heart; for so is the better way. Whosoever obeyeth the gods, to him they gladly hearken."

He said, and stayed his heavy hand on the silver hilt, and thrust the great sword back into the sheath, and was not disobedient to the saying of Athene; and she forthwith was departed to Olympus, to the other gods in the palace of aegis-bearing Zeus.

Then Peleus' son spake again with bitter words to Atreus' son, and in no wise ceased from anger: "Thou heavy with wine, thou with face of dog and heart of deer, never didst thou take courage to arm for battle among thy folk or to lay ambush with the princes of the Achaians; that to thee were even as death. Far better booteth it, forsooth, to seize for thyself the meed of honour of every man through the wide host of the Achaians that speaketh contrary to thee. Folk-devouring king! seeing thou rulest men of naught; else were this despite, thou son of Atreus, thy last. But I will speak my word to thee, and swear a mighty oath therewith: verily by this staff that shall no more put forth leaf or twig, seeing it hath for ever left its trunk among the hills, neither shall it grow green again, because the axe hath stripped it of leaves and bark; and now the sons of the Achaians that exercise judgment bear it in their hands, even they that by Zeus' command watch over the traditions—so shall this be a mighty oath in thine eyes—verily shall longing for Achilles come here-after upon the sons of the Achaians one and all; and then wilt thou in no wise avail to save them, for all thy grief, when multi-tudes fall dying before manslaying Hector. Then shalt thou tear thy heart within thee for anger that thou didst in no wise honour the best of the Achaians."

So said Peleides and dashed to earth the staff studded with golden nails, and himself sat down; and over against him Atreides waxed furious. Then in their midst rose up Nestor, pleasant of speech, the clear-voiced orator of the Pylians, he from whose tongue flowed discourse sweeter than honey. Two generations of mortal men already had he seen perish, that had been of old time born and nurtured with him in goodly Pylos, and he was king among the third. He of good intent made harangue to them and said: "Alas, of a truth sore lamentation cometh upon the land of Achaia. Verily Priam would be glad and Priam's sons, and all the Trojans would have great joy of heart, were they to hear all this tale of strife between you twain that are chiefest of the Danaans in counsel and chiefest in battle. Nay, hearken to me; ye are younger both than I. Of old days held I converse with better men even than you, and never did they make light of me. Yea, I never beheld such warriors, nor shall behold, as were Peirithoos and Dryas shepherd of the host and Kaineous and Exadios and godlike Polyphemos [and Theseus son of Aigeus, like to the immortals]. Mightiest of growth were they of all men upon the earth; mightiest they were and with the mightiest fought they, even the wild tribes of the mountain caves, and destroyed them utterly. And with these held I converse, being come from Pylos, from a distant land afar; for of themselves they summoned me. So I played my part in fight; and with them could none of men that are now on earth do battle. And they laid to heart my counsels and hearkened to my voice. Even so hearken ye also, for better is it to hearken. Neither do thou, though thou art very great, seize from him his damsel, but leave her as she was given at the first by the sons of the Achaians to be a meed of honour; nor do thou, son of Peleus, think to strive with a king, might against might; seeing that no common honour pertaineth to a sceptered king to whom Zeus apportioneth glory. Though thou be strong, and a goddess mother bare thee, yet his is the greater place, for he is king over more. And thou, Atreides, abate thy fury; nay, ·it is even I that beseech thee to let go thine anger with Achilles, who is made unto all the Achaians a mighty bulwark of evil war."

Then lord Agamemnon answered and said: "Yea verily, old man, all this thou sayest is according unto right. But this fellow would be above all others, he would be lord of all and king among all and captain to all; wherein I deem none will hearken to him. Though the immortal gods made him a spearman, do they therefore put revilings in his mouth for him to utter?"

Then goodly Achilles brake in on him and answered: "Yea, for I should be called coward and man of naught, if I yield to thee in every matter, howsoe'er thou bid. To others give now thine orders, not to me [play master; for thee I deem that I shall no more obey]. This, moreover, will I say to thee, and do thou lay it to thy heart. Know that not by violence will I strive for the damsel's sake, neither with thee nor any other; ye gave and ye have taken away. But of all else that is mine beside my fleet black ship, thereof shalt thou not take anything or bear it away against my will. Yea, go to now, make trial, that all these may see; forthwith thy dark blood shall gush about my spear."

3. The Assembly of the Achaians*

In Book II Homer describes an assembly of the Greek army which Agamemnon has called to test the spirit of his men. It reveals much of the political organization and ideas of Homer's world.

Now went the goddess Dawn to high Olympus, foretelling daylight to Zeus and all the immortals; and the king bade the clear-voiced heralds summon to the assembly the flowing-haired Achaians. So did those summon, and these gathered with speed.

But first the council of the great-hearted elders met beside the ship of king Nestor the Pylos-born. And he that had assembled them framed his cunning counsel: "Hearken, my friends. A dream from heaven came to me in my sleep through the ambrosial night, and chiefly to goodly Nestor was very like in shape and bulk and stature. And it stood over my head and charged me saying: 'Sleepest thou, son of wise Atreus tamer of horses? To sleep all night through beseemeth not one that is a counsellor, to whom peoples are entrusted and so many cares belong. But now hearken straightway to me, for I am a messenger to thee from Zeus, who though he be afar yet hath great care for thee and pity. He biddeth thee call to arms the flowing-haired Achaians with all speed, for that now thou mayest take the wide-wayed city of the Trojans. For the immortals that dwell in the palaces of Olympus are no longer divided in counsel, since Hera hath turned the minds of all by her beseeching, and over the Trojans sorrows hang by the will of Zeus. But keep thou this in thy heart.' So spake the dream and was flown away, and sweet sleep left me. So come, let us now call to arms as we may the sons of the Achaians. But first I will speak to make trial of them as is fitting, and will bid them flee with their benched ships; only do ye from this side and from that speak to hold them back."

* The *Iliad, supra.,* pp. 20–27.

13

So spake he and sate him down; and there stood up among them Nestor, who was king of sandy Pylos. He of good intent made harangue to them and said: "My friends, captains and rulers of the Argives, had any other of the Achaians told us this dream we might deem it a false thing, and rather turn away therefrom; but now he hath seen it who of all Achaians avoweth himself far greatest. So come, let us call to arms as we may the sons of the Achaians."

So spake he, and led the way forth from the council, and all the other sceptered chiefs rose with him and obeyed the shepherd of the host; and the people hastened to them. Even as when the tribes of thronging bees issue from some hollow rock, ever in fresh procession, and fly clustering among the flowers of spring, and some on this hand and some on that fly thick; even so from ships and huts before the low beach marched forth their many tribes by companies to the place of assembly. And in their midst blazed forth Rumour, messenger of Zeus, urging them to go; and so they gathered. And the palace of assemblage was in an uproar, and the earth echoed again as the hosts sate them down, and there was turmoil. Nine heralds restrained them with shouting, if perchance they might refrain from clamour, and hearken to their kings, the fosterlings of Zeus. And hardly at the last would the people sit, and keep them to their benches and cease from noise. Then stood up lord Agamemnon bearing his sceptre, that Hephaistos had wrought curiously. Hephaistos gave it to king Zeus son of Kronos, and then Zeus gave it to the messenger-god the slayer of Argus; and king Hermes gave it to Pelops the charioteer, and Pelops again gave it to Atreus shepherd of the host. And Atreus dying left it to Thyestes rich in flocks, and Thyestes in his turn left it to Agamemnon to bear, that over many islands and all Argos he should be lord. Thereon he leaned and spake his saying to the Argives:

"My friends, Danaan warriors, men of Ares' company, Zeus Kronos' son hath bound me with might in grievous blindness of soul; hard of heart is he, for that erewhile he promised me and pledged his nod that not till I had wasted well-walled Ilios should I return; but now see I that he planned a cruel wile and biddeth me return to Argos dishonored, with the loss of many of my folk. So meseems it pleaseth most mighty Zeus, who hath laid low the head of many a city, yea, and shall lay low; for his is highest power. Shame is this even for them that come after to hear; how so goodly and great a folk of the Achaians thus vainly warred a bootless war, and fought scantier enemies, and no end thereof is yet seen. For if perchance we were minded, both Achaians and Trojans, to swear a solemn truce, and to number ourselves, and if the Trojans should gather together all that have their dwellings in the city, and we Achaians should marshal ourselves by tens, and every company choose a Trojan to pour their wine, then would many tens lack a cup-bearer: so much, I say, do the sons of the Achaians outnumber the Trojans that dwell within the city. But allies from many cities, even warriors that wield the spear, are therein, and they hinder me perforce, and for all my will suffer me not to waste the populous citadel of Ilios. Already have nine years of great Zeus passed away, and our ships' timbers have rotted and the tackling is loosed; while there our wives and little children sit in our halls awaiting us; yet is our task utterly unaccomplished wherefor we came hither. So come, even as I shall bid let us all obey. Let us flee with our ships to our dear native land; for now shall we never take wide-wayed Troy."

So spake he, and stirred the spirit in the breasts of all throughout the multitude, as many as had not heard the council. And the assembly swayed like high sea-waves of the Icarian Main that east wind and south wind raise, rushing upon them from the clouds of father Zeus; and even as when the west wind cometh to stir a deep cornfield with violent blast, and the ears bow down, so was all the assembly stirred, and they with shouting hasted toward the ships; and the dust from beneath their feet rose and stood on high. And they bade each man his neighbour to seize the ships and drag them into the bright salt sea, and cleared out the launching ways, and the noise went up to heaven of their hurrying homewards; and they began to take the props from beneath the ships.

Then would the Argives have accomplished their return against the will of fate, but that Hera spake a word to Athene: "Out on it, daughter of aegis-bearing Zeus, unwearied maiden! Shall the Argives thus indeed flee homeward to their dear native land over the sea's broad back? But they would leave to Priam and the Trojans their boast, even Helen of Argos, for whose sake many an Achaian hath perished in Troy, far away from his dear native land. But go thou now amid the host of the mail-clad Achaians; with thy gentle words refrain thou every man, neither suffer them to draw their curved ships down to the salt sea."

So spake she, and the bright-eyed goddess Athene disregarded not; but went darting down from the peaks of Olympus, and came with speed to the fleet ships of the Achaians. There found she Odysseus standing, peer of Zeus in counsel, neither laid he any hand upon his decked black ship, because grief had entered into his heart and soul. And bright-eyed Athene stood by him and said: "Heaven-sprung son of Laertes, Odysseus of many devices, will ye indeed fling yourselves upon your benched ships to flee homeward to your dear native land? But ye would leave to Priam and the Trojans their boast, even Helen of Argos, for whose sake many an Achaian hath perished in Troy, far from his dear native land. But go thou now amid the host of the Achaians, and tarry not; and with thy gentle words refrain every man, neither suffer them to draw their curved ships down to the salt sea."

So said she, and he knew the voice of the goddess speaking to him, and set him to run, and cast away his mantle, the which his herald gathered up, even Eurybates of Ithaca, that waited on him. And himself he went to meet Agamemnon son of Atreus, and at his hand received the sceptre of his sires, imperishable for ever, wherewith he took his way amid the ships of the mail-clad Achaians.

Whenever he found one that was a captain and a man of mark, he stood by his side, and refrained him with gentle words: "Good sir, it is not seemly to affright thee like a coward, but do thou sit thyself and make all thy folk sit down. For thou knowest not yet clearly what is the purpose of Atreus' son; now is he but making trial, and soon he will afflict the sons of the Achaians. And heard we not all of us what he spake in the council? Beware lest in his anger he evilly entreat the sons of the Achaians. For proud is the soul of heaven-fostered kings; because their honour is of Zeus, and the god of counsel loveth them."

But whatever man of the people he saw and found him shouting, him he drave with his sceptre and chode him with loud words: "Good sir, sit still and hearken to the words of others that are thy betters; but thou art no warrior, and a weakling, never reckoned whether in battle or in council. In no wise can we Achaians all be kings here. A multitude of masters is no good thing; let there be one master, one king, to whom the son of crooked-counselling Kronos hath granted it, [even the sceptre and judgments, that he may rule among you]."

So masterfully ranged he the host; and they hasted back to the assembly from ships and huts, with noise as when a wave of the loud-sounding sea roareth on the long beach and the main resoundeth.

Now all the rest sat down and kept their place upon the benches, only Thersites still chattered on, the uncontrolled of speech, whose mind was full of words many and disorderly, wherewith to strive against the chiefs idly and in no good order, but even as he deemed that he should make the Argives laugh. And he was ill-favoured beyond all men that came to Ilios. Bandy-legged was he, and lame of one foot, and his two shoulders rounded, arched down upon his chest; and over them his head was warped, and a scanty stubble sprouted on it. Hateful was he to Achilles above all and to Odysseus, for them he was wont to revile. But now with shrill shout he poured forth his upbraidings upon goodly Agamemnon. With him the Achaians were sore vexed and had indignation in their souls. But he with loud shout spake and reviled Agamemnon: "Atreides, for what art thou now ill content and lacking? Surely thy huts are full of bronze and many women are in thy huts, the chosen spoils that we Achaians give thee first of all, whene'er we take a town. Can it be that thou yet wantest gold as well, such as some one of the horse-taming Trojans may bring from Ilios to ransom his son, whom I perchance or some other Achaian have led captive; or else some young girl, to know in love, whom thou mayest keep apart to thyself? But it is not seemly for one that is their captain to bring the sons of the Achaians to ill. Soft fools, base things of shame, ye women of Achaia and men no more, let us depart home with our ships, and leave this fellow here in Troy-land to gorge him with meeds of honour, that he may see whether our aid avail him aught or no; even he that hath now done dishonour to Achilles, a far better man than he; for he hath taken away his meed of honour and keepeth it by his own violent deed. Of a very surety is there no wrath at all in Achilles' mind, but he is slack; else this despite, thou son of Atreus, were thy last."

So spake Thersites, reviling Agamemnon shepherd of the host. But goodly Odysseus came straight to his side, and looking sternly at him with hard words rebuked him: "Thersites, reckless in words, shrill orator though thou art, refrain thyself, nor aim to strive simply against kings. For I deem that no mortal is baser than thou of all that with the sons of Atreus came before Ilios. Therefore were it well that thou shouldest not have kings in thy mouth as thou talkest, and utter revilings against them and be on the watch for departure. We know not yet clearly how these things shall be, whether we sons of the Achaians shall return for good or for ill. Therefore now dost thou revile continually Agamemnon son of Atreus, shepherd of the host, because the Danaan warriors give him many gifts, and so thou talkest tauntingly. But I will tell thee plain, and that I say shall even be brought to pass: if I find thee again raving as now thou art, then may Odysseus' head no longer abide upon his shoulders, nor may I any more be called father of Telemachos, if I take thee not and strip from thee thy garments, thy mantle and tunic that cover thy nakedness, and for thyself send thee weeping to the fleet ships, and beat thee out of the assembly with shameful blows."

So spake he, and with his staff smote his back and shoulders: and he bowed down and a big tear fell from him, and a bloody weal stood up from his back beneath the golden sceptre. Then he sat down and was amazed, and in pain with helpless look wiped away a tear. But the rest, though they were sorry, laughed lightly at him, and thus would one speak looking at another standing by: "Go to, of a truth Odysseus hath wrought good deeds without number ere now, standing foremost in wise counsels and setting battle in array, but now is this thing the best by far that he hath wrought among the Argives, to wit, that he hath stayed this prating railer from his harangues. Never again, forsooth, will his proud soul henceforth bid him revile the kings with slanderous words."

4. Kingship on Ithaca*

Odysseus has been away from home for twenty years during which time his infant son Telemachus has grown to manhood. Meanwhile the nobles of Ithaca, thinking Odysseus dead, have paid suit to his wife Penelope, wasting his substance and insulting his family. In the First Book Telemachus calls for an assembly. The ensuing debate tells us much about the peculiar nature of Homeric kingship.

Now the wooers clamoured throughout the shadowy halls, and each one uttered a prayer to be her bedfellow. And wise Telemachus first spake among them:

'Wooers of my mother, men despiteful out of measure, let us feast now and make merry and let there be no brawling; for, lo, it is a good thing to list to a minstrel such as him, like to the gods in voice. But in the morning let us all go to the assembly and sit us down, that I may declare my saying outright, to wit that ye leave these halls: and busy yourselves with other feasts, eating your own substance, going in turn from house to house. But if ye deem this a likelier and a better thing, that one man's goods should perish without atonement, then waste ye as ye will; and I will call upon the everlasting gods, if haply Zeus may grant that acts of recompense be made: so should ye hereafter perish within the halls without atonement.'

So spake he, and all that heard him bit their lips and marvelled at Telemachus, in that he spake boldly.

Then Antinous, son of Eupeithes, answered him: "Telemachus, in very truth the gods themselves instruct thee to be proud of speech and boldly to harangue. Never may Cronion make thee king in seagirt Ithaca, which thing is of inheritance thy right!'

Then wise Telemachus answered him, and said: 'Antinous, wilt thou indeed be wroth at the word that I shall say? Yea, at

* The *Odyssey*, translated by S. H. Butcher and A. Lang, Macmillan & Co., Ltd. (London, 1930), pp. 12–13.

the hand of Zeus would I be fain to take even this thing upon me. Sayest thou that this is the worst hap that can befall a man? Nay, verily, it is no ill thing to be a king: the house of such an one quickly waxeth rich and himself is held in greater honour. Howsoever there are many other kings of the Achaeans in seagirt Ithaca, kings young and old; some one of them shall surely have this kingship since goodly Odysseus is dead. But as for me, I will be lord of our own house and thralls, that goodly Odysseus gat me with his spear.'

5.   *The Place of the People**

The world of Homer was aristocratic, but its noble rulers realized the ultimate power of the populace. In Book Sixteen, at another assembly on Ithaca we learn of the respect for the power of the commons already felt in Homeric times.

And the wooers all together went to the assembly-place, and suffered none other to sit with them, either of the young men or of the elders. Then Antinous spake among them, the son of Eupeithes:

'Lo now, how the gods have delivered this man from his evil case! All day long did scouts sit along the windy headlands, ever in quick succession, and at the going down of the sun we never rested for a night upon the shore, but sailing with our swift ship on the high seas we awaited the bright Dawn, as we lay in wait for Telemachus, that we might take and slay the man himself; but meanwhile some god has brought him home. But even here let us devise an evil end for him, even for Telemachus, and let him not escape out of our hands, for methinks that while he lives we shall never achieve this task of ours. For he himself has understanding in counsel and wisdom, and the people no longer show us favour in all things. Nay come, before he assembles all the Acheans to the gathering; for methinks that he

* *Odyssey*, pp. 255–257.

will in no wise be slack, but will be exceeding wroth, and will
stand up and speak out among them all, and tell how we plotted
against him sheer destruction but did not overtake him. Then
will they not approve us, when they hear these evil deeds. Beware then lest they do us a harm, and drive us forth from our
country, and we come to the land of strangers. Nay, but let us
be beforehand and take him in the field far from the city, or by
the way; and let us ourselves keep his livelihood and his possessions, making fair division among us, but the house we would
give to his mother to keep and to whomsoever marries her. But
if this saying likes you not, but ye chose rather that he should
live and keep the heritage of his father, no longer then let us
gather here and eat all his store of pleasant substance, but let
each one from his own hall woo her with his bridal gifts and
seek to win her; so should she wed the man that gives the most
and comes as the chosen of fate.'

So he spake, and they all held their peace. Then Amphinomus made harangue and spake out among them; he was the
famous son of Nisus the prince, the son of Aretias, and he led
the wooers that came from out Dulichium, a land rich in wheat
and in grass, and more than all the rest his words were pleasing
to Penelope, for he was of an understanding mind. And now of
his good will he made harangue, and spake among them:

'Friends, I for one would not choose to kill Telemachus; it
is a fearful thing to slay one of the stock of kings! Nay, first
let us seek to the counsel of the gods, and if the oracles of great
Zeus approve, myself I will slay him and bid all the rest to aid.
But if the gods are disposed to avert it, I bid you to refrain.'

So spake Amphinomus, and his saying pleased them well.
Then straightway they arose and went to the house of Odysseus,
and entering in sat down on the polished seats.

Then the wise Penelope had a new thought, namely, to show
herself to the wooers, so despiteful in ther insolence; for she had
heard of the death of her son that was to be in the halls, seeing
that Medon the henchman had told her of it, who heard their
counsels. So she went on her way to the hall, with the women
her handmaids. Now when that fair lady had come unto the
wooers, she stood by the pillar of the well-builded roof, holding
up her glistening tire before her face, and rebuked Antinous and
spake and hailed him:

'Antinous, full of all insolence, deviser of mischief! and yet

they say that in the land of Ithaca thou art chiefest among thy
peers in counsel and in speech. Nay, no such man dost thou
show thyself. Fool! why indeed dost thou contrive death and
doom for Telemachus, and hast no regard unto suppliants who
have Zeus to witness? Nay but it is an impious thing to contrive
evil one against another. What! knowest thou not of the day
when thy father fled to this house in fear of the people, for verily
they were exceeding wroth against him, because he had followed
with Taphian sea-robbers and harried the Thesprotians, who
were at peace with us? So they wished to destroy thy father and
wrest from him his dear life, and utterly to devour all his great
and abundant livelihood; but Odysseus stayed and withheld
them, for all their desire. His house thou now consumest without atonement, and his wife thou wooest, and wouldst slay his
son, and dost greatly grieve me. But I bid thee cease, and command the others to do likewise.'

2. The Emergence of the Polis

The origin of true political thought is coeval with the rise of that peculiarly Greek institution, the polis. *More than a city-state, it was a way of life and incorporated ideas of government new to the world. The development of the concept of the* polis *may be traced in the works of three poets—Hesiod, Tyrtaeus, and Solon.*

1.   Hesiod: The Works and Days*

Hesiod was a poet from a little town in rural Boeotia who lived about 700 B.C. The following selection from his Works and Days *begins with his account of the five ages of man, a pessimistic view of man's fall from grace which was to become a commonplace in later times. It is followed by the fable of the nightingale and the hawk and an exhortation to justice and fair dealing. The originality of Hesiod is in his connection of justice with the community.*

So there is no way to avoid what Zeus has intended.

Or if you will, I will outline it for you
    in a different story,
well and knowledgeably—store it up
    in your understanding—
the beginnings of things, which were the same for gods
    as for mortals.

In the beginning, the immortals
    who have their homes on Olympos
created the golden generation of mortal people.
These lived in Kronos' time, when he
    was the king in heaven.
They lived as if they were gods,
    their hearts free from all sorrow,
by themselves, and without hard work or pain;
    no miserable
old age came their way; their hands, their feet,
    did not alter.
They took their pleasure in festivals,
    and lived without troubles.
When they died, it was as if they fell asleep.
    All goods
were theirs. The fruitful grainland

* Translated by Richmond Lattimore (Ann Arbor, 1959), pp. 31-49. By permission of the University of Michigan Press.

yielded its harvest to them
of its own accord; this was great and abundant,
    while they at their pleasure
quietly looked after their works,
    in the midst of good things
[prosperous in flocks, on friendly terms
    with the blessed immortals].

Now that the earth has gathered over this generation,
these are called pure and blessed spirits;
    they live upon earth,
and are good, they watch over mortal men
    and defend them from evil;
they keep watch over lawsuits and hard dealings;
    they mantle
themselves in dark mist
    and wander all over the country;
they bestow wealth; for this right
    as of kings was given them.
        Next after these the dwellers upon Olympos created
a second generation, of silver, far worse
    than the other.
They were not like the golden ones either in shape
    or spirit.
A child was a child for a hundred years,
    looked after and playing
by his gracious mother, kept at home,
    a complete booby.
But when it came time for them to grow up
    and gain full measure,
they lived for only a poor short time;
    by their own foolishness
they had troubles, for they were not able
    to keep away from
reckless crime against each other,
    nor would they worship
the gods, nor do sacrifice on the sacred altars
    of the blessed ones,
which is the right thing among the customs of men,
    and therefore
Zeus, son of Kronos, in anger engulfed them,

for they paid no due
honors to the blessed gods who live on Olympos.

But when the earth had gathered over this generation
also—and they too are called blessed spirits
        by men, though under
the ground, and secondary, but still
        they have their due worship—
then Zeus the father created the third generation
        of mortals,
the age of bronze. They were not like
        the generation of silver.
They came from ash spears. They were terrible
        and strong, and the ghastly
action of Ares was theirs, and violence.
        They ate no bread,
but maintained an indomitable and adamantine spirit.
None could come near them; their strength was big,
        and from their shoulders
the arms grew irresistible on their ponderous bodies.
The weapons of these men were bronze,
        of bronze their houses,
and they worked as bronzesmiths. There was not yet
        any black iron.
Yet even these, destroyed beneath the hands
        of each other,
went down into the moldering domain of cold Hades;
nameless; for all they were formidable black death
seized them, and they had to forsake
        the shining sunlight.

Now when the earth had gather over this generation
also, Zeus, son of Kronos, created yet another
fourth generation on the fertile earth,
        and these were better and nobler,
the wonderful generation of hero-men, who are also
called half-gods, the generation before our own
        on this vast earth.
But of these too, evil war and the terrible carnage
took some; some by seven-gated Thebes

    in the land of Kadmos
as they fought together over the flocks of Oidipous;
    others
war had taken in ships over the great gulf
    of the sea,
where they also fought for the sake
    of lovely-haired Helen.
There, for these, the end of death was misted
    about them.
But on others Zeus, son of Kronos, settled a living
    and a country
of their own, apart from human kind,
    at the end of the world.
And there they have their dwelling place,
    and hearts free of sorrow
in the islands of the blessed
    by the deep-swirling stream of the ocean,
prospering heroes, on whom in every year
    three times over
the fruitful grainland bestows its sweet yield.
    These live
far from the immortals, and Kronos
    is king among them.
For Zeus, father of gods and mortals,
    set him free from his bondage,
although the position and the glory still belong
    to the young gods.

After this, Zeus of the wide brows
    established yet one more
generation of men, the fifth, to be
    on the fertile earth.

And I wish that I were not any part
    of the fifth generation
of men, but had died before it came,
    or been born afterward.
For here now is the age of iron. Never by daytime
will there be an end to hard work and pain,
    nor in the night
to weariness, when the gods will send anxieties

to trouble us.
Yet here also there shall be some good things
      mixed with the evils.
But Zeus will destroy this generation of mortals
      also,
in the time when children, as they are born,
      grow gray on the temples,
when the father no longer agrees with the children,
      nor children with their father,
when guest is no longer at one with host,
      nor companion to companion,
when your brother is no longer your friend,
      as he was in the old days.
Men will deprive their parents of all rights,
      as they grow old,
and people will mock them too,
      babbling bitter words against them,
harshly, and without shame in the sight of the gods;
      not even
to their aging parents will they give back
      what once was given.
Strong of hand, one man shall seek
      the city of another.
There will be no favor for the man
      who keeps his oath, for the righteous
and the good man, rather men shall give their praise
      to violence
and the doer of evil. Right will be in the arm.
      Shame will
not be. The vile man will crowd his better out,
      and attack him
with twisted accusations and swear an oath
      to his story.
The spirit of Envy, with grim face
      and screaming voice, who delights
in evil, will be the constant companion
      of wretched humanity,
and at last *Nemesis* and *Aidos, Decency* and *Respect,*
      shrouding
their bright forms in pale mantles, shall go
      from the wide-wayed

earth back on their way to Olympos,
    forsaking the whole race
of mortal men, and all that will be left by them
    to mankind
will be wretched pain. And there shall be no defense
    against evil.

Now I will tell you a fable for the barons;
    they understand it.
This is what the hawk said when he had caught
    a nightingale
with spangled neck in his claws and carried her
    high among the clouds.
She, spitted on the clawhooks, was wailing pitifully,
but the hawk, in his masterful manner,
    gave her an answer:
"What is the matter with you? Why scream?
    Your master has you.
You shall go wherever I take you,
    for all your singing.
If I like, I can let you go. If I like,
    I can eat you for dinner.
He is a fool who tries to match his strength
    with the stronger.
He will lose his battle, and with the shame
    will be hurt also."
So spoke the hawk, the bird who flies so fast
    on his long wings.

But as for you, Perses, listen to justice;
    do not try to practice
violence; violence is bad for a weak man; even a noble
cannot lightly carry the burden of her,
    but she weighs him down
when he loses his way in delusions; that other road
    is the better
which leads toward just dealings. For Justice
    wins over violence
as they come out in the end. The fool knows
    after he's suffered.
The spirit of Oath is one who runs

beside crooked judgments.
There is an outcry when Justice is dragged perforce,
    when bribe-eating
men pull her about, and judge their cases
    with crooked decisions.
She follows perforce, weeping, to the city
    and gatherings of people.
She puts a dark mist upon her and brings a curse
    upon all those
who drive her out, who deal in her
    and twist her in dealing.
        But when men issue straight decisions
    to their own people
and to strangers, and do not step at all
    off the road of rightness,
their city flourishes, and the people
    blossom inside it.
Peace, who brings boys to manhood, is in their land,
    nor does Zeus
of the wide brows ever ordain that hard war
    shall be with them.
Neither famine nor inward disaster comes the way
    of those people
who are straight and just; they do their work
    as if work were a holiday;
the earth gives them great livelihood,
    on their mountains the oaks
bear acorns for them in their crowns,
    and bees in their middles.
Their wool-bearing sheep are weighted down
    with fleecy burdens.
Their women bear them children
    who resemble their parents.
They prosper in good things throughout.
    They need have no traffic
with ships, for their own grain-giving land
    yields them its harvest.
        But when men like harsh violence
    and cruel acts, Zeus
of the wide brows, the son of Kronos,
    ordains their punishment.

Often a whole city is paid punishment
    for one bad man
who commits crimes and plans reckless action.
    On this man's people
the son of Kronos out of the sky
    inflicts great suffering,
famine and plague together, and the people die
    and diminish.
The women bear children no longer, the houses dwindle
by design of Olympian Zeus; or again at other times,
he destroys the wide camped army of a people,
    or wrecks
their city with its walls, or their ships
    on the open water.

You barons also, cannot even you
    understand for yourselves
how justice works? For the immortals
    are close to us, they mingle
with men, and are aware of those who
    by crooked decisions
break other men, and care nothing
    for what the gods think of it.
Upon the prospering earth there are
    thirty thousand immortal
spirits, who keep watch for Zeus and all that men do.
They have an eye on decrees given
    and on harsh dealings,
and invisible in their dark mist they hover
    on the whole earth.
Justice herself is a young maiden.
    She is Zeus's daughter,
and seemly, and respected by all the gods of Olympos.
When any man uses force on her by false impeachment
she goes and sits at the feet of Zeus Kronion,
    her father,
and cries out on the wicked purpose of men,
    so that their people
must pay for the profligacy of their rulers,
    who for their own greedy purposes
twist the courses of justice aslant

by false proclamations.
Beware, you barons, of such spirits.
    Straighten your decisions
you eaters of bribes. Banish from your minds
    the twisting of justice.

2. *Tyrtaeus**

*Tyrtaeus was a Spartan poet of the second half of the seventh
century B.C. The following selections indicate the growing
prominence of the polis in the life of its citizens. The aristocratic concept of individual excellence and prowess has given
way to a new idea. Virtue, courage, excellence, even happiness have become functions of the polis.*

Plutarch *Life of Lycurgus:* When the commons were assembled, he suffered no other to give his opinion, but the people
had the right of giving judgment on an opinion laid before them
by the Elders and Kings. Later, however, when the commons
began to twist and distort the opinions of the Elders and Kings
by addition and subtraction, Kings Polydorus and Theopompus
inserted in the *rhetra* or ordinance the following clause: 'If the
commons choose a crooked opinion, the elderborn and arch-
leaders [that is the Elders and Kings] have powers of dissolu-
tion.'—which means that they may refuse to ratify it and may
withdraw themselves altogether and dismiss the commons, as
trying to divert and change the opinion of the Elders and Kings
contrary to what is best—, and themselves persuaded the people
to accept it in the belief that this was the command of the God,
as indeed Tyrtaeus mentions in the following lines:
    They heard the voice of Phoebus and brought home from
Pytho oracles of the God and words of sure fulfilment; for thus

* Fragments 4, 10, 11, and 12 in *The Loeb Classical Library*, edition of
Elegy and Iambus, translated by J. M. Edmonds (London, 1931). By permission of William Heinemann, Ltd.

the Lord of the Silver Bow, Far-Shooting Apollo of the Golden Hair, gave answer from out his rich sanctuary: The beginning of counsel shall belong to the God-honoured Kings whose care is the delightsome city of Sparta, and to the men of elder birth; after them shall the commons, answering them back with forthright ordinances, both say things honourable and do all that is right, nor give the city any crooked counsel; so shall the common people have victory and might; for this hath Phoebus declared unto their city in these matters. . . .

For 'tis a fair thing for a good man to fall and die fighting in the van for his native land, whereas to leave his city and his rich fields and go a-begging is of all things the most miserable, wandering with mother dear and aged father, with little children and wedded wife. For hateful shall such an one be among all those to whom he shall come in bondage to Want and loathsome Penury, and doth shame his lineage and belie his noble beauty, followed by all evil and dishonour. Now if so little thought be taken of a wanderer, and so little honour, respect, or pity, let us fight with a will for this land, and die for our children and never spare our lives.

Abide then, O young men, shoulder to shoulder and fight; begin not foul flight nor yet be afraid, but make the heart in your breasts both great and stout, and never shrink when you fight the foe. And the elder sort, whose knees are no longer nimble, fly not ye to leave them fallen to earth. For 'tis a foul thing, in sooth, for an elder to fall in the van and lie before the younger, his head white and his beard hoary, breathing forth his stout soul in the dust, with his privities all bloody in his hands, a sight so foul to see and fraught with such ill to the seer, and his flesh also all naked; yet to a young man all is seemly enough, so long as he have the noble bloom of lovely youth, aye a marvel he for men to behold, and desirable unto women, so long as ever he be alive, and fair in like manner when he be fallen in the vanguard. So let each man bite his lip with his teeth and abide firm-set astride upon the ground. . . .

Ye are of the lineage of the invincible Heracles; so be ye of good cheer; not yet is the head of Zeus turned away. Fear ye not a multitude of men, nor flinch, but let every man hold his shield straight towards the van, making Life his enemy and the black Spirits of Death dear as the rays of the sun. For ye know the destroying deeds of lamentable Ares, and well have learnt the disposition of woeful War; ye have tasted both of the fleeing and the pursuing, lads, and had more than your fill of either. Those who abiding shoulder to shoulder go with a will into the mellay and the van, of these are fewer slain, these save the people afterward; as for them that turn to fear, all their valour is lost—no man could tell in words each and all the ills that befall a man if he once come to dishonour. For pleasant it is in dreadful warfare to pierce the midriff of a flying man, and disgraced is the dead that lieth in the dust with a spear-point in his back. So let each man bite his lip and abide firm-set astride upon the ground, covering with the belly of his broad buckler thighs and legs below and breast and shoulders above; let him brandish the massy spear in his right hand, let him wave the dire crest upon his head; let him learn how to fight by doing doughty deeds, and not stand shield in hand beyond the missiles. Nay, let each man close the foe, and with his own long spear, or else with his sword, wound and take an enemy, and setting foot beside foot, resting shield against shield, crest beside crest, helm beside helm, fight his man breast to breast with sword or long spear in hand. And ye also, ye light-armed, crouch ye on either hand beneath the shield and fling your great hurlstones and throw against them your smooth javelins, in your place beside the men of heavier armament. . . .

I would neither call a man to mind nor put him in my tale for prowess in the race or the wrestling, not even had he the stature and strength of a Cyclops and surpassed in swiftness the Thracian Northwind, nor were he a comelier man than Tithonus and a richer than Midas or Cinyras, nor though he were a greater king than Pelops son of Tantalus, and had Adrastus' suasiveness of tongue, nor yet though all fame were his save of warlike strength; for a man is not good in war if he have not endured the sight of bloody slaughter and stood nigh and reached forth to strike the foe. This is prowess, this is the noblest prize and the fairest for a lad to win in the world; a common good this both for the city and all her people, when a man standeth firm in the forefront without ceasing, and making heart and soul to abide, forgetteth foul flight altogether and hearteneth by his words him that he standeth by. Such a man is good in war; he quickly turneth the savage hosts of the enemy, and stemmeth the wave of battle with a will; moreover he that falleth in the van and loseth dear life to the glory of his city and his countrymen and his father, with many a frontwise wound through breast and breastplate and through bossy shield, he is bewailed alike by young and old, and lamented with sore regret by all the city. His grave and his children are conspicuous among men, and his children's children and his line after them; nor ever doth his name and good fame perish, but though he be underground he liveth evermore, seeing that he was doing nobly and abiding in the fight for country's and children's sake when fierce Ares brought him low. But and if he escape the doom of outstretched Death and by victory make good the splendid boast of battle, he hath honour of all, alike young as old, and cometh to his death after happiness; as he groweth old he standeth out among his people, and there's none that will do him hurt either in honour or in right; all yield him place on the benches, alike the young and his peers and his elders. This is the prowess each man should this day aspire to, never relaxing from war.

3. Solon*

Solon (ca. 640–560 B.C.) was an Athenian statesman chosen to settle the class strife which beset Athens at the turn of the sixth century B.C. He put his political ideas in the form of elegiac verse which we have in fragmented form. His view of the polis has evolved to the point where it will become the standard classical view.

But Athens, albeit she will never perish by the destiny of Zeus or the will of the happy Gods immortal—for of such power is the great-hearted Guardian, Daughter of a Mighty Sire, that holdeth Her hands over us—, Her own people, for lucre's sake, are fain to make ruin of this great city by their folly. Unrighteous is the mind of the leaders of the commons, and their

---

* Fragments 4, 5, 6, 9, 10 from *Elegy and Iambus*, translated by J. M. Edmonds, *The Loeb Classical Library* (London, 1931). Vol. 1. By permission of William Heinemann, Ltd.

pride goeth before a fall; for they know not how to hold them
from excess nor to direct in peace the jollity of their present
feasting . . . but grow rich through the suasion of unrighteous
deeds . . . and steal right and left with no respect for possessions sacred or profane, nor have heed of the awful foundations
of Justice, who is so well aware in her silence of what is and what
hath been, and soon or late cometh alway to avenge. This is
a wound that cometh inevitable and forthwith to every city,
and she falleth quickly into an evil servitude, which arouseth
discord and waketh slumbering War that destroyeth the lovely
prime of so many men. For in gatherings dear to the unrighteous
a delightful city is quickly brought low at the hands of them
that are her enemies. Such are the evils which then are rife
among the common folk, and many of the poor go slaves into
a foreign land, bound with unseemly fetters, there to bear perforce the evil works of servitude. So cometh the common evil
into every house, and the street-doors will no longer keep it
out; it leapeth the high hedge and findeth every man, for all
he may go hide himself in his chamber. This it is that my heart
biddeth me tell the Athenians, and how that even as ill-govern-
ment giveth a city much trouble, so good rule maketh all things
orderly and perfect, and often putteth fetters upon the unrighteous; aye, she maketh the rough smooth, checketh excess,
confuseth outrage; she withereth the springing weeds of ruin,
she straighteneth crooked judgments, she mollifieth proud deeds;
she stoppeth the works of faction, she stilleth the wrath of
baneful strife; and of her all is made wise and perfect in the
world of men.

For I gave the common folk such privilege as is sufficient
for them, neither adding nor taking away; and such as had
power and were admired for their riches, I provided that they
too should not suffer undue wrong. Nay, I stood with a strong
shield thrown before the both sorts, and would have neither to
prevail unrighteously over the other.

So best will the people follow their leaders, neither too little
restrained nor yet perforce; for excess breedeth outrage when
much prosperity followeth those whose mind is not perfect.

The strength of snow and of hail is from a cloud, and
thunder cometh of the bright lightning; a city is destroyed of
great men, and the common folk fall into bondage unto a despot
because of ignorance. For him that putteth out too far from

land 'tis not easy to make haven afterward; all such things as these should be thought of ere it be too late.

If ye suffer bitterly through your own fault, blame ye not the Gods for it; for yourselves have ye exalted these men by giving them guards, and therefore it is that ye enjoy foul servitude. Each one of you walketh with the steps of a fox, the mind of all of you is vain; for ye look to a man's tongue and shifty speech, and never to the deed he doeth.

3. The Aristocratic Response: Theognis and Pindar

The institution of the polis *gave rise to two varieties of political thought, the aristocratic and the democratic. Theognis and Pindar represent the response of the Greek aristocracy to the* polis, *an institution which challenged the unquestioned supremacy of the nobility which we find in the Homeric epic.*

1. Theognis*

Theognis was a citizen of Megara, a Dorian city on the Gulf of Corinth. He lived through a period of political turmoil and democratic revolution during the sixth century B.C. *His views are those of the Greek aristocrat disenchanted with the* polis *and its effect on the old aristocratic society.*

Cyrnus, let me cleverly fix my seal on these lines and they shall never be stolen. Nor will evil be changed for good, and everyone will say, "these are the words of Theognis of Negara, famous among all men, although I have not yet been able to please my fellow-townsmen. Nor is that surprising, son of Polypaus, since Zeus himself does not please every man, either when he sends rain or withholds it. But with good intent, Cyrnus, I will teach you the precepts which I learned from good men when I was a child. Be wise and acquire neither honors nor prowess nor wealth by shameful or unjust actions. And know the following as well: do not consort with bad men, but always hold to the good. Eat and drink with them, whose power is great, sit with them and please them. You will learn good from good men, but if you mingle with the bad you will lose such wisdom as you already have. Therefore consort with the good and one day you will say that I give good advice to my friends.

Good men have never yet ruined a city, but when it pleases the bad to act with arrogant violence, corrupting the common people and giving judgments on behalf of unjust men for the sake of their own profit and power, do not then expect that city to remain peaceful, even if at present it enjoys great tranquility, when private gains have become dear to the bad, bringing with them public evil. From such things come factions and civil war and tyrants. May such things never please this city.

Cyrnus, this *polis* is still a *polis*, but its people are different, men who formerly knew neither judgments nor laws but clothed

* Lines 19–38, 43–52, 53–60, 183–192, 429–438, 1171–1176. Translated by Donald Kagan.

themselves in goatskins and wore them till they were rags and pastured themselves outside the city like deer. But now they are the good, son of Polypaus; those who were base are now noble. Who can bear to see such things? Yet they cheat each other as they smile at one another, for they have sound judgment neither of bad things or of good.

We seek thoroughbred rams asses and horses, Cyrnus, and a man wants offspring of good breeding. But in marriage a good man does not decline to marry the bad daughter of a bad father, if he gives him much wealth. Nor does the wife of a bad man refuse to be his bedfellow if he be rich, preferring wealth to goodness. For they value possessions and a good man marries a woman of bad stock and the bad a woman of good. Wealth mixes the breed. So do not wonder, son of Polypaus, that the race of your citizens is obscured since bad things are mixed with good.

It is easier to beget and rear a man than to put good sense into him. No one has ever discovered a way to make a fool wise or a bad man good. If God had given the sons of Asclepius the knowledge to heal the evil nature and mischievous mind of man, great and frequent would be their pay. If thought could be made and put into a man, the son of a good man would never become bad, since he would obey good counsel. But you will never make the bad man good by teaching.

The best things the gods give to men, Cyrnus, is judgment; judgment contains the ends of everything. O happy is the man who has it in his mind; it is much greater than destructive insolence and grievous satiety. There are no evils among mortals worse than these—for every evil, Cyrnus, comes out of them.

2. Pindar*

Pindar was a Theban poet of the early fifth century B.C. *He was the master of the epinician ode, a poem in praise of a victor at one of the Greek athletic festivals. He managed to make such a subject the vehicle for his philosophical, political and esthetic ideas without sacrificing poetic beauty. Thebes, unlike Megara, was a polis in which aristocracy was undisturbed; in the following selections we may discern the views of an aristocrat who has connected the old values with the new institution.*

* *The Odes of Pindar*, Translated by Richmond Lattimore (Chicago, 1947), *Olympia* 2, 9, 13; *Pythia* 2; *Nemea* 3. By permission of the University of Chicago Press.

Olympia 2]

My songs, lords of the lyre,
which of the gods, what hero, what mortal shall we celebrate?
Zeus has Pisa; but Herakles founded the Olympiad
out of spoils of his warfare;
but Theron, for his victory with chariot-four, is the man
we must sing now, him of the kind regard to strangers,
the tower Akragantine,
choice bud of a high line guarding the city.

In strong toil of the spirit
they were the eye of Sicily, they beside the river kept
the sacred house; their doom drew on, bringing wealth and
        delight near
by the valor in their blood.
But, O Kronios, Rhea's son, guarding Olympos' throne
and the games' glory and the Alpheus crossing,
in mild mood for the song's sake
kind keep for them always the land of their fathers

the rest of their generation. Of things come to pass
in justice or unjust, not Time the father
of all can make the end unaccomplished.
But forgetfulness may come still with happiness.
Grief, breaking again out of quiet, dies at last, quenched
under the waxing weight of fair things,

with God's destiny dropping
wealth deep from above. Thus the tale for the queenly
daughters of Kadmos, who endured much; grief falls a dead
        weight
as goods wax in strength. Semele
of the delicate hair, who died in the thunderstroke,
lives on Olympos, beloved of Pallas forever, of Zeus,
best loved of her son with ivy in his hands.

And they say that in the sea
among the daughters of Nereus in the depth, Ino
is given life imperishable for all time. But for mortal men

no limit in death has been set apart
when we shall bring to an end in unbroken good
the sun's child, our day of quiet; stream upon stream
of delights mixed with labor descends upon men.

Thus Destiny, who has from her father
the kindly guidance of these men, yet with wealth sent from
    God
bestows some pain also, to return upon us hereafter.
So his doomed son killed Laios
when they met, and brought to accomplishment
the thing foretold long since at Pytho.

And Erinys looked on him in bitterness
and slew all his strong race at each others' hands.
Yet when Polyneikes fell, Thersandros remained for honor
in the trial of fresh battles,
a branch to shield the house of Adrastos.
Stemmed in his stock, it is fit for Ainesidamos' son
to win songs in his honor and the lyre's sound.

He himself took the prize
at Olympia; to his brother equal in right the impartial
Graces brought blossoms of honor for the twelve-lap chariot
    race
at Pytho, at the Isthmos; success
for the striver washes away the effort of striving.
Wealth elaborate with virtue brings opportunity for various
deeds; it shoulders the cruel depth of care,
star-bright, man's truest
radiance; if a man keep it and know the future,
how, as we die here, the heart uncontrolled
yields retribution; likewise for sins in this kingdom of God
there is a judge under the earth. He gives sentence
in constraint of wrath.

But with nights equal forever,
with sun equal in their days, the good men
have life without labor, disquieting not the earth in strength
    of hand,
never the sea's water

for emptiness of living. Beside the high gods
they who had joy in keeping faith lead a life
without tears. The rest look on a blank face of evil.

But they who endure thrice over
in the world beyond to keep their souls from all sin
have gone God's way to the tower of Kronos; there
winds sweep from the Ocean
across the Island of the Blessed. Gold flowers to flame
on land in the glory of trees; it is fed in the water,
whence they bind bracelets to their arms and go chapleted

under the straight decrees of Rhadamanthys,
whom the husband of Rhea, high throned above all,
our great father, keeps in the chair of state beside him.
They say Peleus is there, and Kadmos,
and his mother with prayer softening Zeus' heart
carried Achilles thither,
who felled Hektor, Troy's unassailable
tall column of strength, who gave death to Kyknos
and the Aithiop, Dawn's child. There are many sharp shafts
        in the quiver
under the crook of my arm.
They speak to the understanding; most men need interpreters.
The wise man knows many things in his blood; the vulgar
        are taught.
They will say anything. They clatter vainly like crows

against the sacred bird of Zeus.
Come, my heart, strain the bow to the mark now. Whom
        shall we strike
in gentleness, slipping merciful arrows? Toward Akragas
we will bend the bow and speak
a word under oath in sincerity of mind.
Not in a hundred years has a city given forth
a man kinder to his friends, more open of hand

than Theron. But envy bestrides praise,
though coupled not with justice; still the revilers'
scandal would put secrecy upon fair deeds

of noble men. For sands escape number,
and of all the joy Theron has brought to others
what man could tell the measure?

Olympia 9]

The Archilochos song
cried aloud at Olympia, the victor hailed in his glory three
    times over
was enough by the Kronian hill to lead in triumph
Epharmostos in revelry with his beloved companions.
But now shower from the Muses' bows that range into wide
    distance,
Zeus, lord of the light in the red thunderbolt,
and with even such arrows
the solemn headland of Elis
that the hero Lydian Pelops of old
won, fairest bridal dower of Hippodameia.

Cast a winged shaft of delight
to Pytho likewise; you will find words that falter not to the
    ground
as you throb the lyre for a man and a wrestler
from famed Opous. Praise the land and her son.
Themis and the lady of salvation, Eunomia, her daughter,
the glorious, keep it for their own; he blossoms in exploits,
Kastalia, beside your spring
and by Alpheus river,
to make the garlands in their bloom lift up
the mother of Lokrian men, land of trees shining.

And I, lighting a city beloved
with blaze of whirling song,
swifter than the proud horse
or winged ship on the sea
will carry the message,
if with hand blessed I garden
this secret close of the Graces.

It is they who minister delightful things. If men are brave, or
    wise, it is by divinity

in them; how else could Herakles'
hands have shaken the club against the trident
when by Pylos' gate Poseidon stood over against him,
and Phoibos strode on him with the silver bow in his hands
    poised;
neither the death-god Hades rested the staff
wherewith he marshals mortal bodies of men perished
down the hollow street. But, my lips,
cast this story from us.
For to revile the gods
is hateful learning, and to vaunt against season carries

an underweb of madness.
Speak not idly such things; let be war and all discord
apart from the immortals. Rather to Protogeneia's city
bring our speech, where, by decree of Zeus of the rippling
    thunder,
Deukalion and Pyrrha, coming down from Parnassos,
founded their house at the first and with no act of love
    established
a stone generation to be their folk.
These were named people thereafter.
Wake for them the high strain of song,
and praise old wine, but the blossoms of poetry

that is young. For they say
the black earth was awash
under the weight of water; but by
Zeus' means, of a sudden the ebb-tide
drained the flood. And from these
came your ancestors, men with brazen shields,
traced back at the outset
to Iapeton's seed, sons of his daughters by the great sons of
    Kronos, kings in the land for all time
until the lord of Olympos,
ravishing from the Epeian land Opous' daughter, lay with
    her
secretly on Mainalian slopes; and thereafter he brought her

to Lokros, lest age, overtaking, doom him
to be childless. The bride carried the mighty
seed; and the hero was glad to see the son for his fostering.
He named him after his mother's sire,
to be called Opous,
a man surpassing in stature and action,
and gave him the city and the people to govern.

There came to him stranger-guests
from Argos and Thebes, Arkadians and Pisatans.
But beyond all newcomers he honored Aktor's son and Aigina's
Menoitios; he whose child, brought with the sons of Atreus,
in the plain of Teuthras stood his ground alone with Achilles
when Telephos, bending back the rest of the valiant Danaans,
hurled them against their own beached ships.
Thus was made plain for any
with wit to see how strong the heart of Patroklos;
and Thetis' son ordained thereafter that never

in grim battle should Patroklos be
marshaled apart from his own
man-wrecking spear's place.
May I find words now to win through
riding the car of the Muses
to the occasion. May daring and compassing power
come upon me. I went, in virtue of proxeny,
to stand by Lampromachos in his garlands of Isthmos, where
    both men won

on a single day their events.
And twice thereafter delight of victory came to him at the
    gates
of Korinth, as in the Nemean valley to Epharmostos.
He likewise at Argos won glory among men, and as a boy
at Athens; in Marathon, torn from beardless antagonists,
he stood the onset of older men for the silver vessels.
He threw these in his speed and craft
with no fall scored against him
and walked through the ring to loud acclamation
in the pride of his youth, splendid, and with achievement of
    splendor.

Before the Parrhasians assembled,
he appeared, a wonder, at the festival of Zeus Lykaios;
as when he won the cloak, warm medicine
of cold winds, at Pellene; the tomb of Iolaos
witnesses to his shining glory, as Eleusis the sea-borne.
Best by nature is best; but many have striven before now
to win by talents acquired
through art the glory.
But the thing unblessed by God is none
the worse for silence, always. There are ways

that surpass others.
But no one discipline sustains
us all. And skills are steep things
to win. As you bring the games' prize,
be bold to cry aloud
this man that is blessed by nature,
strong of hand, nimble, with eyes of valor,
who at your feast, Aias, son of Oileus, has wreathed your altar
    in victory.

Olympia 13]

Thrice Olympionician
the house I praise, gentle to fellow-citizens,
ministrant to strangers. I will know
Korinth the rich, forecourt
of Poseidon of the Isthmos, shining in its young men.
There Law, sure foundation-stone of cities, dwells with
    Justice
and Peace, dispenser of wealth to man, her sisters,
golden daughters of Themis, lady of high counsels.

They will to drive afar
Pride, the rough-spoken, mother of Surfeit.
I have fair things to say, and straightforward
courage urges my lips to speak.
It is vain striving to hide inborn nature.

To you, sons of Alatas, the Hours have brought many times
    bright victory,
as in high achievement you ascended in the sacred contests,
even as, blossoming, they have founded in men's minds

the beginning of many a wise device, from you. To the
    inventor the deed belongs.
Where else did the graces of Dionysos
shine forth with the dithyramb ox-driven?
Who else put curbs to the gear of horses
or set pediments like the double eagle, lord of birds, on the
    gods'
temples? Among you the Muse, sweet-spoken,
among you Ares also,
flowers in your young men's spears of terror.
Lord on high, wide ruling
over Olympia, Zeus father,
begrudge not in all time these words;
and, guiding clear of disaster these people,
for Xenophon steer the wind of his destiny.
Take in his name this festival measure of garlands that he
    brings from the lawn of Pisa,
winner at once in pentathlon and the stade run; a thing
no mortal has matched in time before.

When he came forward at Isthmos,
two wreaths of parsley shaded him.
Nemea will tell no other story.
For Thessalos his father the shining glory
of speed in his feet is laid up by Alpheus' stream,
and at Pytho he had honor in one sun's course of the stade
    and the two-lap race; in the selfsame month
at Athens of the rocks one fleet-running day
laid wreaths of loveliness for three successes on his locks.

Seven times at the maid Hellotis' contests. In the field of
    Poseidon by the sea
for Terpsias and Eritimos with their father
Ptoiodoros, there are songs too long for my singing.
But for all your success at Delphoi

and in the Lion's meadow, I dispute with the rest
the multitude of your splendors. Yet in truth
even I have not power to number
surely the pebbles in the sea.

To each thing belongs
its measure. Occasion is best to know.
I in my own right have sailed with the multitude
and cry aloud the wisdom of your forefathers,
their warcraft in heroic courage
without lies that touch Korinth: Sisyphos most skilled of
     hand, as a god is;
Medeia, who ordained her marriage even in her father's
     despite,
savior of the ship Argo and her seamen;

the show of valor they made
long ago, before the Dardanian battlements,
on either side hewing to the end of strife;
these with the beloved sons of Atreus,
striving to win back Helen; those guarding her
amain. The Danaans shook before Glaukos, who came from
     Lykia. Before them
he vaunted that in the city of Peirene the power abode
and the deep domain and the house of Bellerophon, his fore-
     father,

who beside the Springs, striving to break the serpent Gorgon's
     child,
Pegasos, endured much hardship
until the maiden Pallas gave him
the bridle gold-covered. Out of dream
there was waking, and she spoke: "Do you sleep, king descended
     of Aiolos?
Behold, take this magic for the horse
and dedicate to the father who tames
beasts, a shining bull in sacrifice."

To his dream in darkness
the girl of the black shield seemed to speak
such things, and he sprang upright on his feet.

Gathering up the strange thing that lay beside him,
he sought out, delighted, the prophet in the land
and showed Koiranides all the ending of the matter, how he
    had slept
that night, at his behest, by the goddesses' altar. How the very
    child
of Zeus of the thunder-spear had given into
his hands the conquering gold.
The seer bade him obey
in speed the dream; and, when he had immolated
a bull to him who grips the earth in his wide strength,
to found straightway an altar of Athene of the horses.
God's power makes light possession of things beyond oath
    or hope.
Strong Bellerophon, pondering, caught
with the quiet device drawn to the jaw

the winged horse. Riding, he made weapon play in full
    armor of bronze.
So mounted, out of the cold gulfs
of the high air forlorn, he smote
the archered host of women, the Amazons;
and the Chimaira, breathing flame; and the Solymoi, and
    slew them.
On his fate at the last I will keep silence.
But to Pegasos were given on Olympos
the lordly managers of Zeus.

It becomes me not, spinning
the shaft's straight cast beside the mark, to speed
too many bolts from my hand's strength.
For I came fain helper to the Muses
on their thrones of shining, and to the Oligaithidai.
In brief word I will illumine their assembled success at Isthmos
    and Nemea; and the lordly
herald's sworn glad cry of truth will bear witness
they conquered sixty times in these places.

It has beseemed me before this
to speak of all they have done at Olympia.
Things yet to come shall be told clear as they befall.

Even now I am full of hope, but the end lies
in God. If only his natal divinity walk far,
we shall bring this duty to Zeus and Ares. Under the brow
    of Parnassos there were six
wins; as many at Argos, in Thebes; the king's altar of Zeus
Lykaios will bespeak as many gained in Arkadian gorges;

Pellana and Sikyon, Megara, the fenced grove of the Aiakidai,
Eleusis and Marathon the shining,
the rich cities in their loveliness under the crest of Aitna,
Euboia also; stir with your hand
all Hellas, they will rise to outpass the eyes' vision.
Let me swim out with light feet.
Zeus accomplisher, to all grant grave restraint
and attainment of sweet delight.

Pythia 2]

Great city, O Syracuse, precinct of Ares
that haunts the deeps of battle; nurse divine of horses and
    men that fight in iron,
from shining Thebes I come, bringing you
this melody, message of the chariot course that shakes the
    earth,
wherein Hieron in success of his horses
has bound in garlands that gleam far Ortygia,
site of the river-Artemis, whose aid stood not afar
when, with gentling hands, he guided the intricate reins of
    his young mares.

For the lady of arrows, in both hands bestowing,
and Hermes of the contests set the gleam of glory on his
    head, when to the polished car
and the harness he yokes temperate strength
of horses, invoking also the god of wide strength who shakes
    the trident.
For other kings aforetime other men also have given
the high sound of song, requital of their achievement.
Incessantly the Kyprian songs are of Kinyras,

beloved of the gold-haired god, Apollo, in fulness of heart,

and sacred in the favor of Aphrodite. Grace of friendship
in courteous gaze comes also to bless in requital deeds done.
Son of Deinomenes,
the West Lokrian maiden
at her doors speaks of you; and her gaze, by grace of your
     might,
goes now untroubled, after the hopeless struggles of wartime.
It is by gods' work that they say Ixion,
fixed on his winged wheel, spun in a circle,
cries aloud this message to mortals:
To your benefactor return ever with kind dealing rendered.

He learned that lesson well. By favor of the sons of Kronos,
he was given a life of delight but could not abide blessedness
     long; in his delirious heart
he loved Hera, dedicated to the high couch
of Zeus. That outrage hurled him into conspicuous
ruin. He was a man and endured beyond all others
distress full merited. Two sins flowered
to pain in his heart: a hero, he first
infected the mortal breed with kindred bloodshed, not without
     treachery;

also, in the great secret chambers of Zeus he strove to ravish
the Queen. A man should look at himself and learn well his
     own stature.
The coupling unnatural brought accumulation of evil
on him, even in success; it was a cloud he lay with,
and he in his delusion was given the false loveliness.
A phantom went in the guise of that highest daughter
of Uranian Kronos; a deceit visited upon him
by the hands of Zeus, a fair evil thing. Zeus likewise is wrought
     the crucifixion on the wheel,

Ixion's bane; and, spinning there, limbs fast
to the ineluctable circle, he makes the message a thing that
     all may know.
But she, graceless, spawned
a child of violence.

There was none like her, nor her son; no honor was his
    portion in the usage of god or man.
Nursing him, she named him Kentauros, and he coupled
with the Magnesian mares on the spurs of Pelion;
and a weird breed was engendered
in the favor of either parent:
the mare's likeness in the parts below, and the manlike father
    above.
It is God that accomplishes all term to hopes,
God, who overtakes the flying eagle, outpasses the dolphin
in the sea; who bends under his strength the man with
    thoughts too high,
while to others he gives honor that ages not. My necessity
is to escape the teeth of reproach for excessive blame.
Standing afar, I saw Archilochos the scold,
laboring helpless and fattening on his own cantankerous
hate, naught else; to be rich, with fortune of wisdom also, is
    the highest destiny.

You, in freedom of your heart, can make this plain,
you, that are prince of garlanded streets in their multitude
    and lord of the host. If any man
claims that, for possession of goods and high honor,
some other of those that lived of old in Hellas has overpassed
    you,
that man with loose heart wrestles emptiness.
I shall mount the wreathed ship to speak aloud
your praise. Your youth is staunch in valor to endure
stark battle; whence I say you have found glory that knows
    no measure

in striving against those who rode horses in battle
and the fighting footranks also. But your elder counsels
set me free to speak forth
in your praise, a word without peril
against any man's contention. Hail, then! This melody is
    sent you
like Phoenician ware over the gray sea.
Be fain to behold and welcome the Kastor-chant
on Aiolian strings, by grace
of the seven-stringed lyre.

Learn what you are and be such. See, the ape to children is a
    pretty thing, pretty indeed.
But Rhadamanthys has done well, to reap
a blameless harvest of the mind, without joy of deception at
    the inward heart,
such as ever befalls a man by action of those who whisper.
To both sides the speakers of slander are an evil beyond
    control.
They are minded like foxes, utterly.
But what good then befalls the greedy fox of his slyness?
As when the rest of the gear founders in the sea's
depth, I, the cork at the net, ride not drenched in the brine.

But the treacherous citizen has no force to cast a word of
    power
among the great. Still, fawning on all, he threads his way
    too far.
His confidence is not mine. Be it mine to love my friend,
but against the enemy, hateful indeed, turn with the wolf's
    slash,
treading, as the time may need, my devious path.
Yet in each state the candid man will go far,
when tyrants rule, or the swirling rabble,
or the wise keep the city in ward. Yet, it is ill to strive with
    God

who upholds now one faction, now to the other gives
great glory. Even success softens not the heart
of the envious. Straining
as it were at a pegged line
too far, they stab the spike to rend their own hearts
before attainment of the desire in their minds.
To bear lightly the neck's yoke
brings strength; but kicking
against the goads is the way
of failure. Be it mine that good men will to have me among
    their friends.

Nemea 3]

Lady and Muse, our mother, I entreat you,
in the holy Nemean month, come to the city thronged with
    strangers,
the Dorian island, Aigina; for beside
the waters of Asopos the craftsmen of lovely
choral songs, the young men, await your voice.
Every achievement has a different thirst,
but victory in games longs beyond all for singing
and the skill to glorify garlands and strength proved.

Of such inspiration grant me abundance.
Daughter to the cloudy king of the sky, begin
his stately song. And I shall elaborate it
with voice and in the lyre's strain. Gracious will be the work
of glorification of the land where the Myrmidons lived
in old time, whose legendary assembling place
Aristokleides, under your destiny, lady, stained not
with reproach, weakening under the circling strength

of contestants in the pankration. To heal
the painful blows taken in the deep Nemean plain, he brings
    home the splendor of victory.
Beautiful as he is and with work not shaming his stature,
this son of Aristophanes has come to the uttermost manliness.
    So. Further
you cannot go lightly in the impassable sea, beyond the pillars
    of Herakles,

which the heroic god set down, to mark in fame
journey's end. He broke monsters that rose
up out of the sea, tested the current of every
shoal, to where the end was and the turning-point for home.
He explored the land. My heart, to what alien headland
do you fetch my course along shore?
I say we must bring music to Aiakos and his race.
For highest justice attends the saying: *Praise the good.*

Passions for things alien are not best for a man to have.

Seek nearer home. You have found glory that lends occasion
for fair speech. Among men of old, Peleus
rejoiced in valor, who cut the spear that surpassed all others,
who took Iolkos alone, with no host behind him,
who caught Thetis of the sea in his grasp.
And Telamon of the vast strength
stood by Iolaos to sack Laomedon's city,

and went with him against the Amazons strong in their
    brazen bows,
and the terror that breaks men did not stop the force in his
    heart.
The splendor running in the blood has much weight.
A man can learn and yet see darkly, blow one way, then
    another, walking ever
on uncertain feet, his mind unfinished and fed with scraps
    of a thousand virtues.

But tawny Achilles lived in the house of Philyra
and as yet a boy did great things; in his hands hefting
javelins scantly tipped with iron, wind-light,
he wreaked death in bloody combat upon wild lions;
he struck down boars, and to the house of the Kronian
centaur dragged the gasping carcasses,
at six years, and thereafter for the rest of his time;
and amazed Artemis and stern Athene,

killing deer without hounds or treacherous nets,
for he ran them down in his speed. I tell these tales
out of old time. Under his stone-caverned roof, Chiron
trained Jason, the deeply wise, and thereafter Asklepios,
teaching the gentle-handed way of healing.
He brought to pass the marriage
of Nereus' daughter of the shining breasts, and nursed
her magnificent son, waxing his heart to all things becoming,

so that, carried on the run of the sea winds, beneath Troy
he might stand up against the clamor and shock of spears of
    Lykians, Phrygians,
Dardanians, and come to handstrokes with hard-fighting

Aithiopians; and fix it in his heart that never more might come
   home
their lord, Helenos' valiant kinsman, Memnon.

Thence the shining of the Aiakidai has cast its light afar.
Their blood, Zeus, is yours, and yours the victory that the song
   peals out
in the voices of young singers, a delight for men that live near.
Their music shines forth with Aristokleides also,
who has brought this island again into men's speech of praise,
and likewise by his splendid ambitions the Thearion
of the Pythian god. The end shines through
in the testing of actions where excellence is shown,

as a boy among boys, a man among men, last
among the elders, each part that makes
our mortal life. Human destiny drives
four excellences, with urgency to think of the thing at hand.
This fails not here. Hail, friend. I send you this,
mixed of pale honey
and milk, and a liquid shining is on the mixture,
a draught of song rippled in Aiolian flutes,
late though it come. Among birds the eagle is swift.
Pondering his prey from afar, he plummets suddenly to blood
   the spoil in his claws.
Clamorous daws range the low spaces of the sky.
Aristokleides, by grace of Kleo throned on high, and your own
   will to victory,
from Nemea and Epidauros, from Megara also, the light has
   brightened about you.

4. The Search for Freedom and Responsible Government: Aeschylus and Herodotus

1. Aeschylus

*Aeschylus was the first great tragic poet. His life (525–456 B.C.)
spanned a crucial period in the history of Athens and of Greece. He
took part in the Persian Wars which won freedom from foreign domination for the Greeks. He was an adolescent when the Athenians
expelled the last of their tyrants and established the Constitution of
Cleisthenes, a moderate and responsible democracy. The following
selections illustrate a dominant theme in his work—the hatred of
tyranny.*

a. *The Tyranny of Aegisthus* (Agamemnon)*

In the last scene of the Agamemnon *the king is murdered and the throne usurped by the wife of Agamemnon, Clytemnestra and her paramour Aegisthus. The seizure of a government by coup d'état is analogous to the establishment of tyrannies in historical Greek states. Aeschylus' attitude towards tyranny is manifest in the closing lines of the play.*

Chorus:
  Aegisthus, we acquit you of insults to the dead.
  But since you claim that you alone laid the whole plot,
  And thus, though absent, took his blood upon your hands,
  I tell you plainly, your own life is forfeited;
  Justice will curse you, Argive hands will stone you dead.
Aegisthus:
  So, this is how you lecture, from the lower deck,
  The master on the bridge? Then you shall learn, though old,
  How harsh a thing is discipline, when reverend years
  Lack wisdom. Chains and the distress of hunger are
  A magic medicine, of great power to school the mind.
  Does not this sight bid you reflect? Then do not kick
  Against the goad, lest you should stumble, and be hurt.
Chorus:
  You woman! While he went to fight, you stayed at home;
  Seduced his wife meanwhile; and then, against a man
  Who led an army, *you* could scheme this murder! Pah!
Aegisthus:
  You still use words that have in them the seed of tears.
  Your voice is most unlike the voice of Orpheus: he
  Bound all who heard him with delight; your childish yelps
  Annoy us, and will fasten bonds on you yourselves.
  With hard control you will prove more amenable.
Chorus:
  Control! Are we to see *you* king of Argos—you,
  Who, after plotting the king's murder, did not dare
  To lift the sword yourself?

  * Translated by Philip Vellacott in *The Oresteian Trilogy* (Baltimore, 1956), pp. 98–100. By permission of Penguin Books, Ltd.

Aegisthus:

    To lure him to the trap
    Was plainly woman's work; I, an old enemy,
    Was suspect. Now, helped by his wealth, I will attempt
    To rule in Argos. The refractory shall not
    Be fed fat like show-horses, but shall feel the yoke—
    A heavy one. Hunger and darkness joined will soon
    Soften resistance.

Chorus:

    Then, if you're so bold, why not
    Yourself with your own hands plunder your enemy?
    Instead, a woman, whose life makes this earth unclean
    And flouts the gods of Argos, helped you murder him!
    Oh, does Orestes live? Kind Fortune, bring him home,
    To set against these two his sword invincible!

Aegisthus:

    Then, since your treason's militant, you shall soon learn
    That it is foolish to insult authority.
    Ready, there! Forward, guards! [*armed soldiers rush in*]
    Here's work for you. Each man
    Handle his sword.

Chorus:

    Our swords are ready. We can die.

Aegisthus:

    'Die'! We accept the omen. Fortune hold the stakes!

Clytemnestra:

    Stop, stop, Aegisthus, dearest! No more violence!
    When this first harvest ripens we'll reap grief enough.
    Crime and despair are fed to bursting; let us not
    Plunge deeper still in blood. Elders, I beg of you,
    Yield in good time to Destiny; go home, before
    You come to harm; what we have done was fore-ordained.
    If our long agony finds here fulfilment, we,
    Twice gored by Fate's long talons, welcome it. I speak
    With woman's wisdom, if you choose to understand.

Aegisthus:

    Then are these gross-tongued men to aim their pointed gibes
    At random, and bluff out the fate they've richly earned?

Chorus:

    You'll find no Argive grovel at a blackguard's feet.

Aegisthus:

    Enough! Some later day I'll settle scores with you.

Chorus:
  Not if Fate sets Orestes on the Argos road.
Aegisthus:
  For men in exile hopes are meat and drink; I know.
Chorus:
  Rule on, grow fat defiling Justice—while you can.
Aegisthus:
  You are a fool; in time you'll pay me for those words.
Chorus:
  Brag blindly on—a cock that struts before his hen!
  *During these last lines the Chorus have gone out two by two,
  the last man vanishing with the last insult, leaving Clytemnestra
  and Aegisthus alone.*
Clytemnestra:
  Pay no heed to this currish howling. You and I,
  Joint rulers, will enforce due reverence for our throne.

b. *The Tyranny of Zeus* (Prometheus Bound)*

CHARACTERS

Might

Violence (muta persona)

Hephaestus

Prometheus

Oceanos

Io

Hermes

Chorus of daughters of Oceanos

* Translated by David Grene in *Aeschylus: Four Tragedies* (Chicago, 1950), pp. 139–154. By permission of the University of Chicago Press.

PROMETHEUS BOUND]

SCENE:

A bare and desolate crag in the Caucasus. Enter Might and Violence, demons, servants of Zeus, and Hephaestus, the smith.

Might:

This is the world's limit that we have come to; this is the Scythian country, an untrodden desolation. Hephaestus, it is you that must heed the commands the Father laid upon you to nail this malefactor to the high craggy rocks in fetters unbreakable of adamantine chain. For it was your flower, the brightness of fire that devises all, that he stole and gave to mortal men; this is the sin for which he must pay the Gods the penalty—that he may learn to endure and like the sovereignty of Zeus and quit his man-loving disposition.

Hephaestus:

Might and Violence, in you the command of Zeus has its perfect fulfilment: in you there is nothing to stand in its way. But, for myself, I have not the heart to bind violently a God who is my kin here on this wintry cliff. Yet there is constraint upon me to have the heart for just that, for it is a dangerous thing to treat the Father's words lightly.

High-contriving Son of Themis of Straight Counsel: this is not of your will nor of mine; yet I shall nail you in bonds of indissoluble bronze on this crag far from men. Here you shall hear no voice of mortal; here you shall see no form of mortal. You shall be grilled by the sun's bright fire and change the fair bloom of your skin. You shall be glad when Night comes with her mantle of stars and hides the sun's light; but the sun shall scatter the hoar-frost again at dawn. Always the grievous burden of your torture will be there to wear you down; for he that shall cause it to cease has yet to be born.

Such is the reward you reap of your man-loving disposition. For you, a God, feared not the anger of the Gods, but gave honors to mortals beyond what was just. Wherefore you shall mount guard on this unlovely rock, upright, sleepless, not bending the knee. Many a groan and many a lamentation you shall utter, but they shall not serve you. For the mind of

Zeus is hard to soften with prayer, and every ruler is harsh whose rule is new.

Might:

Come, why are you holding back? Why are you pitying in vain? Why is it that you do not hate a God whom the Gods hate most of all? Why do you not hate him, since it was your honor that he betrayed to men?

Hephaestus:

Our kinship has strange power; that, and our life together.

Might:

Yes. But to turn a deaf ear to the Father's words—how can that be? Do you not fear that more?

Hephaestus:

You are always pitiless, always full of ruthlessness.

Might:

There is no good singing dirges over him. Do not labor uselessly at what helps not at all.

Hephaestus:

O handicraft of mine—that I deeply hate!

Might:

Why do you hate it? To speak simply, your craft is in no way the author of his present troubles.

Hephaestus:

Yet would another had had this craft allotted to him.

Might:

There is nothing without discomfort except the overlordship of the Gods. For only Zeus is free.

Hephaestus:

I know. I have no answer to this.

Might:

Hurry now. Throw the chain around him that the Father may not look upon your tarrying.

Hephaestus:

There are the fetters, there: you can see them.

Might:

Put them on his hands: strong, now with the hammer: strike. Nail him to the rock.

Hephaestus:

It is being done now. I am not idling at my work.

Might:

Hammer it more; put in the wedge; leave it loose nowhere.

He's a cunning fellow at finding a way even out of hopeless difficulties.

Hephaestus:

Look now, his arm is fixed immovably!

Might:

Nail the other safe, that he may learn, for all his cleverness, that he is duller witted than Zeus.

Hephaestus:

No one, save Prometheus, can justly blame me.

Might:

Drive the obstinate jaw of the adamantine wedge right through his breast: drive it hard.

Hephaestus:

Alas, Prometheus, I groan for your sufferings.

Might:

Are you pitying again? Are you groaning for the enemies of Zeus? Have a care, lest some day you may be pitying yourself.

Hephaestus:

You see a sight that hurts the eye.

Might:

I see this rascal getting his deserts. Throw the girth around his sides.

Hephaestus:

I am forced to do this; do not keep urging me.

Might:

Yes, I will urge you, and hound you on as well. Get below now, and hoop his legs in strongly.

Hephaestus:

There now, the task is done. It has not taken long.

Might:

Hammer the piercing fetters with all your power, for the Overseer of our work is severe.

Hephaestus:

Your looks and the refrain of your tongue are alike.

Might:

You can be softhearted. But do not blame my stubbornness and harshness of temper.

Hephaestus:

Let us go. He has the harness on his limbs.

Might (to Prometheus):

Now, play the insolent; now, plunder the Gods' privileges and

give them to creatures of a day. What drop of your sufferings
can mortals spare you? The Gods named you wrongly when
they called you Forethought; you yourself *need* Forethought
to extricate yourself from this contrivance.

(*Prometheus is left alone on the rock.*)

Prometheus:

Bright light, swift-winged winds, springs of the rivers, numberless
laughter of the sea's waves, earth, mother of all, and the all-
seeing circle of the sun: I call upon you to see what I, a God,
suffer at the hands of Gods—
see with what kind of torture
worn down I shall wrestle ten thousand
years of time—
such is the despiteful bond that the Prince
has devised against me, the new Prince
of the Blessed Ones. Oh woe is me!
I groan for the present sorrow,
I groan for the sorrow to come, I groan
questioning when there shall come a time
when He shall ordain a limit to my sufferings.
What am I saying? I have known all before,
all that shall be, and clearly known; to me,
nothing that hurts shall come with a new face.
So must I bear, as lightly as I can,
the destiny that fate has given me;
for I know well against necessity,
against its strength, no one can fight and win.

I cannot speak about my fortune, cannot
hold my tongue either. It was mortal man
to whom I gave great privileges and
for that was yoked in this unyielding harness.
I hunted out the secret spring of fire,
that filled the narthex stem, which when revealed
became the teacher of each craft to men,
a great resource. This is the sin committed
for which I stand accountant, and I pay
nailed in my chains under the open sky.

Ah! Ah!

What sound, what sightless smell approaches me,
God sent, or mortal, or mingled?
Has it come to earth's end
to look on my sufferings,
or what does it wish?
You see me a wretched God in chains,
the enemy of Zeus, hated of all
the Gods that enter Zeus's palace hall,
because of my excessive love for Man.
What is that? The rustle
of birds' wings near? The air whispers
with the gentle strokes of wings.
Everything that comes toward me is occasion for fear.
(*The Chorus, composed of the daughters of Oceanos, enters,
the members wearing some formalized representation of
wings, so that their general appearance is birdlike.*)

Chorus:

Fear not: this is a company of friends
that comes to your mountain with swift
rivalry of wings.
Hardly have we persuaded our Father's
mind, and the quick-bearing winds
speeded us hither. The sound
of stroke of bronze rang through our cavern
in its depths and it shook from us
shamefaced modesty; unsandaled
we have hastened on our chariot of wings.

Prometheus:

Alas, children of teeming Tethys and of him
who encircles all the world with stream unsleeping,
Father Ocean,
look, see with what chains
I am nailed on the craggy heights
of this gully to keep a watch
that none would envy me.

Chorus:

I see, Prometheus: and a mist of fear and tears
besets my eyes as I see your form
wasting away on these cliffs
in adamantine bonds of bitter shame.
For new are the steersmen that rule Olympus:

and new are the customs by which Zeus rules,
customs that have no law to them,
but what was great before he brings to nothingness.
Prometheus:
Would that he had hurled me
underneath the earth and underneath
the House of Hades, host to the dead—
yes, down to limitless Tartarus,
yes, though he bound me cruelly
in chains unbreakable,
so neither God nor any other being
might have found joy in gloating over me.
Now as I hang, the plaything of the winds,
my enemies can laugh at what I suffer.
Chorus:
Who of the Gods is so hard of heart
that he finds joy in this?
Who is that that does not feel
sorrow answering your pain—
save only Zeus? For he malignantly,
always cherishing a mind
that bends not, has subdued the breed
of Uranos, nor shall he cease
until he satisfies his heart,
or someone take the rule from him—that hard-to-capture rule—
by some device of subtlety.
Prometheus:
Yes, there shall come a day for me
when he shall need me, me that now am tortured
in bonds and fetters—he shall need me then,
this president of the Blessed—
to show the new plot whereby he may be spoiled
of his throne and his power.
Then not with honeyed tongues
of persuasion shall he enchant me;
he shall not cow me with his threats
to tell him what I know,
until he free me from my cruel chains
and pay me recompense for what I suffer.
Chorus:
You are stout of heart, unyielding

to the bitterness of pain.
You are free of tongue, too free.
It is my mind that piercing fear has fluttered;
your misfortunes frighten me.
Where and when is it fated
to see you reach the term, to see you reach
the harbor free of trouble at the last?
A disposition none can win, a heart
that no persuasions soften—these are his,
the Son of Kronos.

Prometheus:

I know that he is savage: and his justice
a thing he keeps by his own standard: still
that will of his shall melt to softness yet
when he is broken in the way I know,
and though his temper now is oaken hard
it shall be softened: hastily he'll come
to meet my haste, to join in amity
and union with me—one day he shall come.

Chorus:

Reveal it all to us: tell us the story of what the charge was on
which Zeus caught you and punished you so cruelly with such
dishonor. Tell us, if the telling will not injure you in any way.

Prometheus:

To speak of this is bitterness. To keep silent
bitter no less; and every way is misery.

When first the Gods began their angry quarrel,
and God matched God in rising faction, some
eager to drive old Kronos from his throne
that Zeus might rule—the fools!—others again
earnest that Zeus might never be their king—
I then with the best counsel tried to win
the Titans, sons of Uranos and Earth,
but failed. They would have none of crafty schemes
and in their savage arrogance of spirit
thought they would lord it easily by force.
But she that was my mother, Themis, Earth—
she is but one although her names are many—
had prophesied to me how it should be,
even how the fates decreed it: and she said

the fates allowed the conquerors to conquer
the fates allowed the conquerors to conquor
but by guile only": This is what I told them,
but they would not vouchsafe a glance at me.
Then with those things before me it seemed best
to take my mother and join Zeus's side:
he was as willing as we were:
thanks to my plans the dark receptacle
of Tartarus conceals the ancient Kronos,
him and his allies. These were the services
I rendered to this tyrant and these pains
the payment he has given me in requital.
This is a sickness rooted and inherent
in the nature of a tyranny:
that he that holds it does not trust his friends.

But you have asked on what particular
charge he now tortures me: this I will tell you.
As soon as he ascended to the throne
that was his father's, straightway he assigned
to the several Gods their several privileges
and portioned out the power, but to the unhappy
breed of mankind he gave no heed, intending
to blot the race out and create a new.
Against these plans none stood save I: I dared.
I rescued men from shattering destruction
that would have carried them to Hades' house;
and therefore I am tortured on this rock,
a bitterness to suffer, and a pain
to pitiful eyes. I gave to mortal man
a precedence over myself in pity: I
can win no pity: pitiless is he
that thus chastises me, a spectacle
bringing dishonor on the name of Zeus.

Chorus:

He would be iron-minded and made of stone, indeed, Prometheus, who did not sympathize with your sufferings. I would not have chosen to see them, and now that I see, my heart is pained.

Prometheus:

Yes, to my friends I am pitiable to see.

Chorus:
Did you perhaps go further than you have told us?
Prometheus:
I caused mortals to cease foreseeing doom.
Chorus:
What cure did you provide them with against that sickness?
Prometheus:
I placed in them blind hopes.
Chorus:
That was a great gift you gave to men.
Prometheus:
Besides this, I gave them fire.
Chorus:
And do creatures of a day now possess bright-faced fire?
Prometheus:
Yes, and from it they shall learn many crafts.
Chorus:
Then these are the charges on which—
Prometheus:
Zeus tortures me and gives me no respite.
Chorus:
Is there no limit set for your pain?
Prometheus:
None save when it shall seem good to Zeus.
Chorus:
How will it ever seem good to him? What hope is there? Do
you not see how you have erred? It is not pleasure for me to
say that you have erred, and for you it is a pain to hear. But
let us speak no more of all this and do you seek some means of
deliverance from your trials.
Prometheus:
It is an easy thing for one whose foot
is on the outside of calamity
to give advice and to rebuke the sufferer.
I have known all that you have said: I knew,
I knew when I transgressed nor will deny it.
In helping man I brought my troubles on me;
But yet I did not think that with such tortures
I should be wasted on these airy cliffs,
this lonely mountain top, with no one near.
But do not sorrow for my present suffering;

alight on earth and hear what is to come
that you may know the whole complete: I beg you
alight and join your sorrow with mine: misfortune
wandering the same track lights now upon one
and now upon another.

Chorus:

Willing our ears,
that hear you cry to them, Prometheus,
now with light foot I leave the rushing car
and sky, the holy path of birds, and light
upon this jutting rock: I long
to hear your story to the end.

(*Enter Oceanos, riding on a hippocamp, or sea-monster.*)

Oceanos:

I come
on a long journey, speeding past the boundaries,
to visit you, Prometheus: with the mind
alone, no bridle needed, I direct
my swift-winged bird; my heart is sore
for your misfortunes; you know that. I think
that it is kinship makes me feel them so.
Besides, apart from kinship, there is no one
I hold in higher estimation: that
you soon shall know and know beside that in me
there is no mere word-kindness: tell me
how I can help you, and you will never say
that you have any friend more loyal to you
than Oceanos.

Prometheus:

What do I see? Have you, too, come to gape
in wonder at this great display, my torture?
How did you have the courage to come here
to this land, Iron-Mother, leaving the stream
called after you and the rock-roofed, self-established
caverns? Was it to feast your eyes upon
the spectacle of my suffering and join
in pity for my pain? Now look and see
the sight, this friend of Zeus, that helped set up
his tyranny and see what agonies
twist me, by his instructions!

Oceanos:

    Yes, I see,
Prometheus, and I want, indeed I do,
to advise you for the best, for all your cleverness.
Know yourself and reform your ways to new ways,
for new is he that rules among the Gods.
But if you throw about such angry words,
words that are whetted swords, soon Zeus will hear you,
even though his seat in glory is far removed,
and then your present multitude of pains
will seem like child's play. My poor friend, give up
this angry mood of yours and look for means
of getting yourself free of trouble. Maybe
what I say seems to you both old and commonplace;
but this is what you pay, Prometheus, for
that tongue of yours which talked so high and haughty:
you are not yet humble, still you do not yield
to your misfortunes, and you wish, indeed,
to add some more to them; now, if you follow
me as a schoolmaster you will not kick
against the pricks, seeing that he, the King,
that rules alone, is harsh and sends accounts
to no one's audit for the deeds he does.
Now I will go and try if I can free you:
do you be quiet, do not talk so much.
Since your mind is so subtle, don't you know
that a vain tongue is subject to correction?

Prometheus:

    I envy you, that you stand clear of blame,
yet shared and dared in everything with me!
Now let me be, and have no care for me.
Do what you will, Him you will not persuade;
He is not easily won over: look,
take care lest coming here to me should hurt you.

Oceanos:

    You are by nature better at advising
others than yourself. I take my cue
from deeds, not words. Do not withhold me now
when I am eager to go to Zeus. I'm sure,
I'm sure that he will grant this favor to me,
to free you from your chains.

Prometheus:

> I thank you and will never cease; for loyalty
> is not what you are wanting in. Don't trouble,
> for you will trouble to no purpose, and no help
> to me—if it so be you want to trouble.
> No, rest yourself, keep away from this thing;
> because I am unlucky I would not,
> for that, have everyone unlucky too.
> No, for my heart is sore already when
> I think about my brothers' fortunes—Atlas,
> who stands to westward of the world, supporting
> the pillar of earth and heaven on his shoulders,
> a load that suits no shoulders; and the earthborn
> dweller in caves Cilician, whom I saw
> and pitied, hundred-headed, dreadful monster,
> fierce Typho, conquered and brought low by force.
> Once against all the Gods he stood, opposing,
> hissing out terror from his grim jaws; his eyes
> flashed gorgon glaring lightning as he thought
> to sack the sovereign tyranny of Zeus;
> but upon him came the unsleeping bolt
> of Zeus, the lightning-breathing flame, down rushing,
> which cast him from his high aspiring boast.
> Struck to the heart, his strength was blasted dead
> and burnt to ashes; now a sprawling mass
> useless he lies, hard by the narrow seaway
> pressed down beneath the roots of Aetna: high
> above him on the mountain peak the smith
> Hephaestus works at the anvil. Yet one day
> there shall burst out rivers of fire, devouring
> with savage jaws the fertile, level plains
> of Sicily of the fair fruits; such boiling wrath
> with weapons of fire-breathing surf, a fiery
> unapproachable torrent, shall Typho vomit,
> though Zeus's lightning left him but a cinder.
> But all of this you know: you do not need me
> to be your schoolmaster: reassure yourself
> as you know how: this cup I shall drain myself
> till the high mind of Zeus shall cease from anger.

Oceanos:

Do you not know, Prometheus, that words are healers of the sick temper?

Prometheus:

Yes, if in season due one soothes the heart with them, not tries violently to reduce the swelling anger.

Oceanos:

Tell me, what danger do you see for me in loyalty to you, and courage therein?

Prometheus:

I see only useless effort and a silly good nature.

Oceanos:

Suffer me then to be sick of this sickness, for it is a profitable thing, if one is wise, to seem foolish.

Prometheus:

This shall seem to be my fault.

Oceanos:

Clearly your words send me home again.

Prometheus:

Yes, lest your doings for me bring you enmity.

Oceanos:

His enmity, who newly sits on the all-powerful throne?

Prometheus:

His is a heart you should beware of vexing.

Oceanos:

Your own misfortune will be my teacher, Prometheus.

Prometheus:

Off with you, then! Begone! Keep your present mind.

Oceanos:

These words fall on very responsive ears. Already my four-legged bird is pawing the level track of Heaven with his wings, and he will be glad to bend the knee in his own stable.

Chorus:

STROPHE

I cry aloud, Prometheus, and lament your bitter fate,
my tender eyes are trickling tears:
their fountains wet my cheek.
This is a tyrant's deed; this is unlovely,
a thing done by a tyrant's private laws,
and with this thing Zeus shows his haughtiness
of temper toward the Gods that were of old.

c. The Victory of Freedom (The Persians)*

The following passage indicates Aeschylus' view of the significance of the Greek victory at Salamis.

Hear this accusing groan that rises now
From every Asian land laid bare of men:
    'Who led them forth, but Xerxes?
    Who sealed their death, but Xerxes?
Whose error sent our all to sail in ships,
    And lost it all, but Xerxes'?–
Son of Darius, the invincible
    Leader of Persian bowmen,
    Belov'd by all his people!

Landsmen and seamen both had put their trust
In hulks with canvas wings and sea-blue eyes;
    And ships from home conveyed them,
    And ships at last destroyed them–
Ships, handled by Ionians, beaked with death;
    The king himself escaping
    By weary winter journeys
With his bare life across the plains of Thrace.

And those who were the first to die,
Now, helpless, left behind perforce,
Are swept along the Cychrean shore.
Lift loud your griefs to heaven, and cry
With bitter anguish, vain remorse,
Till heart is weary, flesh is sore.
There, threshed by currents' eddying motion,
Unsightly lie those well-loved forms,
Now feasted on by voiceless swarms,

* Translated by Philip Vellacott in *Prometheus and Other Plays* (Baltimore, 1961), pp. 138–139. By permission of Penguin Books, Ltd.

The children of the untainted ocean.
Here, every house bewails a man,
And parents, childless now, lament
The troubles that the gods have sent
To end in grief their life's long span.

From east to west the Asian race
No more will own our Persian sway,
Nor on the king's compulsion pay
Tribute, nor bow to earth their face
In homage; for the kingly power
Is lost and vanished from this hour.

Now fear no more shall bridle speech;
Uncurbed, the common tongue shall prate
Of freedom; for the yoke of State
Lies broken on the bloody beach
And fields of Salamis, which hide
The ruins of our Persian pride.

d. Responsible Government (The Suppliants)*

The Suppliants *tells the story of the conflict between the brothers Aegyptus and Danaus. The fifty sons of Aegyptus wish to marry the fifty daughters of Danaus and are prepared to force their attention on the unwilling maidens. The girls flee to Argos, their ancestral home, and as suppliants seek sanctuary and protection from the king, Pelasgus. His problem is serious and involves dire consequences for his state. Aeschylus makes clear that although he is king Pelasgus is the responsible ruler of a free people and that he rules by persuasion, not force.*

Chorus:
  May Themis, friend of suppliants, daughter

* Translated by Philip Velacott in *Prometheus and Other Plays* (Baltimore, 1901), pp. 65–66, 72–75. By permission of Penguin Books, Ltd.

Of Zeus who gives to each his due,
See that our flight be harmless.
Old in knowledge, learn from the later born:
If you respect the suppliant,
The sacrifice you pay will be the best
That a man of pure life can offer
On the gracious altars of the gods.

King:

It is not *my* house at whose hearth you sit; and if
The Argive State stands liable to guilt herein,
The people of Argos must together work its cure.
Therefore I'll undertake no pledge till I have shared
This issue in full council with my citizens.

Chorus:

You are the State, *you* are the people.
Ruler unquestioned, you control
The altar that is your country's hearth;
You fear no vote; by your mere nod
You, monarch on one throne, decide all issues:
Therefore, guard against guilt.

King:

Guilt fall upon my enemies. Yet I do not know
How without harm I can assist you; and again,
To ignore such an appeal shows an ungracious heart.
What can I do? Where turn? I fear either to act,
Or not to act, and so let events take their own course.

Chorus:

Beware the watchful eye of Heaven
That looks on mortal grief, and sees
When men in vain sit at their neighbour's hearth,
Denied their lawful just redress.
The anger of Zeus for a suppliant scorned
Remains, and is not softened
By tears of the man on whom it falls.

King:

If by your country's laws the sons of Aegyptus *are*
Your masters, since they claim to be your next of kin,
Who could oppose their plea? By your own laws you must
Be tried, and prove these men have no right over you.

Chorus:

Right or no right, I will not be

Man's chattel won by violence.
I'll stretch my flight from this cruel arrogant rape
Far as the stars stretch over earth.
Choose Justice then for your ally, and give
That holy judgment the gods approve.

King:

To judge is no easy matter; do not choose me for judge.
I have said already, though I am sole king, I cannot
Act in your case without my people. May my citizens
Never, if some mischance befell us, say to me,
'You destroyed Argos for the sake of foreigners.'

Chorus:

Great Zeus, their ancestor and ours,
Sets up his finely-balanced scale,
Looks on both sides, and truly deals
Evil to the evil, blessings to the good.
Since all's now poised impartially,
Why fear to perform justice in my cause?

King:

To save us all, our need is for deep pondering;
An eye to search, as divers search the ocean bed,
Clear-seeing, not distracted, that this dilemma may
Achieve an end happy and harmless; first, for Argos
And for myself, that war and plunder may not strike
Us in reprisal; and that we may not surrender
You who are suppliants at the altars of our gods,
And so bring Vengeance, that destroying spirit, to plague
Our lives, who never, even in death, lets go his prey.
Is it not clear we must think deeply, or we perish?

Chorus:

Think! And befriend us
Justly, religiously;
Do not betray the fugitives
Whom godless men drove from their homes!
Do not see me dragged
Away from this shrine of many gods,
O King, all-powerful in Argos!

* * *

Re-enter Danaus.

Danaus:

    Good news, my children! Argos in full assembly has
    Reached absolute decisions favourable to us.

Chorus:

    Welcome, my father, dearest of all messengers!
    Tell us this one thing—what does their decision say?
    What action is laid down by the prevailing vote?

Danaus:

    The Argives have decided—and without dispute,
    With one clear voice that made my old heart young again;
    Why, the air was thick with the right hands of the whole city—
    And this was their decision: we are to live in Argos
    As free, inviolate guests, promised security
    From mortal malice. Neither Argive nor foreigner
    Can touch us. Should our enemies use force, the man
    Who, being a citizen, does not come to our help
    Will suffer loss of civic rights and banishment.
    So eloquently King Pelasgus spoke for us,
    Warning his people thus: 'Do not in future time
    Feed full the vengeance of the god of suppliants.
    Here is a twofold claim, of guests and citizens;
    If we reject them, there will rise to threaten us
    Twofold pollution, like a fiend insatiable
    Gorging on ruin.' At this, impatient of delay,
    The Argives raised their hands and voted as I have said.
    The king used every subtle and persuasive turn
    Of the orator's art: Zeus brought the issue to success.

Chorus:

    Come, now, let us recite
    A prayer for the men of Argos,
    That good may reward the good they have done to us.
    May Zeus, the stranger's friend,
    Look upon and fulfil the grateful vows
    Offered by strangers for their hosts,
    That our words may attain the desired end.

* * *

    Let the council-seats of their old men
    Be graced with venerable beards;

Thus let their city be well governed,
While they pay due reverence to Zeus,
And above all to Zeus the God of Strangers,
Who establishes Right by immemorial law.

* * *

May their council, holding lifelong office,
Watch with wise forethought and deliberation
The people, whose power rules the State.
To foreigners in their city may they grant
Lawful appeal and honouring of contracts,
Before the sword is drawn or harm inflicted.

And may they always honour
The gods who keep their country
With the ritual they learnt from their fathers on their own soil,
With bearing of laurel boughs and sacrifice of oxen.
For the law of reverence to parents—
This duty is written third
In the laws of Justice, whom all must honour.

e. Persuasion and Moderation

The last play of the Oresteia *trilogy tells of Orestes, who has
killed his mother, Clytemnestra, to avenge the murder of his
father. He seeks justice in Athens, pursued by the chorus of
Furies. There he is tried by a new tribunal, the Areopagus,
established by Athena. Aeschylus' account of its nature and
purposes demonstrates his belief in the positive moral role of a
polis such as that of Cleisthenes' Athens. The jury produces a
tie vote which is broken by Athena in favor of Orestes. The
enraged furies are tamed by Persuasion, the weapon of democracy, and converted into the Eumenides, the "well-dis-
posed."*

* Translated by Philip Vellacott in *The Oresteian Trilogy* (Baltimore,
1956), pp. 170–171, 176–180. By permission of Penguin Books, Ltd.

Athene:

    Citizens of Athens! As you now try this first case
    Of bloodshed, hear the constitution of your court.
    From this day forward this judicial council shall
    For Aegeus' race hear every trial of homicide.
    Here shall be their perpetual seat, on Ares' Hill.
    Here, when the Amazon army came to take revenge
    On Theseus, they set up their camp, and fortified
    This place with walls and towers as a new fortress-town
    To attack the old, and sacrifice to Ares; whence
    This rock is named Areopagus. Here, day and night,
    Shall Awe, and Fear, Awe's brother, check my citizens
    From all misdoing, while they keep my laws unchanged
    If you befoul a shining spring with an impure
    And muddy dribble, you will come in vain to drink.
    So, do not taint pure laws with new expediency.
    Guard well and reverence that form of government
    Which will eschew alike licence and slavery;
    And from your polity do not wholly banish fear.
    For what man living, freed from fear, will still be just
    Hold fast such upright fear of the law's sanctity,
    And you will have a bulwark of your city's strength,
    A rampart round your soil, such as no other race
    Possesses between Scythia and the Peloponnese.
    I here establish you a court inviolable,
    Holy, and quick to anger, keeping faithful watch
    That men may sleep in peace.

* * *

Athene:

               Then, goddesses, I offer you
    A home in Athens, where the gods most love to live,
    Where gifts and honours shall deserve your kind good-will.

Chorus:

    O shame and grief, that such a fate
    should fall to me, whose wisdom grew
    Within me when the world was new!
    Must I accept, beneath the ground,
    A nameless and abhorred estate?
    O ancient Earth, see my disgrace!
    While anguish runs through flesh and bone

My breathless rage breaks every bound.
O Night, my mother, hear me groan,
Outwitted, scorned and overthrown
By new gods from my ancient place!
Athene:
I will not weary in offering you friendly words.
You shall not say that you, an elder deity,
Were by a younger Power and by these citizens
Driven dishonoured, homeless, from this land. But if
Holy Persuasion bids your heart respect my words
And welcome soothing eloquence, then stay with us!
If you refuse, be sure you will have no just cause
To turn with spleen and malice on our peopled streets.
A great and lasting heritage awaits you here;
Thus honour is assured and justice satisfied.
Chorus:
What place, divine Athene, do you offer me?
Athene:
One free from all regret. Acceptance lies with you.
Chorus:
Say I accept it: what prerogatives are mine?
Athene:
Such that no house can thrive without your favour sought.
Chorus:
You promise to secure for me this place and power?
Athene:
I will protect and prosper all who reverence you.
Chorus:
Your word is pledged for ever?
Athene:
Do I need to promise
What I will not perform?
Chorus:
                    My anger melts. Your words
   Move me.
Athene:
In Athens you are in the midst of friends.
Chorus:
What blessings would you have me call upon this land?
Athene:
Such as bring victory untroubled with regret;
Blessing from earth and sea and sky; blessing that breathes

In wind and sunlight through the land; that beast and field
Enrich my people with unwearied fruitfulness,
And armies of brave sons be born to guard their peace.
Sternly weed out the impious, lest their rankness choke
The flower of goodness. I would not have just men's lives
Troubled with villainy. These blessings *you* must bring;
I will conduct their valiant arms to victory,
And make the name of Athens honoured through the world.

Chorus:
I will consent to share Athene's home,
To bless this fortress of the immortal Powers
    Which mighty Zeus and Ares
    Chose for their habitation,
The pride and glory of the gods of Greece,
    And guardian of their altars.
    This prayer I pray for Athens,
Pronounce this prophecy with kind intent:
Fortune shall load her land with healthful gifts
    From her rich earth engendered
    By the sun's burning brightness.

Athene:
I will do my part, and win
Blessing for my city's life,
Welcoming within our walls
These implacable and great
Goddesses. Their task it is
To dispose all mortal ways.
He who wins their enmity
Lives accurst, not knowing whence
Falls the wounding lash of life.
Secret guilt his father knew
Hails him to their judgement-seat,
Where, for all his loud exclaims,
Death, his angry enemy,
Silent grinds him into dust.

Chorus:
I have yet more to promise. No ill wind
Shall carry blight to make your fruit-trees fade;
    No bud-destroying canker
    Shall creep across your frontiers,
Nor sterile sickness threaten your supply.

May Pan give twin lambs to your thriving ewes
   In their expected season;
    And may the earth's rich produce
Honour the generous Powers with grateful gifts.
Athene:
   Guardians of our city's wall,
   Hear the blessings they will bring!
   Fate's Avengers wield a power
   Great alike in heaven and hell;
   And their purposes on earth
   They fulfil for all to see,
   Giving, after their deserts,
   Songs to some, to others pain
   In a prospect blind with tears.
Chorus:
   I pray that no untimely chance destroy
    Your young men in their pride;
   And let each lovely virgin, as a bride,
    Fulfil her life with joy.
   For all these gifts, you sovereign gods, we pray,
    And you, our sisters three,
    Dread Fates, whose just decree
   Chooses for every man his changeless way,
   You who in every household have your place,
    Whose visitations fall
    With just rebuke on all—
   Hear us, most honoured of the immortal race!
Athene:
   Now, for the love that you perform
   To this dear land, my heart is warm.
   Holy Persuasion too I bless,
   Who softly strove with harsh denial,
   Till Zeus the Pleader came to trial
   And crowned Persuasion with success.
   Now good shall strive with good; and we
   And they shall share the victory.
Chorus:
   Let civil war, insatiate of ill,
    Never in Athens rage;
   Let burning wrath, that murder must assuage,
    Never take arms to spill,

In this my heritage,
The blood of man till dust has drunk its fill.
   Let all together find
      Joy in each other;
And each both love and hate with the same mind
      As his blood-brother;
For this heals many hurts of humankind.

Athene:
These gracious words and promised deeds
Adorn the path where wisdom leads.
Great gain for Athens shall arise
From these grim forms and threatening eyes.
Then worship them with friendly heart,
For theirs is friendly. Let your State
Hold justice as her chiefest prize;
And land and city shall be great
And glorious in every part.

Chorus:
City, rejoice and sing,
Who, blest and flourishing
With wealth of field and street,
Wise in your hour, and dear
To the goddess you revere,
Sit by the judgement-seat
Of heaven's all-judging king,
Who guards and governs well
Those favoured ones who dwell
Under her virgin wing.

2.   Herodotus*

The historian of the Persian Wars lived in Athens during the Periclean period. His political views, however, are those of the generation of Aeschylus. The following passages show his respect for the polis, his hatred of tyranny, and his respect for freedom under law.

a. The Greek and Oriental Views of Happiness (1, 30–33)

On this account, as well as to see the world, Solon set out upon his travels, in the course of which he went to Egypt to the court of Amasis, and also came on a visit to Croesus at Sardis. Croesus received him as his guest, and lodged him in the royal palace. On the third or fourth day after, he bade his servants conduct Solon over his treasuries, and show him all their greatness and magnificence. When he had seen them all, and, so far as time allowed, inspected them, Croesus addressed this question to him, "Stranger of Athens, we have heard much of your wisdom and of your travels through many lands, from love of knowledge and a wish to see the world. I am curious therefore to inquire of you, whom, of all the men that you have seen, you consider the most happy?" This he asked because he thought himself the happiest of mortals: but Solon answered him without flattery, according to his true sentiments, "Tellus of Athens, sire." Full of astonishment at what he heard, Croesus demanded sharply, "And wherefore do you deem Tellus happiest?" To which the other replied, "First, because his country was flourishing in his days, and he himself had sons both beautiful and good, and he lived to see children born to each of them, and these children all grew up; and further because, after a life spent in what our people look upon as comfort, his end was surpassingly glorious. In a battle between the Athenians and their neighbours near Eleusis, he came to the assistance of his countrymen, routed the

* Translated by George Rawlinson.

87

foe, and died upon the field most gallantly. The Athenians gave him a public funeral on the spot where he fell, and paid him the highest honours."

Thus did Solon admonish Croesus by the example of Tellus, enumerating the manifold particulars of his happiness. When he had ended, Croesus inquired a second time, who after Tellus seemed to him the happiest, expecting that, at any rate, he would be given the second place. "Cleobis and Bito," Solon answered, "they were of Argive race: their fortune was enough for their wants, and they were besides endowed with so much bodily strength that they had both gained prizes at the Games. Also this tale is told of them: There was a great festival in honour of the goddess Hera at Argos, to which their mother must needs be taken in a car. Now the oxen did not come home from the field in time: so the youths, fearful of being too late, put the yoke on their own necks, and themselves drew the car in which their mother rode. Five miles they drew her, and stopped before the temple. This deed of theirs was witnessed by the whole assembly of worshippers, and then their life closed in the best possible way. Herein, too, God showed forth most evidently, how much better a thing for man death is than life. For the Argive men stood thick around the car and extolled the vast strength of the youths; and the Argive women extolled the mother who was blessed with such a pair of sons; and the mother herself, overjoyed at the deed and at the praises it had won, standing straight before the image, besought the goddess to bestow on Cleobis and Bito, the sons who had so mightily honoured her, the highest blessing to which mortals can attain. Her prayer ended, they offered sacrifice, and partook of the holy banquet, after which the two youths fell asleep in the temple. They never woke more, but so passed from the earth. The Argives, looking on them as among the best of men, caused statues of them to be made, which they gave to the shrine at Delphi."

When Solon had thus assigned these youths the second place, Croesus broke in angrily, "What, stranger of Athens, is my happiness, then, valued so little by you, that you do not even put me on a level with private men?"

"Croesus," replied the other, "you asked a question concerning the condition of man, of one who knows that the power above us is full of jealousy, and fond of troubling our lot. A long life gives one to witness much, and experience much oneself, that one would not choose. Seventy years I regard as the limit of the life of man. In these seventy years are contained, without reckoning intercalary months, 25,200 days. Add an intercalary month to every other year, that the seasons may come round at the right time, and there will be, besides the seventy years, thirty-five such months, making an addition of 1,050 days. The whole number of the days contained in the seventy years will thus be 26,250, whereof not one but will produce events unlike the rest. Hence man is wholly accident. For yourself, Croesus, I see that you are wonderfully rich, and the lord of many nations; but with respect to your question, I have no answer to give, until I hear that you have closed your life happily. For assuredly he who possesses great store of riches is no nearer happiness than he who has what suffices for his daily needs, unless luck attend upon him, and so he continue in the enjoyment of all his good things to the end of life. For many of the wealthiest men have been unfavoured of fortune, and many whose means were moderate, have had excellent luck. Men of the former class excel those of the latter but in two respects; these last excel the former in many. The wealthy man is better able to content his desires, and to bear up against a sudden buffet of calamity. The other has less ability to withstand these evils (from which, however, his good luck keeps him clear), but he enjoys all these following blessings: he is whole of limb, a stranger to disease, free from misfortune, happy in his children, and comely to look upon. If, in addition to all this, he end his life well, he is of a truth the man of whom you are in search, the man who may rightly be termed happy. Call him, however, until he die, not happy but fortunate. Scarcely, indeed, can any man unite all these advantages: as there is no country which contains within it all that it needs, but each, while it possesses some things, lacks others, and the best country is that which contains the most; so no single human being is complete in every respect—something is always lacking. He who unites the greatest number of advantages, and retaining them to the day of his death, then dies peaceably, that man alone, sire, is, in my judgment, entitled to bear the name of 'happy.' But in every matter we must mark well the end; for oftentimes God gives men a gleam of happiness, and then plunges them into ruin."

Such was the speech which Solon addressed to Croesus, a speech which brought him neither largess nor honour. The

king saw him depart with much indifference, since he thought
that a man must be an arrant fool who made no account of present good, but bade men always wait and mark the end.

b. The Constitutional Debate (3, 80–83)

*In Book III Herodotus describes a discussion which he says
took place among the Persians after a civil war. The arguments in favor of democracy, oligarchy, and monarchy are
more likely than not to reflect Greek political ideas of the
fifth century.*

And now when five days were gone, and the hubbub had
settled down, the conspirators met together to consult about
the situation of affairs. At this meeting speeches were made, to
which many of the Greeks gave no credence, but they were
made nevertheless. Otanes recommended that the management
of public affairs should be entrusted to the whole nation. "To
me," he said, "it seems advisable, that we should no longer have
a single man to rule over us—the rule of one is neither good nor
pleasant. You cannot have forgotten to what lengths Cambyses
went in his haughty tyranny, and the haughtiness of the Magi
you have experienced. How indeed is it possible that monarchy
should be a well-adjusted thing, when it allows a man to do as
he likes without being answerable? Such licence is enough to
stir strange and unwonted thoughts in the heart of the worthiest
of men. Give a person this power, and straightway his manifold good things puff him up with pride, while envy is so
natural to human kind that it cannot but arise in him. But pride
and envy together include all wickedness; both leading on to
deeds of savage violence. True it is that kings, possessing as they
do all that heart can desire, ought to be void of envy, but the
contrary is seen in their conduct towards the citizens. They
are jealous of the most virtuous among their subjects, and wish
their death; while they take delight in the meanest and basest,
being ever ready to listen to the tales of slanderers. A king,

besides, is beyond all other men inconsistent with himself. Pay him court in moderation, and he is angry because you do not show him more profound respect—show him profound respect, and he is offended again, because (as he says) you fawn on him. But the worst of all is, that he sets aside the laws of the land, puts men to death without trial, and rapes women. The rule of the many, on the other hand, has, in the first place, the fairest of names, equality before the law; and further it is free from all those outrages which a king is wont to commit. There, places are given by lot, the magistrate is answerable for what he does, and measures rest with the commonality. I vote, therefore, that we do away with monarchy, and raise the people to power. For the people are all in all."

Such were the sentiments of Otanes. Megabyzus spoke next, and advised the setting up of an oligarchy. "In all that Otanes has said to persuade you to put down monarchy," he observed, "I fully concur; but his recommendation that we should call the people to power seems to me not the best advice. For there is nothing so void of understanding, nothing so full of wantonness as the unwieldy rabble. It were folly not to be borne for men, while seeking to escape the wantonness of a tyrant, to give themselves up to the wantonness of a rude unbridled mob. The tyrant, in all his doings, at least knows what he is about, but a mob is altogether devoid of knowledge; for how should there be any knowledge in a rabble, untaught, and with no natural sense of what is right and fit? It rushes wildly into state affairs with all the fury of a stream swollen in the winter, and confuses everything. Let the enemies of the Persians be ruled by democracies; but let us choose out from the citizens a certain number of the worthiest, and put the government into their hands. For thus both we ourselves shall be among the governors, and power being entrusted to the best men, it is likely that the best counsels will prevail in the state."

This was the advice which Megabyzus gave, and after him Darius came forward, and spoke as follows, "All that Megabyzus said against democracy was well said, I think; but about oligarchy he did not speak advisedly; for take these three forms of government, democracy, oligarchy, and monarchy, and let them each be at their best, I maintain that monarchy far surpasses the other two. What government can possibly be better than that of the very best man in the whole state? The counsels

of such a man are like himself, and so he governs the mass of the
people to their heart's content; while at the same time his measures against evil-doers are kept more secret than in other states.
Contrariwise, in oligarchies, where men vie with each other in
the service of the commonwealth, fierce enmities are apt to arise
between man and man, each wishing to be leader, and to carry
his own measures; whence violent quarrels come, which lead to
open strife, often ending in bloodshed. Then monarchy is sure
to follow; and this too shows how far that rule surpasses all others.
Again, in a democracy, it is impossible but that there will be
malpractices: these malpractices, however, do not lead to en-
mities, but to close friendships, which are formed among those
engaged in them, who must hold well together to carry on their
villanies. And so things go on until a man stands forth as champion of the commonalty, and puts down the evil-doers. Straightway the author of so great a service is admired by all, and from
being admired soon comes to be appointed king; so that here
too it is plain that monarchy is the best government. Lastly, to
sum up all in a word, whence, I ask, was it that we got the freedom which we enjoy?—did democracy give it us, or oligarchy,
or a monarch? As a single man recovered our freedom for us,
my sentence is that we keep to the rule of one. Even apart from
this, we ought not to change the laws of our forefathers when
they work fairly; for to do so, is not well."

c. Tyranny (5, 92)

*Late in the sixth century Sparta tried to restore Hippias, the
deposed tyrant of Athens, to his throne. In the following
passage the Corinthian spokesman refuses to cooperate. He
defends his position with an account of the horrors of
tyranny.*

Such was the address of the Spartans. The greater number of
the allies listened without being persuaded. None however broke
silence, but Sosicles the Corinthian, who exclaimed:

"Surely the heaven will soon be below, and the earth above, and men will henceforth live in the sea, and fish take their place upon the dry land, since you, Lacedaemonians, propose to put down free governments in the cities of Greece, and to set up tyrannies in their stead. There is nothing in the whole world so unjust, nothing so bloody, as a tyranny. If, however, it seems to you a desirable thing to have the cities under despotic rule, begin by putting a tyrant over yourselves, and then establish despots in the other states. While you continue yourselves, as you have always been, unacquainted with tyranny, and take such excellent care that Sparta may not suffer from it, to act as you are now doing is to treat your allies unworthily. If you knew what tyranny was as well as ourselves, you would be better advised than you now are in regard to it. . . .

Cypselus thereby became master of Corinth. Having thus got the tyranny, he showed himself a harsh ruler—many of the Corinthians he drove into banishment, many he deprived of their fortunes, and a still greater number of their lives. His reign lasted thirty years, and was prosperous to its close; insomuch that he left the government to Periander, his son. This prince at the beginning of his reign was of a milder temper than his father; but after he corresponded by means of messengers with Thrasybulus, tyrant of Miletus, he became even more sanguinary. On one occasion he sent a herald to ask Thrasybulus what mode of government it was safest to set up in order to rule with honour. Thrasybulus led the messenger without the city, and took him into a field of corn, through which he began to walk, while he asked him again and again concerning his coming from Corinth, ever as he went breaking off and throwing away all such ears of corn as overtopped the rest. In this way he went through the whole field, and destroyed all the best and richest part of the crop; then, without a word, he sent the messenger back. On the return of the man to Corinth, Periander was eager to know what Thrasybulus had counselled, but the messenger reported that he had said nothing; and he wondered that Periander had sent him to so strange a man, who seemed to have lost his senses, since he did nothing but destroy his own property. And upon this he told how Thrasybulus had behaved at the interview. Periander, perceiving what the action meant, and knowing that Thrasybulus advised the destruction of all the leading citizens, treated his subjects from this time forward with the very great-

est cruelty. Where Cypselus had spared any, and had neither
put them to death nor banished them, Periander completed what
his father had left unfinished. One day he stripped all the
women of Corinth stark naked, for the sake of his own wife
Melissa. He had sent messengers into Thesprotia to consult the
oracle of the dead upon the Acheron concerning a pledge which
had been given into his charge by a stranger, and Melissa appeared, but refused to speak or tell where the pledge was. 'She
was chill,' she said, 'having no clothes; the garments buried
with her were of no manner of use, since they had not been
burnt. And this should be her token to Periander, that what
she said was true—the oven was cold when he baked his loaves
in it.' When this message was brought him, Periander knew
the token for he had had intercourse with the dead body of
Melissa; wherefore he straightway made proclamation, that all
the wives of the Corinthians should go forth to the temple of
Hera. So the women apparelled themselves in their bravest, and
went forth, as if to a festival. Then, with the help of his guards,
whom he had placed for the purpose, he stripped them one and
all, making no difference between the free women and the slaves;
and, taking their clothes to a pit, he called on the name of
Melissa, and burnt the whole heap. This done, he sent a second
time to the oracle, and Melissa's ghost told him where he would
find the stranger's pledge. Such, Lacedaemonians, is tyranny,
and such are the deeds which spring from it. We Corinthians
marvelled greatly when we first knew of your having sent for
Hippias, and now it surprises us still more to hear you speak
as you do. We adjure you, by the common gods of Greece,
plant not despots in her cities. If however you are determined,
if you persist, against all justice, in seeking to restore Hippias,
know, at least, that the Corinthians will not approve your
conduct."

d. The Blessings of Freedom (5, 78)

Thus did the Athenians increase in strength. And it is plain
enough, not from this instance only, but from many everywhere,
that freedom is an excellent thing; since even the Athenians,
who, while they continued under the rule of tyrants, were not

a whit more valiant than any of their neighbours, no sooner shook off the yoke than they became decidedly the first of all. These things show that, while undergoing oppression, they let themselves be beaten, since then they worked for a master; but so soon as they got their freedom, each man was eager to do the best he could for himself. So fared it now with the Athenians.

e. *Tyranny versus Freedom under Law* (7, *101–105*)

Now after Xerxes had sailed down the whole line and was gone ashore, he sent for Demaratus the son of Ariston, who had accompanied him in his march upon Greece, and addressed him thus:

"Demaratus, it is my pleasure at this time to ask you certain things which I wish to know. You are a Greek, and, as I hear from the other Greeks with whom I converse, no less than from your own lips, you are a native of a city which is not the meanest or the weakest in their land. Tell me, therefore, what do you think? Will the Greeks lift a hand against us? My own judgment is, that even if all the Greeks and all the barbarians of the west were gathered together in one place, they would not be able to abide my onset, not being really of one mind. But I would like to know what you think."

Thus Xerxes questioned; and the other replied in his turn, "O King, do you wish me to give you a true answer, or do you wish for a pleasant one?"

Then the King bade him speak the plain truth, and promised that he would not on that account hold him in less favour than heretofore.

So Demaratus, when he heard the promise, spoke as follows, "O King, since you bid me at all risks speak the truth, and not say what will one day prove me to have lied to you, thus I answer. Want has at all times been a fellow-dweller with us in our land, while Valour is an ally whom we have gained by dint of wisdom and strict laws. Her aid enables us to drive out want and escape tyranny. Brave are all the Greeks who dwell in any Dorian land, but what I am about to say does not concern all, but only the Lacedaemonians. First then, come what may, they

will never accept your terms, which would reduce Greece to
slavery; and further, they are sure to join battle with you,
though all the rest of the Greeks should submit to your will. As
for their numbers, do not ask how many they are, that their
resistance should be a possible thing; for if 1,000 of them should
take the field, they will meet you in battle, and so will any
number, be it less than this, or be it more."

When Xerxes heard this answer of Demaratus, he laughed
and answered, "What wild words, Demaratus! 1,000 men join
battle with such an army as this! Come then, will you—who
were once, as you say, their king—engage to fight this very
day with ten men? I think not. And yet, if all your fellow citizens be indeed such as you say they are, you ought, as their
king, by your own country's usages, to be ready to fight with
twice the number. If then each one of them be a match for ten
of my soldiers, I may well call upon you to be a match for twenty.
So would you assure the truth of what you have now said.
If, however, you Greeks, who vaunt yourselves so much, are
of a truth men like those whom I have seen about my court,
as you, Demaratus, and the others with whom I converse, if, I
say, you are really men of this sort and size, how is the speech
that you have uttered more than a mere empty boast? For, to
go to the very verge of likelihood,—how could 1,000 men, or
10,000, or even 50,000, particularly if they were all alike free,
and not under one lord, how could such a force, I say, stand
against an army like mine? Let them be 5,000, and we shall have
more than 1,000 men to each one of theirs. If, indeed, like our
troops, they had a single master, their fear of him might make
them courageous beyond their natural bent, or they might be
urged by lashes against an enemy which far outnumbered them.
But left to their own free choice, assuredly they will act differently. For my own part, I believe, that if the Greeks had to contend with the Persians only, and the numbers were equal on
both sides, the Greeks would find it hard to stand their ground.
We too have among us such men as those of whom you spoke—
not many indeed, but still we possess a few. For instance, some
of my body-guard would be willing to engage singly with three
Greeks. But this you did not know, and therefore it was you
talked so foolishly."

Demaratus answered him, "I knew, O King, at the outset,
that if I told you the truth, my speech would displease your

ears. But as you required me to answer you with all possible truthfulness, I informed you what the Spartans will do. And in this I speak not from any love that I bear them—for you know what my love towards them is likely to be at the present time, when they have robbed me of my rank and my ancestral honours, and made me a homeless exile, whom your father received, bestowing on me both shelter and sustenance. What likelihood is there that a man of understanding should be unthankful for kindness shown him, and not cherish it in his heart? For myself, I pretend not to cope with ten men, or with two, nay, had I the choice, I would rather not fight even with one. But, if need appeared, or if there were any great cause urging me on, I would contend with right good-will against one of those persons who boast themselves a match for any three Greeks. So likewise the Lacedaemonians, when they fight singly, are as good men as any in the world, and when they fight in a body, are the bravest of all. For though they be free men, they are not in all respects free; Law is the master whom they own, and this master they fear more than your subjects fear you. Whatever it commands they do; and its commandment is always the same: it forbids them to flee in battle, whatever the number of their foes, and requires them to stand firm, and either to conquer or die. If in these words, O King, I seem to you to speak foolishly, I am content from this time forward evermore to hold my peace. I had not now spoken unless compelled by you. But I pray that all may turn out according to your wishes."

Such was the answer of Demaratus, and Xerxes was not angry with him at all, but only laughed, and sent him away with words of kindness.

5. *Democratic Political Theory*

It is no easy task to present a coherent picture of Greek democratic theory, for the political philosophers were not democrats and we have no lengthy, reasoned defence of democracy. The theory must be put together from stray bits and pieces, the speeches of politicians, the statements of enemies of democracy, an occasional statement by a historian and from the constitution of democratic Athens itself. One very useful source is the judgment of its enemies on democracy, for in their criticisms they often describe the views with which they disagree.

1.   The "Old Oligarch"*

This is a pamphlet which has come down to us among the works of Xenophon but which is clearly not his work. It was written toward the beginning of the Peloponnesian War by an anonymous critic of Athenian democracy conventionally called the "Old Oligarch."

The Constitution of the Athenians]

Now, as for the constitution of the Athenians, and the type or manner of constitution which they have chosen, I praise it not, in so far as the very choice involves the welfare of the baser folk as opposed to that of the better class. I repeat, I withhold my praise so far; but, given the fact that this is the type agreed upon, I propose to show that they set about its preservation in the right way; and that those other transactions in connection with it, which are looked upon as blunders by the rest of the Hellenic world, are the reverse.

In the first place, I maintain, it is only just that the poorer classes and the common people of Athens should be better off than the men of birth and wealth, seeing that it is the people who man the fleet, and have brought the city her power. The steersman, the boatswain, the lieutenant, the look-out man at the prow, the shipwright—these are the people who supply the city with power far rather than her heavy infantry and men of birth and quality. This being the case, it seems only just that offices of state should be thrown open to every one both in the ballot and the show of hands, and that the right of speech should belong to any one who likes, without restriction. For, observe, there are many of these offices which, according as they are in good or in bad hands, are a source of safety or of danger to the People, and in these the People prudently abstains from sharing; as, for instance, it does not think it incumbent on itself to share in the functions of the general or of the commander of cavalry. The commons recognises the fact that in forgoing the personal exercise of these offices, and leaving them to the control of the more powerful citizens, it secures the balance of advantage to

* Translated by Henry G. Dakyns.

99

itself. It is only those departments of government which bring
pay and assist the private estate that the People cares to keep in
its own hands.

In the next place, in regard to what some people are puzzled
to explain—the fact that everywhere greater consideration is
shown to the base, to poor people and to common folk, than
to persons of good quality,—so far from being a matter of surprise, this, as can be shown, is the keystone of the preservation
of the democracy. It is these poor people, this common folk,
this worse element, whose prosperity, combined with the growth
of their numbers, enhances the democracy. Whereas, a shift-
ing of fortune to the advantage of the wealthy and the better
classes implies the establishment on the part of the commons
of a strong power in opposition to itself. In fact, all the world
over, the cream of society is in opposition to the democracy.
Naturally, since the smallest amount of intemperance and injustice, together with the highest scrupulousness in the pursuit of excellence, is to be found in the ranks of the better class, while
within the ranks of the People will be found the greatest amount
of ignorance, disorderliness, rascality,—poverty acting as a
stronger incentive to base conduct, not to speak of lack of education and ignorance, traceable to the lack of means which
afflicts the average of mankind.

The objection may be raised that it was a mistake to allow the
universal right of speech and a seat in council. These should have
been reserved for the cleverest, the flower of the community. But
here, again, it will be found that they are acting with wise deliberation in granting to even the baser sort the right of speech,
for supposing only the better people might speak, or sit in council,
blessings would fall to the lot of those like themselves, but to the
commons the reverse of blessings. Whereas now, any one who
likes, any base fellow, may get up and discover something to the
advantage of himself and his equals. It may be retorted, "And
what sort of advantage either for himself or for the People can
such a fellow be expected to hit upon?" The answer to which is,
that in their judgment the ignorance and the baseness of this
fellow, together with his goodwill, are worth a great deal more
to them than your superior person's virtue and wisdom, coupled
with animosity. What it comes to, therefore, is that a state
founded upon such institutions will not be the best state; but,
given a democracy, these are the right means to secure its pres-

ervation. The People, it must be borne in mind, does not demand that the city should be well governed and itself a slave. It desires to be free and to be master. As to bad legislation it does not concern itself about that. In fact, what you believe to be bad legislation is the very source of the People's strength and freedom. But if you seek for good legislation, in the first place you will see the cleverest members of the community laying down the laws for the rest. And in the next place, the better class will curb and chastise the lower orders; the better class will deliberate in behalf of the state, and not suffer crack-brained fellows to sit in council, or to speak or vote in the assemblies. No doubt; but under the weight of such blessings the People will in a very short time be reduced to slavery.

Another point is the extraordinary amount of license granted to slaves and resident aliens at Athens, where a blow is illegal, and a slave will not step aside to let you pass him in the street. I will explain the reason of this peculiar custom. Supposing it were legal for a slave to be beaten by a free citizen, or for a resident alien or freedman to be beaten by a citizen, it would frequently happen that an Athenian might be mistaken for a slave or an alien and receive a beating; since the Athenian People is not better clothed than the slave or alien, nor in personal appearance is there any superiority. Or if the fact itself that slaves in Athens are allowed to indulge in luxury, and indeed in some cases to live magnificently, be found astonishing, this too, it can be shown, is done of set purpose. Where you have a naval power dependent upon wealth we must perforce be slaves to our slaves, in order that we may get in our slave-rents, and let the real slave go free. Where you have wealthy slaves it ceases to be advantageous that my slave should stand in awe of you. In Lacedaemon my slave stands in awe of you. But if your slave is in awe of me there will be a risk of his giving away his own moneys to avoid running a risk in his own person. It is for this reason then that we have established an equality between our slaves and free men; and again between our resident aliens and full citizens, because the city stands in need of her resident aliens to meet the requirements of such a multiplicity of arts and for the purposes of her navy. That is, I repeat, the justification of the equality conferred upon our resident aliens.

The common people put a stop to citizens devoting their time to athletics and to the cultivation of music, disbelieving in the beauty of such training, and recognising the fact that these are things the cultivation of which is beyond its power. On the same principle, in the case of the choregia, the management of athletics, and the command of ships, the fact is recognised that it is the rich man who trains the chorus, and the People for whom the chorus is trained; it is the rich man who is naval commander or superintendent of athletics, and the People that profits by their labours. In fact, what the People looks upon as its right is to pocket the money. To sing and run and dance and man the vessels is well enough, but only in order that the People may be the gainer, while the rich are made poorer. And so in the courts of justice, justice is not more an object of concern to the jurymen than what touches personal advantage.

To speak next of the allies, and in reference to the point that emissaries from Athens come out, and, according to common opinion, calumniate and vent their hatred upon the better sort of people, this is done on the principle that the ruler cannot help being hated by those whom he rules; but that if wealth and respectability are to wield power in the subject cities the empire of the Athenian People has but a short lease of existence. This explains why the better people are punished with infamy, robbed of their money, driven from their homes, and put to death, while the baser sort are promoted to honour. On the other hand, the better Athenians protect the better class in the allied cities. And why? Because they recognise that it is to the interest of their own class at all times to protect the best element in the cities. It may be urged that if it comes to strength and power the real strength of Athens lies in the capacity of her allies to contribute their money quota. But to the democratic mind it appears a higher advantage still for the individual Athenian to get hold of the wealth of the allies, leaving them only enough to live upon and to cultivate their estates, but powerless to harbour treacherous designs.

Again, it is looked upon as a mistaken policy on the part of the Athenian democracy to compel her allies to voyage to Athens in order to have their cases tried. On the other hand, it is easy to reckon up what a number of advantages the Athenian People derives from the practice impugned. In the first place, there is the steady receipt of salaries throughout the year derived from the court fees. Next, it enables them to manage the affairs of the allied states while seated at home without the expense of naval expeditions. Thirdly, they thus preserve the partisans of the democracy, and ruin her opponents in the law courts. Whereas, supposing the several allied states tried their cases at home, being inspired by hostility to Athens, they would destroy those of their own citizens whose friendship to the Athenian People was most marked. But besides all this the democracy derives the following advantages from hearing the cases of her allies in Athens. In the first place, the one per cent levied in Piraeus is increased to the profit of the state; again, the owner of a lodging-house does better, and so, too, the owner of a pair of beasts, or of slaves to be let out on hire; again, heralds and criers are a class of people who fare better owing to the sojourn of foreigners at Athens. Further still, supposing the allies had not to resort to Athens for the hearing of cases, only the official representative of the imperial state would be held in honour, such as the general, or trierarch, or ambassador. Whereas now every single individual among the allies is forced to pay flattery to the People of Athens because he knows that he must betake himself to Athens and win or lose his case at the bar, not of any stray set of judges, but of the sovereign People itself, such being the law and custom at Athens. He is compelled to behave as a suppliant in the courts of justice, and when some juryman comes into court, to grasp his hand. For this reason, therefore, the allies find themselves more and more in the position of slaves to the people of Athens.

Furthermore, owing to the possession of property beyond the limits of Attica, and the exercise of magistracies which take them into regions beyond the frontier, they and their attendants have insensibly acquired the art of navigation. A man who is perpetually voyaging is forced to handle the oar, he and his domestic alike, and to learn the terms familiar in seamanship. Hence a stock of skilful mariners is produced, bred upon a wide experience of voyaging and practice. They have learned their business, some in piloting a small craft, others a merchant vessel, while others have been drafted off from these for service on a ship-of-war. So that the majority of them are able to row the moment they set foot on board a vessel, having been in a state of preliminary practice all their lives.

As to the heavy infantry, an arm the deficiency of which at Athens is well recognised, this is how the matter stands. They recognise the fact that, in reference to the hostile power, they are themselves inferior, and must be, even if their heavy infantry were more numerous. But relatively to the allies, who bring in the tribute, their strength even on land is enormous. And they

are persuaded that their heavy infantry is sufficient for all purposes, provided they retain this superiority. Apart from all else,
to a certain extent fortune must be held responsible for the
actual condition. The subjects of a power which is dominant
by land have it open to them to form contingents from several
small states and to muster in force for battle. But with the subjects of a naval power it is different. As far as they are groups
of islanders it is impossible for their states to meet together for
united action, for the sea lies between them, and the dominant
power is master of the sea. And even if it were possible for them
to assemble in some single island unobserved, they would only
do so to perish by famine. And as to the states subject to Athens
which are not islanders, but situated on the continent, the larger
are held in check by need and the small ones absolutely by fear,
since there is no state in existence which does not depend upon
imports and exports, and these she will forfeit if she does not
lend a willing ear to those who are masters by sea. In the next
place, a power dominant by sea can do certain things which a
land power is debarred from doing; as, for instance, ravage the
territory of a superior, since it is always possible to coast along to
some point, where either there is no hostile force to deal with
or merely a small body; and in case of an advance in force on the
part of the enemy they can take to their ships and sail away.
Such a performance is attended with less difficulty than that experienced by the relieving force on land. Again, it is open to a
power so dominating by sea to leave its own territory and sail
off on as long a voyage as you please. Whereas the land power
cannot place more than a few days' journey between itself and
its own territory, for marches are slow affairs; and it is not possible for an army on the march to have food supplies to last for
any great length of time. Such an army must either march
through friendly territory or it must force a way by victory in
battle. The voyager meanwhile has it in his power to disembark
at any point where he finds himself in superior force, or, at the
worst, to coast by until he reaches either a friendly district or
an enemy too weak to resist. Again, those diseases to which the
fruits of the earth are liable as visitations from heaven fall severely
on a land power, but are scarcely felt by the naval power, for
such sicknesses do not visit the whole earth everywhere at once.
So that the ruler of the sea can get in supplies from a thriving
district. And if one may descend to more trifling particulars, it
is to this same lordship of the sea that the Athenians owe the

discovery, in the first place, of many of the luxuries of life through intercourse with other countries. So that the choice things of Sicily and Italy, of Cyprus and Egypt and Lydia, of Pontus or Peloponnese, or wheresoever else it be, are all swept, as it were, into one centre, and all owing, as I say, to their maritime empire. And again, in process of listening to every form of speech, they have selected this from one place and that from another—for themselves. So much so that while the rest of the Hellenes employ each pretty much their own peculiar mode of speech, habit of life, and style of dress, the Athenians have adopted a composite type, to which all sections of Hellas, and the foreigner alike, have contributed.

As regards sacrifices and temples and festivals and sacred enclosures, the People sees that it is not possible for every poor citizen to do sacrifice and hold festival, or to set up temples and to inhabit a large and beautiful city. But it has hit upon a means of meeting the difficulty. They sacrifice—that is, the whole state sacrifices—at the public cost a large number of victims; but it is the People that keeps holiday and distributes the victims by lot among its members. Rich men have in some cases private gymnasia and baths with dressing-rooms, but the People takes care to have built at the public cost a number of palaestras, dressing-rooms, and bathing establishments for its own special use, and the mob gets the benefit of the majority of these, rather than the select few or the well-to-do.

As to wealth, the Athenians are exceptionally placed with regard to Hellenic and foreign communities alike, in their ability to hold it. For, given that some state or other is rich in timber for shipbuilding, where is it to find a market for the product except by persuading the ruler of the sea? Or, suppose the wealth of some state or other to consist of iron, or may be of bronze, or of linen yarn, where will it find a market except by permission of the supreme maritime power? Yet these are the very things, you see, which I need for my ships. Timber I must have from one, and from another iron, from a third bronze, from a fourth linen yarn, from a fifth wax. Besides which they will not suffer their antagonists in those parts to carry these products elsewhere, or they will cease to use the sea. Accordingly I, without one stroke of labour, extract from the land and possess all these good things, thanks to my supremacy on the sea; while not a single other state possesses the two of them. Not timber, for instance, **and yarn** together, the same city. But where yarn is abundant,

the soil will be light and devoid of timber. And in the same way
bronze and iron will not be products of the same city. And so for
the rest, never two, or at best three, in one state, but one thing
here and another thing there. Moreover, above and beyond what
has been said, the coastline of every mainland presents, either
some jutting promontory, or adjacent island, or narrow strait of
some sort, so that those who are masters of the sea can come to
moorings at one of these points and wreak vengeance on the
inhabitants of the mainland.

There is just one thing which the Athenians lack. Supposing
they were the inhabitants of an island, and were still, as now,
rulers of the sea, they would have had it in their power to work
whatever mischief they liked, and to suffer no evil in return (as
long as they kept command of the sea), neither the ravaging of
their territory nor the expectation of an enemy's approach.
Whereas at present the farming portion of the community and
the wealthy landowners are ready to cringe before the enemy
overmuch, while the People, knowing full well that, come what
may, not one stock or stone of their property will suffer, nothing will be cut down, nothing burnt, lives in freedom from
alarm, without fawning at the enemy's approach. Besides this,
there is another fear from which they would have been exempt
in an island home—the apprehension of the city being at any
time betrayed by their oligarchs and the gates thrown open, and
an enemy bursting suddenly in. How could incidents like these
have taken place if an island had been their home? Again, had
they inhabited an island there would have been no stirring of
sedition against the People; whereas at present, in the event of
faction, those who set it on foot base their hopes of success
on the introduction of an enemy by land. But a people inhabit-
ing an island would be free from all anxiety on that score. Since,
however, they did not chance to inhabit an island from the first,
what they now do is this—they deposit their property in the
islands, trusting to their command of the sea, and they suffer
the soil of Attica to be ravaged without a sigh. To expend pity
on that, they know, would be to deprive themselves of other
blessings still more precious.

Further, states oligarchically governed are forced to ratify
their alliances and solemn oaths, and if they fail to abide by
their contracts, the offence, by whomsoever committed, lies
nominally at the door of the oligarchs who entered upon the
contract. But in the case of engagements entered into by a de-

mocracy it is open to the People to throw the blame on the single individual who spoke in favour of some measure, or put it to the vote, and to maintain to the rest of the world, "I was not present, nor do I approve of the terms of the agreement." Inquiries are made in a full meeting of the People, and should any of these things be disapproved of, they can at once discover countless excuses to avoid doing whatever they do not wish. And if any mischief should spring out of any resolutions which the People has passed in council, the People can readily shift the blame from its own shoulders. "A handful of oligarchs acting against the interests of the People have ruined us." But if any good result ensue, they, the People, at once take the credit of that to themselves.

In the same spirit it is not allowed to caricature on the comic stage or otherwise libel the People, because they do not care to hear themselves ill spoken of. But if any one has a desire to satirise his neighbour he has full leave to do so. And this because they are well aware that, as a general rule, the person caricatured does not belong to the People, or the masses. He is more likely to be some wealthy or well-born person, or man of means and influence. In fact, but few poor people and of the popular stamp incur the comic lash, or if they do they have brought it on themselves by excessive love of meddling or some covetous self-seeking at the expense of the People, so that no particular annoyance is felt at seeing such folk satirised.

What, then, I venture to assert is, that the People of Athens has no difficulty in recognising which of its citizens are of the better sort and which the opposite. And so recognising those who are serviceable and advantageous to itself, even though they be base, the People loves them; but the good folk they are disposed the rather to hate. This virtue of theirs, the People holds, is not engrained in their nature for any good to itself, but rather for its injury. In direct opposition to this, there are some persons who, being born of the People, are yet by natural instinct not commoners. For my part I pardon the People its own democracy, as, indeed, it is pardonable in any one to do good to himself. But the man who, not being himself one of the People, prefers to live in a state democratically governed rather than in an oligarchical state may be said to smooth his own path towards iniquity. He knows that a bad man has a better chance of slipping through the fingers of justice in a democratic than in an oligarchical state.

108 DEMOCRATIC POLITICAL THEORY

I repeat that my position concerning the constitution of the Athenians is this: the type of constitution is not to my taste, but given that a democratic form of government has been agreed upon, they do seem to me to go the right way to preserve the democracy by the adoption of the particular type which I have set forth.

But there are other objections brought, as I am aware, against the Athenians, by certain people, and to this effect. It not seldom happens, they tell us, that a man is unable to transact a piece of business with the senate or the People, even if he sit waiting a whole year. Now this does happen at Athens, and for no other reason save that, owing to the immense mass of affairs they are unable to work off all the business on hand and dismiss the applicants. And how in the world should they be able, considering in the first place that they, the Athenians, have more festivals to celebrate than any other state throughout the length and breadth of Hellas? During these festivals, of course, the transaction of any sort of affairs of state is still more out of the question. In the next place, only consider the number of cases they have to decide, what with private suits and public causes and scrutinies of accounts, more than the whole of the rest of mankind put together; while the senate has multifarious points to advise upon concerning peace and war, concerning ways and means, concerning the framing and passing of laws, and concerning the matters affecting the state perpetually occurring, and endless questions touching the allies; besides the receipt of the tribute, the superintendence of dockyards and temples. Can, I ask again, any one find it at all surprising that, with all these affairs on their hands, they are unequal to doing business with all the world?

But some people tell us that if the applicant will only address himself to the senate or the People with a bribe in his hand he will do a good stroke of business. And for my part I am free to confess to these gainsayers that a good many things may be done at Athens by dint of money; and I will add, that a good many more still might be done, if the money flowed still more freely and from more pockets. One thing, however, I know full well, that as to transacting with every one of these applicants all he wants, the state could not do it, not even if all the gold and silver in the world were the inducement offered.

Here are some of the cases which have to be decided on. Some one fails to fit out a ship: judgment must be given. Another puts up a building on a piece of public land: again judgment must be given. Or, to take another class of cases: adjudication has to be made between the patrons of choruses for the Dionysia, the Thargelia, the Panathenaea, the Prometheia, and the Hephaestia, year after year. Also as between the trierarchs, 400 of whom are appointed each year, of these, too, any who choose must have their cases adjudicated on, year after year. But that is not all. There are various magistrates to examine and approve and decide between; there are orphans whose status must be examined; and guardians of prisoners to appoint. These, be it borne in mind, are all matters of yearly occurrence; while at intervals there are exemptions and abstentions from military service which call for adjudication, or in connection with some other extraordinary misdemeanour, some case of outrage and violence of an exceptional character, or some charge of impiety. A whole string of others I simply omit; I am content to have named the most important part with the exception of the assessments of tribute which occur, as a rule, at intervals of four years.

I put it to you, then: can any one suppose that all, or any, of these may dispense with adjudication? If so, will any one say which ought, and which ought not, to be adjudicated on, there and then? If, on the other hand, we are forced to admit that these are all fair cases for adjudication, it follows of necessity that they should be decided during the twelve-month; since even now the boards of judges sitting right through the year are powerless to stay the tide of evildoing by reason of the multitude of the people.

So far so good. "But," some one will say, "try the cases you certainly must, but lessen the number of the judges." But if so, it follows of necessity that unless the number of courts themselves are diminished in number there will only be a few judges sitting in each court, with the further consequence that in dealing with so small a body of judges it will be easier for a litigant to present an invulnerable front to the court, and to bribe the whole body, to the great detriment of justice.

But besides this we cannot escape the conclusion that the Athenians have their festivals to keep, during which the courts cannot sit. As a matter of fact these festivals are twice as numerous as those of any other people. But I will reckon them as merely equal to those of the state which has the fewest.

This being so, I maintain that it is not possible for business affairs at Athens to stand on any very different footing from the present, except to some slight extent, by adding here and deducting there. Any large modification is out of the question, short of damaging the democracy itself. No doubt many expedients might be discovered for improving the constitution, but if the problem be to discover some adequate means of improving the constitution, while at the same time the democracy is to remain intact, I say it is not easy to do this, except, as I have just stated, to the extent of some trifling addition here or deduction there.

There is another point in which it is sometimes felt that the Athenians are ill advised, in their adoption, namely, of the less respectable party, in a state divided by faction. But if so, they do it advisedly. If they chose the more respectable, they would be adopting those whose views and interests differ from their own, for there is no state in which the best element is friendly to the people. It is the worst element which in every state favours the democracy—on the principle that like favours like. It is simple enough then. The Athenians choose what is most akin to themselves. Also on every occasion on which they have attempted to side with the better classes, it has not fared well with them, but within a short interval the democratic party has been enslaved, as for instance in Boeotia; or, as when they chose the aristocrats of the Milesians, and within a short time these revolted and cut the people to pieces; or, as when they chose the Lacedaemonians as against the Messenians, and within a short time the Lacedaemonians subjugated the Messenians and went to war against Athens.

I seem to overhear a retort, "No one, of course, is deprived of his civil rights at Athens unjustly." My answer is, that there are some who are unjustly deprived of their civil rights, though the cases are certainly rare. But it will take more than a few to attack the democracy at Athens, since you may take it as an established fact, it is not the man who has lost his civil rights justly that takes the matter to heart, but the victims, if any, of injustice. But how in the world can any one imagine that many are in a state of civil disability at Athens, where the People and the holders of office are one and the same? It is from iniquitous exercise of office, from iniquity exhibited either in speech or action, and the like circumstances, that citizens are punished with deprivation of civil rights in Athens. Due reflection on these matters will serve to dispel the notion that there is any danger at Athens from persons visited with disfranchisement.

2. *Plato on Democracy (Selections from* Republic, *557–566)* *

And then democracy comes into being after the poor have conquered their opponents, slaughtering some and banishing some, while to the remainder they give an equal share of freedom and power; and this is the form of government in which the magistrates are commonly elected by lot.

Yes, he said, that is the nature of democracy, whether the revolution has been effected by arms, or whether fear has caused the opposite party to withdraw.

And now what is their manner of life, and what sort of a government have they? for as the government is, such will be the man.

Clearly, he said.

In the first place, are they not free; and is not the city full of freedom and frankness—a man may say and do what he likes?

'Tis said so, he replied.

And where freedom is, the individual is clearly able to order for himself his own life as he pleases?

Clearly.

Then in this kind of State there will be the greatest variety of human natures?

There will.

This, then, seems likely to be the fairest of States, being like an embroidered robe which is spangled with every sort of flower. And just as women and children think a variety of colours to be of all things most charming, so there are many men to whom this State, which is spangled with the manners and characters of mankind, will appear to be the fairest of States.

Yes.

Yes, my good Sir, and there will be no better in which to look for a government.

Why?

Because of the liberty which reigns there—they have a complete assortment of constitutions; and he who has a mind to establish a State, as we have been doing, must go to a democracy as he would to a bazaar at which they sell them, and pick out

* Translated by Benjamin Jowett.

the one that suits him; then, when he has made his choice, he may found his State.

He will be sure to have patterns enough.

And there being no necessity, I said, for you to govern in this State, even if you have the capacity, or to be governed, unless you like, or go to war when the rest go to war, or to be at peace when others are at peace, unless you are so disposed—there being no necessity also, because some law forbids you to hold office or be a dicast, that you should not hold office or be a dicast, if you have a fancy—is not this a way of life which for the moment is supremely delightful?

For the moment, yes.

And is not their humanity to the condemned in some cases quite charming? Have you not observed how, in a democracy, many persons, although they have been sentenced to death or exile, just stay where they are and walk about the world—the gentleman parades like a hero, and nobody sees or cares?

Yes, he replied, many and many a one.

See too, I said, the forgiving spirit of democracy, and the 'don't care' about trifles, and the disregard which she shows of all the fine principles which we solemnly laid down at the foundation of the city—as when we said that, except in the case of some rarely gifted nature, there never will be a good man who has not from his childhood been used to play amid things of beauty and make of them a joy and a study—how grandly does she trample all these fine notions of ours under her feet, never giving a thought to the pursuits which make a statesman, and promoting to honour any one who professes to be the people's friend.

Yes, she is of a noble spirit.

These and other kindred characteristics are proper to democracy, which is a charming form of government, full of variety and disorder, and dispensing a sort of equality to equals and unequals alike. . . .

Again, let us see how the democratical man grows out of the oligarchical: the following, as I suspect, is commonly the process.

What is the process?

When a young man who has been brought up as we were just now describing, in a vulgar and miserly way, has tasted drones' honey and has come to associate with fierce and crafty natures who are able to provide for him all sorts of refinements and varieties of pleasure—then, as you may imagine, the change will begin of the oligarchical principle within him into the democratical?

Inevitably.

And as in the city like was helping like, and the change was effected by an alliance from without assisting one division of the citizens, so too the young man is changed by a class of desires coming from without to assist the desires within him, that which is akin and alike again helping that which is akin and alike?

Certainly.

And if there be any ally which aids the oligarchical principle within him, whether the influence of a father or of kindred, advising or rebuking him, then there arises in his soul a·faction and an opposite faction, and he goes to war with himself.

It must be so.

And there are times when the democratical principle gives way to the oligarchical, and some of his desires die, and others are banished; a spirit of reverence enters into the young man's soul and order is restored.

Yes, he said, that sometimes happens.

And then, again, after the old desires have been driven out, fresh ones spring up, which are akin to them, and because he their father does not know how to educate them, wax fierce and numerous.

Yes, he said, that is apt to be the way.

They draw him to his old associates, and holding secret intercourse with them, breed and multiply in him.

Very true.

At length they seize upon the citadel of the young man's soul, which they perceive to be void of all accomplishments and fair pursuits and true words, which make their abode in the minds of men who are dear to the gods, and are their best guardians and sentinels.

None better.

False and boastful conceits and phrases mount upwards and take their place.

They are certain to do so.

And so the young man returns into the country of the lotus-eaters, and takes up his dwelling there in the face of all men; and if any help be sent by his friends to the oligarchical part of him, the aforesaid vain conceits shut the gate of the king's fastness; and they will neither allow the embassy itself to enter, nor if private advisers offer the fatherly counsel of the aged will they listen to them or receive them. There is a battle and they gain the day, and then modesty, which they call silliness, is ignominiously thrust into exile by them, and temperance, which they nickname unmanliness, is trampled in the mire and cast forth; they persuade men that moderation and orderly expenditure are vulgarity and meanness, and so, by the help of a rabble of evil appetites, they drive them beyond the border.

Yes, with a will.

And when they have emptied and swept clean the soul of him who is now in their power and who is being initiated by them in great mysteries, the next thing is to bring back to their house insolence and anarchy and waste and impudence in bright array having garlands on their heads, and a great company with them, hymning their praises and calling them by sweet names; insolence they term breeding, and anarchy liberty, and waste magnificence, and impudence courage. And so the young man passes out of his original nature, which was trained in the school of necessity, into the freedom and libertinism of useless and unnecessary pleasures.

Yes, he said, the change in him is visible enough.

After this he lives on, spending his money and labour and time on unnecessary pleasures quite as much as on necessary ones; but if he be fortunate, and is not too much disordered in his wits, when years have elapsed, and the heyday of passion is over—supposing that he then re-admits into the city some part of the exiled virtues, and does not wholly give himself up to their successors—in that case he balances his pleasures and lives in a sort of equilibrium, putting the government of himself into the hands of the one which comes first and wins the turn; and when he has had enough of that, then into the hands of another; he despises none of them but encourages them all equally.

Very true, he said.

Neither does he receive or let pass into the fortress any true word of advice; if any one says to him that some pleasures are the satisfactions of good and noble desires, and others of evil desires, and that he ought to use and honour some and chastise and master the others—whenever this is repeated to him he shakes his head and says that they are all alike, and that one is as good as another.

Yes, he said; that is the way with him.

Yes, I said, he lives from day to day indulging the appetite of the hour; and sometimes he is lapped in drink and strains of the flute; then he becomes a water-drinker, and tries to get thin; then he takes a turn at gymnastics; sometimes idling and neglecting everything, then once more living the life of a philosopher; often he is busy with politics, and starts to his feet and says and does whatever comes into his head; and, if he is emulous of any one who is a warrior, off he is in that direction, or of men of business, once more in that. His life has neither law nor order; and this distracted existence he terms joy and bliss and freedom; and so he goes on.

Yes, he replied, he is all liberty and equality.

Yes, I said; his life is motley and manifold and an epitome of the lives of many;—he answers to the State which we described as fair and spangled. And many a man and many a woman will take him for their pattern, and many a constitution and many an example of manners is contained in him.

Just so.

Let him then be set over against democracy; he may truly be called the democratic man. . . .

The last extreme of popular liberty is when the slave bought with money, whether male or female, is just as free as his or her purchaser; nor must I forget to tell of the liberty and equality of the two sexes in relation to each other.

Why not, as Aeschylus says, utter the word which rises to our lips?

That is what I am doing, I replied; and I must add that no one who does not know would believe, how much greater is the liberty which the animals who are under the dominion of man have in a democracy than in any other State: for truly, the she-dogs, as the proverb says, are as good as their she-mistresses, and the horses and asses have a way of marching along with all the rights and dignities of freemen; and they will run at any body who comes in their way if he does not leave the road clear for them: and all things are just ready to burst with liberty.

When I take a country walk, he said, I often experience what you describe. You and I have dreamed the same thing.

And above all, I said, and as the result of all, see how sensitive the citizens become; they chafe impatiently at the least touch of authority and at length, as you know, they cease to care even for the laws, written or unwritten; they will have no one over them.

Yes, he said, I know it too well.

Such, my friend, I said, is the fair and glorious beginning out of which springs tyranny.

Glorious indeed, he said. But what is the next step?

The ruin of oligarchy is the ruin of democracy; the same disease magnified and intensified by liberty overmasters democracy—the truth being that the excessive increase of anything often causes a reaction in the opposite direction; and this is the case not only in the seasons and in vegetable and animal life, but above all in forms of government.

True.

The excess of liberty, whether in States or individuals, seems only to pass into excess of slavery.

Yes, the natural order.

And so tyranny naturally arises out of democracy, and the most aggravated form of tyranny and slavery out of the most extreme form of liberty?

As we might expect.

That, however, was not, as I believe, your question—you rather desired to know what is that disorder which is generated alike in oligarchy and democracy, and is the ruin of both?

Just so, he replied.

Well, I said, I meant to refer to the class of idle spendthrifts, of whom the more courageous are the leaders and the more timid the followers, the same whom we were comparing to drones, some stingless, and others having stings.

A very just comparison.

These two classes are the plagues of every city in which they are generated, being what phlegm and bile are to the body. And the good physician and lawgiver of the State ought, like the wise bee-master, to keep them at a distance and prevent, if possible, their ever coming in; and if they have anyhow found a way in, then he should have them and their cells cut out as speedily as possible.

Yes, by all means, he said.

Then, in order that we may see clearly what we are doing, let us imagine democracy to be divided, as indeed it is, into three classes; for in the first place freedom creates rather more drones in the democratic than there were in the oligarchical State.

That is true.

And in the democracy they are certainly more intensified.

How so?

Because in the oligarchical State they are disqualified and

driven from office, and therefore they cannot train or gather strength; whereas in a democracy they are almost the entire ruling power, and while the keener sort speak and act, the rest keep buzzing about the bema and do not suffer a word to be said on the other side; hence in democracies almost everything is managed by the drones.

Very true, he said.

Then there is another class which is always being severed from the mass.

What is that?

They are the orderly class, which in a nation of traders is sure to be the richest.

Naturally so.

They are the most squeezable persons and yield the largest amount of honey to the drones.

Why, he said, there is little to be squeezed out of people who have little.

And this is called the wealthy class, and the drones feed upon them.

That is pretty much the case, he said.

The people are a third class, consisting of those who work with their own hands; they are not politicians, and have not much to live upon. This, when assembled, is the largest and most powerful class in a democracy.

True, he said; but then the multitude is seldom willing to congregate unless they get a little honey.

And do they not share? I said. Do not their leaders deprive the rich of their estates and distribute them among the people; at the same time taking care to reserve the larger part for themselves?

Why, yes, he said, to that extent the people do share.

And the persons whose property is taken from them are compelled to defend themselves before the people as they best can?

What else can they do?

And then, although they may have no desire of change, the others charge them with plotting against the people and being friends of oligarchy?

True.

And the end is that when they see the people, not of their own accord, but through ignorance, and because they are deceived by informers, seeking to do them wrong, then at last they are forced to become oligarchs in reality; they do not wish to be, but the sting of the drones torments them and breeds revolution in them.

That is exactly the truth.

Then come impeachments and judgments and trials of one another.

True.

The people have always some champion whom they set over them and nurse into greatness.

Yes, that is their way.

This and no other is the root from which a tyrant springs; when he first appears above ground he is a protector.

Yes, that is quite clear.

How then does a protector begin to change into a tyrant? Clearly when he does what the man is said to do in the tale of the Arcadian temple of Lycaean Zeus.

What tale?

The tale is that he who has tasted the entrails of a single human victim minced up with the entrails of other victims is destined to become a wolf. Did you never hear it?

O yes.

And the protector of the people is like him; having a mob entirely at his disposal, he is not restrained from shedding the blood of kinsmen; by the favourite method of false accusation he brings them into court and murders them, making the life of man to disappear, and with unholy tongue and lips tasting the blood of his fellow citizen; some he kills and others he banishes, at the same time hinting at the abolition of debts and partition of lands: and after this, what will be his destiny? Must he not either perish at the hands of his enemies, or from being a man become a wolf—that is, a tyrant?

3. *Aristotle on Democracy* (Politics, *1317b–1318a; 1318b–1319b; 1310a)* *

The basis of a democratic state is liberty; which, according to the common opinion of men, can only be enjoyed in such a

* Translated by Benjamin Jowett.

state;—this they affirm to be the great end of every democracy. One principle of liberty is for all to rule and be ruled in turn, and indeed democratic justice is the application of numerical not proportionate equality; whence it follows that the majority must be supreme, and that whatever the majority approve must be the end and the just. Every citizen, it is said, must have equality, and therefore in a democracy the poor have more power than the rich, because there are more of them, and the will of the majority is supreme. This, then, is one note of liberty which all democrats affirm to be the principle of their state. Another is that a man should live as he likes. This, they say, is the privilege of a free-man, since, on the other hand, not to live as a man likes is the mark of a slave. This is the second characteristic of democracy, whence has arisen the claim of men to be ruled by none, if possible, or, if this is impossible, to rule and be ruled in turns; and so it contributes to the freedom based upon equality.

Such being our foundation and such the principle from which we start, the characteristics of democracy are as follows:—the election of officers by all out of all; and that all should rule over each, and each in his turn over all; that the appointment to all offices, or to all but those which require experience and skill, should be made by lot; that no property qualification should be required for offices, or only a very low one; that a man should not hold the same office twice, or not often, or in the case of few except military offices: that the tenure of all offices, or of as many as possible, should be brief; that all men should sit in judgement, or that judges selected out of all should judge, in all matters, or in most and in the greatest and most important—such as the scrutiny of accounts, the constitution, and private contracts; that the assembly should be supreme over all causes, or at any rate over the most important, and the magistrates over none or only over a very few. Of all magistracies, a council is the most democratic when there is not the means of paying all the citizens, but when they are paid even this is robbed of its power; for the people then draw all cases to themselves, as I said in the previous discussion. The next characteristic of democracy is payment for services; assembly, law-courts, magistrates, everybody receives pay, when it is to be had; or when it is not to be had for all, then it is given to the law-courts and to the stated assemblies, to the council and to the magistrates, or at least to any of them who are compelled to have their meals together. And whereas oligarchy is characterized by birth, wealth, and education, the notes of democracy appear to be the opposite of these—low birth, poverty, mean employment. Another note is that no magistracy is perpetual, but if any such have survived some ancient change in the constitution it should be stripped of its power, and the holders should be elected by lot and no longer by vote. These are the points common to all democracies; but democracy and demos in their truest form are based upon the recognized principle of democratic justice, that all should count equally; for equality implies that the poor should have no more share in the government than the rich, and should not be the only rulers, but that all should rule equally according to their numbers. And in this way men think that they will secure equality and freedom in their state. . . .

Of the four kinds of democracy, as was said in the previous discussion, the best is that which comes first in order; it is also the oldest of them all. I am speaking of them according to the natural classification of their inhabitants. For the best material of democracy is an agricultural population; there is no difficulty in forming a democracy where the mass of the people live by agriculture or tending of cattle. Being poor, they have no leisure, and therefore do not often attend the assembly, and not having the necessaries of life they are always at work, and do not covet the property of others. Indeed, they find their employment pleasanter than the cares of government or office where no great gains can be made out of them, for the many are more desirous of gain than of honour. A proof is that even the ancient tyrannies were patiently endured by them, as they still endure oligarchies, if they are allowed to work and are not deprived of their property; for some of them grow quickly rich and the others are well enough off. Moreover, they have the power of electing the magistrates and calling them to account; their ambition, if they have any, is thus satisfied; and in some democracies, although they do not all share in the appointment of offices, except through representatives elected in turn out of the whole people, as at Mantinea;—yet, if they have the power of deliberating, the many are contented. Even this form of government may be regarded as a democracy, and was such at Mantinea. Hence it is both expedient and customary in the afore-mentioned type of democracy that all should elect to offices, and conduct scrutinies, and sit in the law-courts, but that the great offices should be filled up by election and from persons having a qualification; the greater requiring a greater qualification, or, if there be no offices for which a qualification is required, then those who are marked out by special ability should be appointed. Under such a form of government the citizens are sure to be governed well (for the offices will always be held by the best persons; the people are willing enough to elect them and are not jealous of the good). The good and the notables will then be satisfied, for they will not be governed by men who are their inferiors, and the persons elected will rule justly, because others will call them to account. Every man should be responsible to others, nor should any one be allowed to do just as he pleases; for where absolute freedom is allowed there is nothing to restrain the evil which is inherent in every man. But the principle of responsibility secures that which is the greatest good in states; the right persons rule and are prevented from doing wrong, and the people have their due. It is evident that this is the best kind of democracy, and why? Because the people are drawn from a certain class. Some of the ancient laws of most states were, all of them, useful with a view to making the people husbandmen. They provided either that no one should possess more than a certain quantity of land, or that, if he did, the land should not be within a certain distance from the town or the acropolis. Formerly in many states there was a law forbidding any one to sell his original allotment of land. There is a similar law attributed to Oxylus, which is to the effect that there should be a certain portion of every man's land on which he could not borrow money. A useful corrective to the evil of which I am speaking would be the law of the Aphytaeans, who, although they are numerous, and do not possess much land, are all of them husbandmen. For their properties are reckoned in the census, not entire, but only in such small portions that even the poor may have more than the amount required.

Next best to an agricultural, and in many respects similar, are a pastoral people, who live by their flocks; they are the best trained of any for war, robust in body and able to camp out. The people of whom other democracies consist are far inferior to them, for their life is inferior; there is no room for moral excellence in any of their employments, whether they be mechanics or traders or labourers. Besides, people of this class can readily come to the assembly, because they are continually moving about in the city and in the agora; whereas husbandmen are scattered over the country and do not meet, or equally feel the want of assembling together. Where the territory also happens to extend to a distance from the city, there is no difficulty in making an excellent democracy or constitutional government; for the people are compelled to settle in the country, and even if there is a town population the assembly ought not to meet, in democracies, when the country people cannot come. We have thus explained how the first and best form of democracy should be constituted; it is clear that the other or inferior sorts will deviate in a regular order, and the population which is excluded will at each stage be of a lower kind.

The last form of democracy, that in which all share alike, is one which cannot be borne by all states, and will not last long unless well regulated by laws and customs. The more general causes which tend to destroy this or other kinds of government have been pretty fully considered. In order to constitute such a democracy and strengthen the people, the leaders have been in the habit of including as many as they can, and making citizens not only of those who are legitimate, but even of the illegitimate, and of those who have only one parent a citizen, whether father or mother; for nothing of this sort comes amiss to such a democracy. This is the way in which demagogues proceed. Whereas the right thing would be to make no more additions when the number of the commonalty exceeds that of the notables and of the middle class—beyond this not to go. When in excess of this point, the constitution becomes disorderly, and the notables grow excited and impatient of the democracy, as in the insurrection at Cyrene; for no notice is taken of a little evil, but when it increases it strikes the eye. Measures like those which Cleisthenes passed when he wanted to increase the power of the democracy at Athens, or such as were taken by the founders of popular government at Cyrene, are useful in the extreme form of democracy. Fresh tribes and brotherhoods should be established; the private rites of families should be restricted and converted into public ones; in short, every contrivance should be adopted which will mingle the citizens with one another and get rid of old connexions. Again, the measures which are taken by tyrants appear all of them to be democratic; such, for instance, as the licence permitted to slaves (which may be to a certain extent advantageous) and also that of women and children, and the allowing everybody to live as he likes. Such a government will have many supporters, for most persons would rather live in a disorderly than in a sober manner. . . .

* * *

And in democracies of the more extreme type there has arisen a false idea of freedom which is contradictory to the true interests of the state. For two principles are characteristic of democracy, the government of the majority and freedom. Men think that what is just is equal; and that equality is the supremacy of the popular will; and that freedom means the doing what a man likes. In such democracies every one lives as he pleases, or in the words of Euripides, 'according to his fancy.' But this is all wrong; men should not think it slavery to live according to the rule of the constitution; for it is their salvation.

4. *Pericles on Athenian Democracy— The Funeral Oration (Thucydides* 2, 35-46)*

In 430 B.C. Pericles recited the customary oration over those Athenians who had fallen in the first year of the Pelopon-nesian War. He used the occasion to offer a defense and justification of the democracy of Athens.

Most of my predecessors in this place have commended him who made this speech part of the law, telling us that it is well that it should be delivered at the burial of those who fall in battle. For myself, I should have thought that the worth which had dis-played itself in deeds, would be sufficiently rewarded by hon-ours also shown by deeds; such as you now see in this funeral prepared at the people's cost. And I could have wished that the reputations of many brave men were not to be imperilled in the mouth of a single individual, to stand or fall according as he spoke well or ill. For it is hard to speak properly upon a subject where it is even difficult to convince your hearers that you are speaking the truth. On the one hand, the friend who is

* Translated by Richard Crawley.

familiar with every fact of the story, may think that some point
has not been set forth with that fulness which he wishes and
knows it to deserve; on the other, he who is a stranger to the
matter may be led by envy to suspect exaggeration if he hears
anything above his own nature. For men can endure to hear
others praised only so long as they can severally persuade themselves of their own ability to equal the actions recounted: when
this point is passed, envy comes in and with it incredulity. However, since our ancestors have stamped this custom with their
approval, it becomes my duty to obey the law and to try to satisfy your several wishes and opinions as best I may.

I shall begin with our ancestors: it is both just and proper
that they should have the honour of the first mention on an occasion like the present. They dwelt in the country without break
in the succession from generation to generation, and handed it
down free to the present time by their valour. And if our more
remote ancestors deserve praise, much more do our own fathers,
who added to their inheritance the empire which we now possess, and spared no pains to be able to leave their acquisitions to
us of the present generation. Lastly, there are few parts of our
dominions that have not been augmented by those of us here,
who are still more or less in the vigour of life; while the mother
country has been furnished by us with everything that can enable her to depend on her own resources whether for war or
for peace. That part of our history which tells of the military
achievements which gave us our several possessions, or of the
ready valour with which either we or our fathers stemmed the
tide of Hellenic or foreign aggression, is a theme too familiar to
my hearers for me to dilate on, and I shall therefore pass it by.
But what was the road by which we reached our position, what
the form of government under which our greatness grew, what
the national habits out of which it sprang; these are questions
which I may try to solve before I proceed to my panegyric upon
these men; since I think this to be a subject upon which on the
present occasion a speaker may properly dwell, and to which
the whole assemblage, whether citizens or foreigners, may listen
with advantage.

Our constitution does not copy the laws of neighbouring
states; we are rather a pattern to others than imitators ourselves.
Its administration favours the many instead of the few; this is
why it is called a democracy. If we look to the laws, they afford
equal justice to all in their private differences; if to social stand-

ing, advancement in public life falls to reputation for capacity, class considerations not being allowed to interfere with merit; nor again does poverty bar the way, if a man is able to serve the state, he is not hindered by the obscurity of his condition. The freedom which we enjoy in our government extends also to our ordinary life. There, far from exercising a jealous surveillance over each other, we do not feel called upon to be angry with our neighbour for doing what he likes, or even to indulge in those injurious looks which cannot fail to be offensive, although they inflict no positive penalty. But all this ease in our private relations does not make us lawless as citizens. Against this fear is our chief safeguard, teaching us to obey the magistrates and the laws, particularly such as regard the protection of the injured, whether they are actually on the statute book, or belong to that code which, although unwritten, yet cannot be broken without acknowledged disgrace.

Further, we provide plenty of means for the mind to refresh itself from business. We celebrate games and sacrifices all the year round, and the elegance of our private establishments forms a daily source of pleasure and helps to banish the spleen; while the magnitude of our city draws the produce of the world into our harbour, so that to the Athenian the fruits of other countries are as familiar a luxury as those of his own.

'If we turn to our military policy, there also we differ from our antagonists. We throw open our city to the world, and never by alien acts exclude foreigners from any opportunity of learning or observing, although the eyes of an enemy may occasionally profit by our liberality; trusting less in system and policy than to the native spirit of our citizens; while in education, where our rivals from their very cradles by a painful discipline seek after manliness, at Athens we live exactly as we please, and yet are just as ready to encounter every legitimate danger. In proof of this it may be noticed that the Lacedaemonians do not invade our country alone, but bring with them all their confederates; while we Athenians advance unsupported into the territory of a neighbour, and fighting upon a foreign soil usually vanquish with ease men who are defending their homes. Our united force was never yet encountered by any enemy, because we have at once to attend to our marine and to despatch our citizens by land upon a hundred different services; so that, wherever they engage with some such fraction of our strength, a success against a detachment is magnified into a victory over the

nation, and a defeat into a reverse suffered at the hands of our
entire people. And yet if with habits not of labour but of ease,
and courage not of art but of nature, we are still willing to
encounter danger, we have the double advantage of escaping
the experience of hardships in anticipation and of facing them
in the hour of need as fearlessly as those who are never free
from them.

Nor are these the only points in which our city is worthy of
admiration. We cultivate refinement without extravagance and
knowledge without effeminacy; wealth we employ more for use
than for show, and place the real disgrace of poverty not in own-
ing to the fact but in declining the struggle against it. Our public
men have, besides politics, their private affairs to attend to, and
our ordinary citizens, though occupied with the pursuits of industry, are still fair judges of public matters; for, unlike any
other nation, regarding him who takes no part in these duties
not as unambitious but as useless, we Athenians are able to judge
at all events if we cannot originate, and instead of looking on
discussion as a stumbling-block in the way of action, we think
it an indispensable preliminary to any wise action at all. Again,
in our enterprises we present the singular spectacle of daring
and deliberation, each carried to its highest point, and both
united in the same persons; although usually decision is the fruit
of ignorance, hesitation of reflexion. But the palm of courage
will surely be adjudged most justly to those, who best know the
difference between hardship and pleasure and yet are never
tempted to shrink from danger. In generosity we are equally
singular, acquiring our friends by conferring not by receiving
favours. Yet, of course, the doer of the favour is the firmer friend
of the two, in order by continued kindness to keep the recipient
in his debt; while the debtor feels less keenly from the very
consciousness that the return he makes will be a payment, not a
free gift. And it is only the Athenians who, fearless of consequences, confer their benefits not from calculations of expedi-
ency, but in the confidence of liberality.

In short, I say that as a city we are the school of Hellas;
while I doubt if the world can produce a man, who where he
has only himself to depend upon, is equal to so many emergencies, and graced by so happy a versatility as the Athenian. And
that this is no mere boast thrown out for the occasion, but
plain matter of fact, the power of the state acquired by these
habits proves. For Athens alone of her contemporaries is found

when tested to be greater than her reputation, and alone gives no occasion to her assailants to blush at the antagonist by whom they have been worsted, or to her subjects to question her title by merit to rule. Rather, the admiration of the present and succeeding ages will be ours, since we have not left our power without witness, but have shown it by mighty proofs; and far from needing a Homer for our panegyrist, or other of his craft whose verses might charm for the moment only for the impression which they gave to melt at the touch of fact, we have forced every sea and land to be the highway of our daring, and everywhere, whether for evil or for good, have left imperishable monuments behind us. Such is the Athens for which these men, in the assertion of their resolve not to lose her, nobly fought and died; and well may every one of their survivors be ready to suffer in her cause.

'Indeed if I have dwelt at some length upon the character of our country, it has been to show that our stake in the struggle is not the same as theirs who have no such blessings to lose, and also that the panegyric of the men over whom I am now speaking might be by definite proofs established. That panegyric is now in a great measure complete; for the Athens that I have celebrated is only what the heroism of these and their like have made her, men whose fame, unlike that of most Hellenes, will be found to be only commensurate with their deserts. And if a test of worth be wanted, it is to be found in their closing scene, and this not only in the cases in which it set the final seal upon their merit, but also in those in which it gave the first intimation of their having any. For there is justice in the claim that steadfastness in his country's battles should be as a cloak to cover a man's other imperfections; since the good action has blotted out the bad, and his merit as a citizen more than outweighed his demerits as an individual. But none of these allowed either wealth with its prospect of future enjoyment to unnerve his spirit, or poverty with its hope of a day of freedom and riches to tempt him to shrink from danger. No, holding that vengeance upon their enemies was more to be desired than any personal blessings, and reckoning this to be the most glorious of hazards, they joyfully determined to accept the risk, to make sure of their vengeance and to let their wishes wait; and while committing to hope the uncertainty of final success, in the business before them they thought fit to act boldly and trust in themselves. Thus choosing to die resisting, rather than to live submitting, they fled only from dishonour, but met danger face to face, and after one brief moment, while at the summit of their fortune, escaped, not from their fear, but from their glory.

So died these men as became Athenians. You, their survivors, must determine to have as unaltering a resolution in the field, though you may pray that it may have a happier issue. And not contented with ideas derived only from words of the advantages which are bound up with the defence of your country, though these would furnish a valuable text to a speaker even before an audience so alive to them as the present, you must yourselves realise the power of Athens, and feed your eyes upon her from day to day, till love of her fills your hearts; and then when all her greatness shall break upon you, you must reflect that it was by courage, sense of duty, and a keen feeling of honour in action that men were enabled to win all this, and that no personal failure in an enterprise could make them consent to deprive their country of their valour, but they laid it at her feet as the most glorious contribution that they could offer. For this offering of their lives made in common by them all they each of them individually received that renown which never grows old, and for a sepulchre, not so much that in which their bones have been deposited, but that noblest of shrines wherein their glory is laid up to be eternally remembered upon every occasion on which deed or story shall fall for its commemoration. For heroes have the whole earth for their tomb; and in lands far from their own, where the column with its epitaph declares it, there is enshrined in every breast a record unwritten with no tablet to preserve it, except that of the heart. These take as your model, and judging happiness to be the fruit of freedom and freedom of valour, never decline the dangers of war. For it is not the miserable that would most justly be unsparing of their lives; these have nothing to hope for: it is rather they to whom continued life may bring reverses as yet unknown, and to whom a fall, if it came, would be most tremendous in its consequences. And surely, to a man of spirit, the degradation of cowardice must be immeasurably more grievous than the unfelt death which strikes him in the midst of his strength and patriotism!

Comfort, therefore, not condolence, is what I have to offer to the parents of the dead who may be here. Numberless are the chances to which, as they know, the life of man is subject; but fortunate indeed are they who draw for their lot a death so glorious as that which has caused your mourning, and to whom life has been so exactly measured as to terminate in the happiness in which it has been passed. Still I know that this is a hard saying, especially when those are in question of whom you will constantly be reminded by seeing in the homes of others blessings of which once you also boasted: for grief is felt not so much for the want of what we have never known, as for the loss of that to which we have been long accustomed. Yet you who are still of an age to beget children must bear up in the hope of having others in their stead; not only will they help you to forget those whom you have lost, but will be to the state at once a reinforcement and a security; for never can a fair or just policy be expected of the citizen who does not, like his fellows, bring to the decision the interests and apprehensions of a father. While those of you who have passed your prime must congratulate yourselves with the thought that the best part of your life was fortunate, and that the brief span that remains will be cheered by the fame of the departed. For it is only the love of honour that never grows old; and honour it is, not gain, as some would have it, that rejoices the heart of age and helplessness.

Turning to the sons or brothers of the dead, I see an arduous struggle before you. When a man is gone, all are wont to praise him, and should your merit be ever so transcendent, you will still find it difficult not merely to overtake, but even to approach their renown. The living have envy to contend with, while those who are no longer in our path are honoured with a goodwill into which rivalry does not enter. On the other hand, if I must say anything on the subject of female excellence to those of you who will now be in widowhood, it will be all comprised in this brief exhortation. Great will be your glory in not falling short of your natural character, and greatest will be hers who is least talked of among the men whether for good or for bad.

My task is now finished. I have performed it to the best of my ability, and in words, at least, the requirements of the law are now satisfied. If deeds be in question, those who are here interred have received part of their honours already, and for the rest, their children will be brought up till manhood at the public expense: the state thus offers a valuable prize, as the garland of victory in this race of valour, for the reward both of

those who have fallen and their survivors. And where the rewards
for merit are greatest, there are found the best citizens.

And now that you have brought to a close your lamentations
for your relatives, you may depart.

5. The Funeral Oration of Aspasia
(Plato: Menexenus, 238-239)*

In the Menexenus *Plato puts into the mouth of Aspasia, the
mistress of Pericles, a funeral oration in which a common
theme of such performance, the defense of the democratic
constitution, is touched upon. Whether intended seriously
or satirically it surely gives us a good idea of what was the
kind of argument used for such a purpose.*

Thus born into the world and thus educated, the ancestors
of the departed lived and made themselves a government, which
I ought briefly to commemorate. For government is the nurture
of man, and the government of good men is good, and of bad
men bad. And I must show that our ancestors were trained under
a good government, and for this reason they were good, and
our contemporaries are also good, among whom our departed
friends are to be reckoned. Then as now, and indeed always, from
that time to this, speaking generally, our government was an
aristocracy—a form of government which receives various names,
according to the fancies of men, and is sometimes called democracy, but is really an aristocracy or government of the best which
has the approval of the many. For kings we have always had,
first hereditary and then elected, and authority is mostly in the
hands of the people, who dispense offices and power to those who
appear to be most deserving of them. Neither is a man rejected
from weakness or poverty or obscurity of origin, nor honoured
by reason of the opposite, as in other states, but there is one
principle—he who appears to be wise and good is a governor

* Translated by Benjamin Jowett.

and ruler. The basis of this our government is equality of birth;
for other states are made up of all sorts and unequal conditions
of men, and therefore their governments are unequal; there are
tyrannies and there are oligarchies, in which the one party are
slaves and the others masters. But we and our citizens are brethren, the children all of one mother, and we do not think it right
to be one another's masters or servants; but the natural equality
of birth compels us to seek for legal equality, and to recognize
no superiority except in the reputation of virtue and wisdom.

6. Euripides on Democracy (The Suppliant Women, 399–462)*

*In this scene a herald from Thebes confronts Theseus, king
of an anachronistically democratic Athens. They hold a
brief conversation in which the herald challenges and Theseus
defends democracy.*

(*Enter a Herald from Thebes.*)

Herald:
  What man is master in this land? To whom
  Must I give the word I bring from Creon, ruler
  In Cadmus' country since Eteocles
  Fell at his brother Polynices' hand
  Beside the seven-mouthed gates?
Theseus:
                One moment, stranger.
  Your start was wrong, seeking a master here.
  This city is free, and ruled by one man.
  The people reign, in annual succession.
  They do not yield the power to the rich;
  The poor man has an equal share in it.

* Translated by Frank Jones in *The Complete Greek Tragedies*, David
Grene and Richmond Lattimore, eds. (Chicago, 1958). By permission of the
University of Chicago Press.

Herald:
   That one point gives the better of the game
   To me. The town I come from is controlled
   By one man, not a mob. And there is no one
   To puff it up with words, for private gain,
   Swaying it this way, that way. Such a man
   First flatters it with wealth of favors; then
   He does it harm, but covers up his blunders
   By blaming other men, and goes scot-free.
   The people is no right judge of arguments;
   Then how can it give right guidance to a city?
   A poor man, working hard, could not attend
   To public matters, even if ignorance
   Were not his birthright. When a wretch, a nothing,
   Obtains respect and power from the people
   By talk, his betters sicken at the sight.
Theseus:
   What bombast from a herald! Waster of words,
   If it is argument you want—and you yourself
   Have set the battle going—listen. Nothing
   Is worse for a city than an absolute ruler.
   In earliest times, before there are common laws,
   One man has power and makes the law his own:
   Equality is not yet. With written laws,
   People of few resources and the rich
   Both have the same recourse to justice. Now
   A man of means, if badly spoken of,
   Will have no better standing than the weak;
   And if the lesser is in the right, he wins
   Against the great. This is the call of freedom:
   "What man has good advice to give the city,
   And wishes to make it known?" He who responds
   Gains glory; the unwilling may hold their peace.
   For the city, what can be more fair than that?
   Again, when the people is master in the land,
   It welcomes youthful townsmen as its subjects;
   But when one man is king, he finds this hateful,
   And if he thinks that any of the nobles
   Are wise, he fears for his despotic power
   And kills them. How can a city become strong
   If someone takes away, cuts off new ventures

Like ears of corn in a spring field? What use
To build a fortune, if your work promotes
The despot's welfare, not your family's?
Why bring up girls as gentlewomen, fit
For marriage, if tyrants may take them for their joy—
A grief to parents? I would rather die
Than see my children forced to such a union.
   These are the darts I shoot at what you say.
What have you come to ask of this, our country?
You talk too much; you would regret your visit
Had not a city sent you. Messengers
Should state their mission promptly, then return.
I hope that henceforth, to my city, Creon
Sends a less wordy messenger than you.

7. *Lysias—The Funeral Oration* (Funeral Oration, *17–19*) *

Lysias, an alien resident at Athens in the late fifth and early fourth centuries, was a professional speech-writer and a loyal democrat. The following passage puts forward several crucial principles of democratic theory as it was understood in classical Athens.

Now in many ways it was natural to our ancestors, moved by a single resolve, to fight the battles of justice: for the very beginning of their life was just. They had not been collected, like most nations, from every quarter, and had not settled in a foreign land after driving out its people: they were born of the soil, and possessed in one and the same country their mother and their fatherland. They were the first and the only people in that time to drive out the ruling classes of their state and to establish a democracy, believing the liberty of all to be the strongest bond of

* Translated by W. R. Lamb in *Lysias, The Loeb Classical Library*. By permission of William Heinemann, Ltd.

agreement; by sharing with each other the hopes born of their perils they had freedom of soul in their civic life, and used law for honouring the good and punishing the evil. For they deemed that it was the way of wild beasts to be held subject to one another by force, but the duty of men to delimit justice by law, to convince by reason, and to serve these two in act by submitting to the sovereignty of law and the instruction of reason.

8. Aeschines (Against Timarchus, 4-8)*

Aeschines, an Athenian orator of the fourth century, here argues for the close connection of democracy and the rule of law.

I am aware, fellow citizens, that the statement which I am about to make first is something that you will undoubtedly have heard from other men on other occasions; but I think the same thought is especially timely on this occasion, and from me. It is acknowledged, namely, that there are in the world three forms of government, autocracy, oligarchy, and democracy: autocracies and oligarchies are administered according to the tempers of their lords, but democratic states according to established laws. And be assured, fellow citizens, that in a democracy it is the laws that guard the person of the citizen and the constitution of the state, whereas the despot and the oligarch find their protection in suspicion and in armed guards. Men, therefore, who administer an oligarchy, or any government based upon inequality, must be on their guard against those who attempt revolution by the law of force; but you, who have a government based upon equality and law, must guard against those whose words violate the laws or whose lives have defied them; for then only will you be strong, when you cherish the laws, and when the revolutionary attempts of lawless men shall have

* Translated by C. D. Adams in *Aeschines, The Loeb Classical Library.* By permission of William Heinemann, Ltd.

ceased. And it behooves us, I think, not only when we are en-
acting laws, to consider always how the laws that we make
may be good and advantageous to the democracy, but when
once we have enacted them, it equally behooves us, if all is to
be well with the state, to obey the laws that we have enacted,
and to punish those who do not obey them.

Consider fellow citizens, how much attention that ancient
lawgiver, Solon, gave to morality, as did Draco and the other
lawgivers of those days. First, you recall, they laid down laws
to protect the morals of our children, and they expressly prescribed what were to be the habits of the freeborn boy, and
how he was to be brought up; then they legislated for the lads,
and next for the other age-groups in succession, including in
their provision, not only private citizens, but also the public
men. And when they had inscribed these laws, they gave them
to you in trust, and made you their guardians.

Now it is my desire, in addressing you on this occasion, to
follow in my speech the same order which the lawgiver followed in his laws. For you shall hear first a review of the laws
that have been laid down to govern the orderly conduct of
your children, then the laws concerning the lads, and next those
concerning the other ages in succession, including not only private citizens, but the public men as well. For so, I think, my
argument will most easily be followed. And at the same time I
wish, fellow citizens, first to describe to you in detail the laws
of the state, and then in contrast with the laws to examine the
character and habits of Timarchus. For you will find that the life
he has lived has been contrary to all the laws.

9. *Demosthenes:* Against Leptines, *105–108**

Demosthenes was the greatest orator of the fourth century and a leading democratic politician. The following passage is an example of a favorite theme of the orators, the difference between Spartan oligarchy and Athenian democracy.

Now I have been quite seriously informed that with regard to the absolute prohibition of all rewards, whatever a man's services may be, our opponents are prepared to use some such argument as this. The Lacedaemonians, who are a well-organized state, and the Thebans grant no such reward to any of their citizens, and yet possibly there are some good men among them. In my opinion, men of Athens, all such arguments are provocative, and intended to persuade you to abolish the immunities, but just they are certainly not. For I am quite aware that the Thebans and the Lacedaemonians and ourselves do not observe the same laws and customs, nor the same form of government. For in the first place, if this is their argument, they are about to do exactly what a man cannot do at Sparta—praise the laws of Athens or of any other state; nay, so far from that, he is obliged to praise, as well as do, whatever accords with his native constitution. Then again, though the Lacedaemonians do not hold with these customs, yet there are other honours at Sparta, which our citizens to a man would shrink from introducing here. What, then, are those honours? Not to take each singly, I will describe one which comprises all the rest. Whenever a man for his good conduct is elected to the Senate, or Gerusia, as they call it, he is absolute master of the mass of citizens. For at Sparta the prize of merit is to share with one's peers the supremacy in the State; but with us the people is supreme, and any other form of supremacy is forbidden by imprecations and laws and other safe-

* Translated by J. H. Vince in *The Loeb Classical Library*. By permission of William Heinemann, Ltd.

guards, but we have crowns of honour and immunities and free maintenance and similar rewards, which anyone may win, if he is a good citizen. And both these customs are right enough, the one at Sparta and the other here. Why? Because in an oligarchy harmony is attained by the equality of those who control the State, but the freedom of a democracy is guarded by the rivalry with which good citizens compete for the rewards offered by the people.

10. *Demosthenes:* The Funeral Speech, 25-26*

While it stands to reason that many influences helped to make them what they were, not least was their virtue ascribable to our form of government. For though absolute governments dominated by a few create fear in their citizens, they fail to awaken the sense of shame. Consequently, when the test of war comes, everyone lightheartedly proceeds to save himself, knowing full well that if only he succeeds in appeasing his masters by presents or any other civility whatsoever, even though he becomes guilty of the most revolting conduct, only slight reproach will attach to him thereafter. Democracies, however, possess many other just and noble features, to which right-minded men should hold fast, and in particular it is impossible to deter freedom of speech, which depends upon speaking the truth, from exposing the truth. For neither is it possible for those who commit a shameful act to appease all the citizens, so that even the lone individual, uttering the deserved reproach, makes the guilty wince: for even those who would never speak an accusing word themselves are pleased at hearing the same, provided another utters it. Through fear of such condemnation, all these men, as was to be expected, for shame at the thought of subsequent reproaches, manfully faced the threat arising from our foes and chose a noble death in preference to life and disgrace.

* Translated by N. W. and N. J. De Witt in *The Loeb Classical Library.* By permission of William Heinemann, Ltd.

11. *Demosthenes:* Against Timocrates, 59, 75–76*

THE LAW

[Nor shall it be lawful to propose a law applying to a particular man, unless the same be applicable to all Athenian citizens, except by the votes of not less than six thousand citizens voting in the affirmative by ballot.]

It forbids the introduction of any law that does not affect all citizens alike,—an injunction conceived in the true spirit of democracy. As every man has an equal share in the constitution generally, so this statute asserts his equal share in the laws. . . .

Again, we may discern how monstrously he has acted in making his law retrospective, by asking ourselves what is the real difference between government by law and oligarchy; and why we regard those who prefer to live under laws as honest, sober-minded persons, and those who submit to oligarchical rule as cowards and slaves. The outstanding difference you will find to be really this: under oligarchical government everybody is entitled to undo the past, and to prescribe future transactions according to his own pleasure; whereas the laws of a free state prescribe what shall be done in the future, such laws having been enacted by convincing people that they will be beneficial to those who live under them. Timocrates however, legislating in a democratically governed city, has introduced into his law the characteristic iniquity of oligarchy; and in dealing with past transactions has presumed to claim for himself an authority higher than that of the convicting jury.

* Translated by J. H. Vince in *The Loeb Classical Library.* By permission of William Heinemann, Ltd.

12. *Pericles and Alcibiades on the Law* (*Xenophon:* Memorabilia, *1, 2, 40–46*)*

Indeed, there is a story told of Alcibiades, that, when he was less than twenty years old, he had a talk about laws with Pericles, his guardian, the first citizen in the State.

"Tell me, Pericles," he said, "can you teach me what a law is?"

"Certainly," he replied.

"Then pray teach me. For whenever I hear men praised for keeping the laws, it occurs to me that no one can really deserve that praise who does not know what a law is."

"Well, Alcibiades, there is no great difficulty about what you desire. You wish to know what a law is. Laws are all the rules approved and enacted by the majority in assembly, whereby they declare what ought and what ought not to be done."

"Do they suppose it is right to do good or evil?"

"Good, of course, young man,—not evil."

"But if, as happens under an oligarchy, not the majority, but a minority meet and enact rules of conduct, what are these?"

"Whatsoever the sovereign power in the State, after deliberation, enacts and directs to be done is known as a law."

"If, then, a despot, being the sovereign power, enacts what the citizens are to do, are his orders also a law?"

"Yes, whatever a despot as ruler enacts is also known as a law."

"But force, the negation of law, what is that, Pericles? Is it not the action of the stronger when he constrains the weaker to do whatever he chooses, not by persuasion, but by force?"

"That is my opinion."

"Then whatever a despot by enactment constrains the citizens to do without persuasion, is the negation of law?"

"I think so: and I withdraw my answer that whatever a despot enacts without persuasion is a law."

"And when the minority passes enactments, not by persuading the majority, but through using its power, are we to call that force or not?"

* Translated by E. C. Marchant in *The Loeb Classical Library.* By permission of William Heinemann, Ltd.

"Everything, I think, that men constrain others to do 'without persuasion,' whether by enactment or not, is not law, but force."

"It follows then, that whatever the assembled majority, through using its power over the owners of property, enacts without persuasion is not law, but force?"

"Alcibiades," said Pericles, "at your age, I may tell you, we, too, were very clever at this sort of thing. For the puzzles we thought about and exercised our wits on were just such as you seem to think about now."

"Ah, Pericles," cried Alcibiades, "if only I had known you intimately when you were at your cleverest in these things!"

13. Demosthenes on the Law
(Against Aristogeiton, 20–22; 15–16) *

I shall say nothing novel or extravagant or peculiar, but only what you all know to be true as well as I do. For if any of you cares to inquire what is the motive-power that calls together the Council, draws the people into the Assembly, fills the law-courts, makes the old officials resign readily to the new, and enables the whole life of the State to be carried on and preserved, he will find that it is the laws and the obedience that all men yield to the laws; since, if once they were done away with and every man were given licence to do as he liked, not only does the constitution vanish, but our life would not differ from that of the beasts of the field. You see what the defendant is, when the laws are in force: what do you think he would do, if the laws were done away with? Since then it is admitted that, next after the gods, the laws preserve the State, it is the duty of all of you to act just as if you were sitting here making up a contribution to your club. If a man obeys the laws, respect and commend him for paying his contribution in full to the welfare of his fatherland; if he disobeys them, punish him. For everything done at the bidding of the laws is a contribution made to the State and the community. Whoever leaves it unpaid, men of Athens, is depriving

* Translated by J. H. Vince in *The Loeb Classical Library*. By permission of William Heinemann, Ltd.

you of many great, honourable, and glorious benefits which he is destroying to the best of his ability. . . .

The whole life of men, Athenians, whether they dwell in a large state or a small one, is governed by nature and by the laws. Of these, nature is something irregular and incalculable, and peculiar to each individual; but the laws are something universal, definite, and the same for all. Now nature, if it be evil, often chooses wrong, and that is why you will find men of an evil nature committing errors. But the laws desire what is just and honourable and salutary; they seek for it, and when they find it, they set it forth as a general commandment, equal and identical for all. The law is that which all men ought to obey for many reasons, but above all because every law is an invention and gift of the gods, a tenet of wise men, a corrective of errors voluntary and involuntary, and a general covenant of the whole State, in accordance with which all men in that State ought to regulate their lives. . . . For there are two objects, men of Athens, for which all laws are framed—to deter any man from doing what is wrong, and, by punishing the transgressor, to make the rest better men. . . .

14. Protagoras in Defense of the Athenian Democracy (*Plato:* Protagoras, *320–328*)*

In the dialogue bearing his name Protagoras is made to defend his own profession as teacher of political virtue by arguing that political virtue can be taught. He does so by means of a myth and a reasoned exposition. Together they form the best statement of the ultimate assumptions underlying Greek democracy in our possession.

Once upon a time there were gods only, and no mortal creatures. But when the time came that these also should be created, the gods fashioned them out of earth and fire and various mix-

* Translated by Benjamin Jowett.

tures of both elements in the interior of the earth; and when they were about to bring them into the light of day, they ordered Prometheus and Epimetheus to equip them, and to distribute to them severally their proper qualities. Epimetheus said to Prometheus: 'Let me distribute, and do you inspect.' This was agreed, and Epimetheus made the distribution. There were some to whom he gave strength without swiftness, while he equipped the weaker with swiftness; some he armed, and others he left unarmed; and devised for the latter some other means of preservation, making some large, and having their size as a protection, and others small, whose nature was to fly in the air or burrow in the ground; this was to be their way of escape. Thus did he compensate them with the view of preventing any race from becoming extinct. And when he had provided against their destruction by one another, he contrived also a means of protecting them against the seasons of heaven; clothing them with close hair and thick skins sufficient to defend them against the winter cold and able to resist the summer heat, so that they might have a natural bed of their own when they wanted to rest; also he furnished them with hoofs and hair and hard and callous skins under their feet. Then he gave them varieties of food,—herb of the soil to some, to others fruits of trees, and to others roots, and to some again he gave other animals as food. And some he made to have few young ones, while those who were their prey were very prolific; and in this manner the race was preserved. Thus did Epimetheus, who, not being very wise, forgot that he had distributed among the brute animals all the qualities which he had to give,—and when he came to man, who was still unprovided, he was terribly perplexed. Now while he was in this perplexity, Prometheus came to inspect the distribution, and he found that the other animals were suitably furnished, but that man alone was naked and shoeless, and had neither bed nor arms of defence. The appointed hour was approaching when man in his turn was to go forth into the light of day; and Prometheus, not knowing how he could devise his salvation, stole the mechanical arts of Hephaestus and Athene, and fire with them (they could neither have been acquired nor used without fire), and gave them to man. Thus man had the wisdom necessary to the support of life, but political wisdom he had not; for that was in the keeping of Zeus, and the power of Prometheus did not extend to entering into the citadel of heaven, where Zeus dwelt, who moreover had terrible sentinels; but he

did enter by stealth into the common workshop of Athene and
Hephaestus, in which they used to practise their favourite arts,
and carried off Hephaestus' art of working by fire, and also the
art of Athene, and gave them to man. And in this way man was
supplied with the means of life. But Prometheus is said to have
been afterwards prosecuted for theft, owing to the blunder of
Epimetheus.

Now man, having a share of the divine attributes, was at first
the only one of the animals who had any gods, because he alone
was of their kindred; and he would raise altars and images of
them. He was not long in inventing articulate speech and names;
and he also constructed houses and clothes and shoes and beds,
and drew sustenance from the earth. Thus provided, mankind
at first lived dispersed, and there were no cities. But the consequence was that they were destroyed by the wild beasts, for
they were utterly weak in comparison of them, and their art was
only sufficient to provide them with the means of life, and did
not enable them to carry on war against the animals: food they
had, but not as yet the art of government, of which the art of
war is a part. After a while the desire of self-preservation gathered them into cities; but when they were gathered together,
having no art of government, they evil intreated one another,
and were again in process of dispersion and destruction. Zeus
feared that the entire race would be exterminated, and so he
sent Hermes to them, bearing reverence and justice to be the
ordering principles of cities and the bonds of friendship and conciliation. Hermes asked Zeus how he should impart justice and
reverence among men:—Should he distribute them as the arts
are distributed; that is to say, to a favoured few only, one skilled
individual having enough of medicine or of any other art for
many unskilled ones? 'Shall this be the manner in which I am to
distribute justice and reverence among men, or shall I give them
to all?' 'To all,' said Zeus; 'I should like them all to have a share;
for cities cannot exist, if a few only share in the virtues, as in
the arts. And further, make a law by my order, that he who has
no part in reverence and justice shall be put to death, for he is
a plague of the state.'

And this is the reason, Socrates, why the Athenians and mankind in general, when the question relates to carpentering or any
other mechanical art, allow but a few to share in their delibera-
tions; and when any one else interferes, then, as you say, they
object, if he be not of the favoured few; which, as I reply, is

very natural. But when they meet to deliberate about political
virtue, which proceeds only by way of justice and wisdom, they
are patient enough of any man who speaks of them, as is also
natural, because they think that every man ought to share in
this sort of virtue, and that states could not exist if this were
otherwise. I have explained to you, Socrates, the reason of this
phenomenon.

And that you may not suppose yourself to be deceived in
thinking that all men regard every man as having a share of
justice or honesty and of every other political virtue, let me give
you a further proof, which is this. In other cases, as you are
aware, if a man says that he is a good flute-player, or skilful in
any other art in which he has no skill, people either laugh at
him or are angry with him, and his relations think that he is mad
and go and admonish him; but when honesty is in question, or
some other political virtue, even if they know that he is dis-
honest, yet, if the man comes publicly forward and tells the
truth about his dishonesty, then, what in the other case was
held by them to be good sense, they now deem to be madness.
They say that all men ought to profess honesty whether they
are honest or not, and that a man is out of his mind who says
anything else. Their notion is, that a man must have some degree
of honesty; and that if he has none at all he ought not to be in
the world.

I have been showing that they are right in admitting every
man as a counsellor about this sort of virtue, as they are of opinion that every man is a partaker of it. And I will now endeavour
to show further that they do not conceive this virtue to be given
by nature, or to grow spontaneously, but to be a thing which
may be taught; and which comes to man by taking pains. No
one would instruct, no one would rebuke, or be angry with
those whose calamities they suppose to be due to nature or
chance; they do not try to punish or to prevent them from being
what they are; they do but pity them. Who is so foolish as to
chastise or instruct the ugly, or the diminutive, or the feeble?
And for this reason. Because he knows that good and evil of
this kind is the work of nature and of chance; whereas if a man
is wanting in those good qualities which are attained by study
and exercise and teaching, and has only the contrary evil qualities, other men are angry with him, and punish and reprove
him—of these evil qualities one is impiety, another injustice, and

they may be described generally as the very opposite of political virtue. In such cases any man will be angry with another, and reprimand him,—clearly because he thinks that by study and learning, the virtue in which the other is deficient may be acquired. If you will think, Socrates, of the nature of punishment, you will see at once that in the opinion of mankind virtue may be acquired; no one punishes the evil-doer under the notion, or for the reason, that he has done wrong,—only the unreasonable fury of a beast acts in that manner. But he who desires to inflict rational punishment does not retaliate for a past wrong which cannot be undone; he has regard to the future, and is desirous that the man who is punished, and he who sees him punished, may be deterred from doing wrong again. He punishes for the sake of prevention, thereby clearly implying that virtue is capable of being taught. This is the notion of all who retaliate upon others either privately or publicly. And the Athenians, too, your own citizens, like other men, punish and take vengeance on all whom they regard as evil doers; and hence, we may infer them to be of the number of those who think that virtue may be acquired and taught. Thus far, Socrates, I have shown you clearly enough, if I am not mistaken, that your countrymen are right in admitting the tinker and the cobbler to advise about politics, and also that they deem virtue to be capable of being taught and acquired.

There yet remains one difficulty which has been raised by you about the sons of good men. What is the reason why good men teach their sons the knowledge which is gained from teachers, and make them wise in that, but do nothing towards improving them in the virtues which distinguish themselves? And here, Socrates, I will leave the apologue and resume the argument. Please to consider: Is there or is there not some one quality of which all the citizens must be partakers, if there is to be a city at all? In the answer to this question is contained the only solution of your difficulty; there is no other. For if there be any such quality, and this quality or unity is not the art of the carpenter, or the smith, or the potter, but justice and temperance and holiness and, in a word, manly virtue—if this is the quality of which all men must be partakers, and which is the very condition of their learning or doing anything else, and if he who is wanting in this, whether he be a child only or a grown-up man or woman, must be taught and punished, until

by punishment he becomes better, and he who rebels against
instruction and punishment is either exiled or condemned to
death under the idea that he is incurable—if what I am saying
be true, good men have their sons taught other things and not
this, do consider how extraordinary their conduct would appear
to be. For we have shown that they think virtue capable of
being taught and cultivated both in private and public; and, notwithstanding, they have their sons taught lesser matters, ignorance of which does not involve the punishment of death: but
greater things, of which the ignorance may cause death and
exile to those who have no training or knowledge of them—aye,
and confiscation as well as death, and, in a word, may be the
ruin of families—those things, I say, they are supposed not to
teach them,—not to take the utmost care that they should learn.
How improbable is this, Socrates!

Education and admonition commence in the first years of
childhood, and last to the very end of life. Mother and nurse
and father and tutor are vying with one another about the improvement of the child as soon as ever he is able to understand
what is being said to him: he cannot say or do anything without
their setting forth to him that this is just and that is unjust; this
is honourable, that is dishonourable; this is holy, that is unholy;
do this and abstain from that. And if he obeys, well and good;
if not, he is straightened by threats and blows, like a piece of
bent or warped wood. At a later stage they send him to teachers,
and enjoin them to see to his manners even more than to his
reading and music; and the teachers do as they are desired. And
when the boy has learned his letters and is beginning to understand what is written, as before he understood only what was
spoken, they put into his hands the works of great poets, which
he reads sitting on a bench at school; in these are contained many
admonitions, and many tales, and praises, and encomia of ancient
famous men, which he is required to learn by heart, in order
that he may imitate or emulate them and desire to become like
them. Then, again, the teachers of the lyre take similar care
that their young disciple is temperate and gets into no mischief;
and when they have taught him the use of the lyre, they introduce him to the poems of other excellent poets, who are the
lyric poets; and these they set to music, and make their har-
monies and rhythms quite familiar to the children's souls, in
order that they may learn to be more gentle, and harmonious,

and rhythmical, and so more fitted for speech and action; for
the life of man in every part has need of harmony and rhythm.
Then they send them to the master of gymnastic, in order that
their bodies may better minister to the virtuous mind, and that
they may not be compelled through bodily weakness to play
the coward in war or on any other occasion. This is what is
done by those who have the means, and those who have the
means are the rich; their children begin to go to school soonest
and leave off latest. When they have done with masters, the state
again compels them to learn the laws, and live after the pattern which they furnish, and not after their own fancies; and
just as in learning to write, the writing-master first draws lines
with a style for the use of the young beginner, and gives him
the tablet and makes him follow the lines, so the city draws the
laws, which were the invention of good lawgivers living in the
olden time; these are given to the young man, in order to guide
him in his conduct whether he is commanding or obeying; and
he who transgresses them is to be corrected, or, in other words,
called to account, which is a term used not only in your country,
but also in many others, seeing that justice calls men to account.
Now when there is all this care about virtue private and public,
why, Socrates, do you still wonder and doubt whether virtue
can be taught? Cease to wonder, for the opposite would be far
more surprising.

But why then do the sons of good fathers often turn out ill?
There is nothing very wonderful in this; for, as I have been
saying, the existence of a state implies that virtue is not any
man's private possession. If so—and nothing can be truer—then
I will further ask you to imagine, as an illustration, some other
pursuit or branch of knowledge which may be assumed equally
to be the condition of the existence of a state. Suppose that
there could be no state unless we were all flute-players, as far
as each had the capacity, and everybody was freely teaching
everybody the art, both in private and public, and reproving the
bad player as freely and openly as every man now teaches justice and the laws, not concealing them as he would conceal the
other arts, but imparting them—for all of us have a mutual interest in the justice and virtue of one another, and this is the reason
why every one is so ready to teach justice and the laws;—suppose,
I say, that there were the same readiness and liberality among
us in teaching one another flute-playing, do you imagine, Soc-

rates, that the sons of good flute-players would be more likely
to be good than the sons of bad ones? I think not. Would not
their sons grow up to be distinguished or undistinguished according to their own natural capacities as flute-players, and the
son of a good player would often turn out to be a bad one, and
the son of a bad player to be a good one, and all flute-players
would be good enough in comparison of those who were ignorant
and unacquainted with the art of flute-playing? In like manner I
would have you consider that he who appears to you to be the
worst of those who have been brought up in laws and humani-
ties, would appear to be a just man and a master of justice if
he were to be compared with men who had no education, or
courts of justice, or laws, or any restraints upon them which
compelled them to practise virtue—with the savages, for example,
whom the poet Pherecrates exhibited on the stage at the last
year's Lenaean festival. If you were living among men such as
the man-haters in his Chorus, you would be only too glad to
meet with Eurybates and Phrynondas, and you would sorrow-
fully long to revisit the rascality of this part of the world. And
you, Socrates, are discontented, and why? Because all men are
teachers of virtue, each one according to his ability; and you
say, Where are the teachers? You might as well ask, Who teaches
Greek? For of that too there will not be any teachers found.
Or you might ask, Who is to teach the sons of our artisans this
same art which they have learned of their fathers? He and his
fellow-workmen have taught them to the best of their ability,—
but who will carry them further in their arts? And you would
certainly have a difficulty, Socrates, in finding a teacher of them;
but there would be no difficulty in finding a teacher of those
who are wholly ignorant. And this is true of virtue or of anything else; if a man is better able than we are to promote virtue
ever so little, we must be content with the result. A teacher of
this sort I believe myself to be, and above all other men to have
the knowledge which makes a man noble and good; and I give
my pupils their money's-worth, and even more, as they themselves confess. And therefore I have introduced the following
mode of payment:—When a man has been my pupil, if he likes
he pays my price, but there is no compulsion; and if he does not
like, he has only to go into a temple and take an oath of the
value of the instructions, and he pays no more than he declares
to be their value.

Such is my Apologue, Socrates, and such is the argument by which I endeavour to show that virtue may be taught, and that this is the opinion of the Athenians. And I have also attempted to show that you are not to wonder at good fathers having bad sons, or at good sons having bad fathers, of which the sons of Polycleitus afford an example, who are the companions of our friends here, Paralus and Xanthippus, but are nothing in comparison with their father; and this is true of the sons of many other artists. As yet I ought not to say the same of Paralus and Xanthippus themselves, for they are young and there is still hope of them.

6. *Thucydides*

Thucydides, the historian of the Peloponnesian War, is interesting to the student of political thought for at least two reasons. He was a witness to the greatness of the Athenian democracy and also to its collapse. This provides him with a unique opportunity to report and criticize its political theory and practice. At the same time, he was a political thinker of no little talent and insight. For him history was past politics and the historian's purpose to provide material for the use of future politicians with the genius to use it.

* Translated by Richard Crawley throughout this chapter.

1.   *Methods and Purpose* (*1, 22–23*)

On the whole, . . . the conclusions I have drawn from the proofs quoted may, I believe, safely be relied on. Assuredly they will not be disturbed either by the lays of a poet displaying the exaggeration of his craft, or by the compositions of the chroniclers that are attractive at truth's expense; the subjects they treat of being out of the reach of evidence, and time having robbed most of them of historical value by enthroning them in the region of legend. Turning from these, we can rest satisfied with having proceeded upon the clearest data, and having arrived at conclusions as exact as can be expected in matters of such antiquity. To come to this war; despite the known disposition of the actors in a struggle to overrate its importance, and when it is over to return to their admiration of earlier events, yet an examination of the facts will show that it was much greater than the wars which preceded it.

With reference to the speeches in this history, some were delivered before the war began, others while it was going on; some I heard myself, others I got from various quarters; it was in all cases difficult to carry them word for word in one's memory, so my habit has been to make the speakers say what was in my opinion demanded of them by the various occasions, of course adhering as closely as possible to the general sense of what they really said. And with reference to the narrative of events, far from permitting myself to derive it from the first source that came to hand, I did not even trust my own impressions, but it rests partly on what I saw myself, partly on what others saw for me, the accuracy of the report being always tried by the most severe and detailed tests possible. My conclusions have cost me some labour from the want of coincidence between accounts of the same occurrences by different eye-witnesses, arising sometimes from imperfect memory, sometimes from undue partiality for one side or the other. The absence of romance in my history will, I fear, detract somewhat from its interest; but if it be judged useful by those inquirers who desire an exact knowledge of the past as an aid to the interpretation of the future, which in the course of human things must resemble if it does not re-

flect it, I shall be content. In fine, I have written my work, not
as an essay which is to win the applause of the moment, but as
a possession for all time.

2. The Plague at Athens (2, 49-53)

*In the second year of the war a fearful plague broke out in
Athens. Thucydides describes it in clinical detail, for diag-
nostic and prognostic purposes. Not content with its purely
physical manifestations he comments on its social and political
consequences as well.*

It first began, it is said, in the parts of Ethiopia above Egypt,
and thence descended into Egypt and Libya and into most of
the king's country. Suddenly falling upon Athens, it first attacked the population in Piræus,—which was the occasion of
their saying that the Peloponnesians had poisoned the reservoirs,
their being as yet no wells there—and afterwards appeared in
the upper city, when the deaths became much more frequent.
All speculation as to its origin and its causes, if causes can be
found adequate to produce so great a disturbance, I leave to
other writers, whether lay or professional; for myself, I shall
simply set down its nature, and explain the symptoms by which
perhaps it may be recognised by the student, if it should ever
break out again. This I can the better do, as I had the disease
myself, and watched its operation in the case of others.

That year then is admitted to have been otherwise unprec-
edentedly free from sickness; and such few cases as occurred, all
determined in this. As a rule, however, there was no ostensible
cause; but people in good health were all of a sudden attacked
by violent heats in the head, and redness and inflammation in the
eyes, the inward parts, such as the throat or tongue, becoming
bloody and emitting an unnatural and fetid breath. These symptoms were followed by sneezing and hoarseness, after which the
pain soon reached the chest, and produced a hard cough. When
it fixed in the stomach, it upset it; and discharges of bile of every

kind named by physicians ensued, accompanied by very great distress. In most cases also an ineffectual retching followed, producing violent spasms, which in some cases ceased soon after, in others much later. Externally the body was not very hot to the touch, nor pale in its appearance, but reddish, livid, and breaking out into small pustules and ulcers. But internally it burned so that the patient could not bear to have on him clothing or linen even of the very lightest description; or indeed to be otherwise than stark naked. What they would have liked best would have been to throw themselves into cold water; as indeed was done by some of the neglected sick, who plunged into the rain-tanks in their agonies of unquenchable thirst; though it made no difference whether they drank little or much. Besides this, the miserable feeling of not being able to rest or sleep never ceased to torment them. The body meanwhile did not waste away so long as the distemper was at its height, but held out to a marvel against its ravages; so that when they succumbed, as in most cases, on the seventh or eighth day to the internal inflammation, they had still some strength in them. But if they passed this stage, and the disease descended further into the bowels, inducing a violent ulceration there accompanied by severe diarrhea, this brought on a weakness which was generally fatal. For the disorder first settled in the head, ran its course from thence through the whole of the body, and even where it did not prove mortal, it still left its mark on the extremities; for it settled in the privy parts, the fingers and the toes, and many escaped with the loss of these, some too with that of their eyes. Others again were seized with an entire loss of memory on their first recovery, and did not know either themselves or their friends.

But while the nature of the distemper was such as to baffle all description, and its attacks almost too grievous for human nature to endure, it was still in the following circumstance that its difference from all ordinary disorders was most clearly shown. All the birds and beasts that prey upon human bodies, either abstained from touching them (though there were many lying unburied), or died after tasting them. In proof of this, it was noticed that birds of this kind actually disappeared; they were not about the bodies, or indeed to be seen at all. But of course the effects which I have mentioned could best be studied in a domestic animal like the dog.

Such then, if we pass over the varieties of particular cases, which were many and peculiar, were the general features of the distemper. Meanwhile the town enjoyed an immunity from all the ordinary disorders; or if any case occurred, it ended in this. Some died in neglect, others in the midst of every attention. No remedy was found that could be used as a specific; for what did good in one case, did harm in another. Strong and weak constitutions proved equally incapable of resistance, all alike being swept away, although dieted with the utmost precaution. By far the most terrible feature in the malady was the dejection which ensued when any one felt himself sickening, for the despair into which they instantly fell took away their power of resistance, and left them a much easier prey to the disorder; besides which, there was the awful spectacle of men dying like sheep, through having caught the infection in nursing each other. This caused the greatest mortality. On the one hand, if they were afraid to visit each other, they perished from neglect; indeed many houses were emptied of their inmates for want of a nurse: on the other, if they ventured to do so, death was the consequence. This was especially the case with such as made any pretensions to goodness: honour made them unsparing of themselves in their attendance in their friends' houses, where even the members of the family were at last worn out by the moans of the dying, and succumbed to the force of the disaster. Yet it was with those who had recovered from the disease that the sick and the dying found most compassion. These knew what it was from experience, and had now no fear for themselves; for the same man was never attacked twice—never at least fatally. And such persons not only received the congratulations of others, but themselves also, in the elation of the moment, half entertained the vain hope that they were for the future safe from any disease whatsoever.

An aggravation of the existing calamity was the influx from the country into the city, and this was especially felt by the new arrivals. As there were no houses to receive them, they had to be lodged at the hot season of the year in stifling cabins, where the mortality raged without restraint. The bodies of dying men lay one upon another, and half-dead creatures reeled about the streets and gathered round all the fountains in their longing for water. The sacred places also in which they had quartered themselves were full of corpses of persons that had died there, just as they were; for as the disaster passed all bounds, men, not knowing what was to become of them, became utterly careless of everything, whether sacred or profane. All the burial rites before in use were entirely upset, and they buried the bodies as best they could. Many from want of the proper appliances, through so many of their friends having died already, had recourse to the most shameless sepultures: sometimes getting the start of those who had raised a pile, they threw their own dead body upon the stranger's pyre and ignited it; sometimes they tossed the corpse which they were carrying on the top of another that was burning, and so went off.

Nor was this the only form of lawless extravagance which owed its origin to the plague. Men now coolly ventured on what they had formerly done in a corner, and not just as they pleased, seeing the rapid transitions produced by persons in prosperity suddenly dying and those who before had nothing succeeding to their property. So they resolved to spend quickly and enjoy themselves, regarding their lives and riches as alike things of a day. Perseverance in what men called honour was popular with none, it was so uncertain whether they would be spared to attain the object; but it was settled that present enjoyment, and all that contributed to it, was both honourable and useful. Fear of gods or law of man there was none to restrain them. As for the first, they judged it to be just the same whether they worshipped them or not, as they saw all alike perishing; and for the last, no one expected to live to be brought to trial for his offences, but each felt that a far severer sentence had been already passed upon them all and hung ever over their heads, and before this fell it was only reasonable to enjoy life a little.

3. *Civil War at Corcyra*

In 427 civil war broke out on the island of Corcyra. Thucydides describes it in the same clinical detail as he does the plague at Athens, and for the same reasons.

During seven days that Eurymedon stayed with his sixty ships, the Corcyræans were engaged in butchering those of their fellow-citizens whom they regarded as their enemies: and although the crime imputed was that of attempting to put down the democracy, some were slain also for private hatred, others by their debtors because of the monies owed to them. Death thus raged in every shape; and, as usually happens at such times, there was no length to which violence did not go; sons were killed by their fathers, and suppliants dragged from the altar or slain upon it; while some were even walled up in the temple of Dionysus and died there.

So bloody was the march of the revolution, and the impression which it made was the greater as it was one of the first to occur. Later on, one may say, the whole Hellenic world was convulsed; struggles being everywhere made by the popular chiefs to bring in the Athenians, and by the oligarchs to introduce the Lacedaemonians. In peace there would have been neither the pretext nor the wish to make such an invitation; but in war, with an alliance always at the command of either faction for the hurt of their adversaries and their own corresponding advantage, opportunities for bringing in the foreigner were never wanting to the revolutionary parties. The sufferings which revolution entailed upon the cities were many and terrible, such as have occurred and always will occur, as long as the nature of mankind remains the same; though in a severer or milder form, and varying in their symptoms, according to the variety of the particular cases. In peace and prosperity states and individuals have better sentiments, because they do not find themselves suddenly confronted with imperious necessities; but war takes away the easy supply of daily wants, and so proves a rough master, that brings most men's characters to a level with their fortunes. Revolution thus ran its course from city to city, and the places which it arrived at last, from having heard what had been done before, carried to a still greater excess the refinement of their inventions, as manifested in the cunning of their enterprises and the atrocity of their reprisals. Words had to change their ordinary meaning and to take that which was now given them. Reckless audacity came to be considered the courage of a loyal ally; prudent hesitation, specious cowardice; moderation was held to be a cloak for unmanliness; ability to see all sides of a question inaptness to act on any. Frantic violence became the attribute of manliness; cautious plotting, a justifiable means of self-defence. The advocate of extreme measures was always trustworthy; his opponent a man to be suspected. To succeed in a plot was to have a shrewd head, to divine a plot a still shrewder; but to try to provide against having to do either was to break up your party and to be afraid of your adversaries. In fine, to forestall an intending criminal, or to suggest the idea of a crime where it was wanting, was equally commended, until even blood became a weaker tie than party, from the superior readiness of those united by the latter to dare everything without reserve; for such associations had not in view the blessings derivable from established institutions but were formed by ambition for their overthrow; and the confidence of their members in each other rested less on any religious sanction than upon complicity in crime. The fair proposals of an adversary were met with jealous precautions by the stronger of the two, and not with a generous confidence. Revenge also was held of more account than self-preservation. Oaths of reconciliation, being only profferred on either side to meet an immediate difficulty, only held good so long as no other weapon was at hand; but when opportunity offered, he who first ventured to seize it and to take his enemy off his guard, thought this perfidious vengeance sweeter than an open one, since, considerations of safety apart, success by treachery won him the palm of superior intelligence. Indeed it is generally the case that men are readier to call rogues clever than simpletons honest, and are as ashamed of being the second as they are proud of being the first. The cause of all these evils was the lust for power arising from greed and ambition; and from these passions proceeded the violence of parties once engaged in contention. The leaders in the cities, each provided with the fairest professions, on the one side with the cry of political equality of the people, on the other of a moderate aristocracy, sought prizes for themselves in those public interests which they pretended to cherish, and, recoiling from no means in their struggles for ascendancy, engaged in the direct excesses; in their acts of vengeance they went to even greater lengths, not stopping at what justice or the good of the state demanded, but making the party caprice of the moment their only standard, and invoking with equal readiness the condemnation of an unjust verdict or the authority of the strong arm to glut the animosities of the hour. Thus religion was in honour with neither party; but the use of fair phrases to arrive at guilty ends was in high reputation. Meanwhile the moderate part of the citizens perished between the two, either for not joining in the quarrel, or because envy would not suffer them to escape.

Thus every form of iniquity took root in the Hellenic countries by reason of the troubles. The ancient simplicity into which honour so largely entered was laughed down and disappeared; and society became divided into camps in which no man trusted his fellow. To put an end to this, there was neither promise to be depended upon, nor oath that could command respect; but all parties dwelling rather in their calculation upon the hopelessness of a permanent state of things, were more intent upon self-defence than capable of confidence. In this contest the blunter wits were most successful. Apprehensive of their own deficiencies and of the cleverness of their antagonists, they feared to be worsted in debate and to be surprised by the combinations of their more versatile opponents, and so at once boldly had recourse to action: while their adversaries, arrogantly thinking that they should know in time, and that it was unnecessary to secure by action what policy afforded, often fell victims to their want of precaution.

Meanwhile Corcyra gave the first example of most of the crimes alluded to; of the reprisals exacted by the governed who had never experienced equitable treatment or indeed aught but insolence from their rulers—when their hour came; of the iniquitous resolves of those who desired to get rid of their accustomed poverty, and ardently coveted their neighbours' goods; and lastly, of the savage and pitiless excesses into which men who had begun the struggle not in a class but in a party spirit, were hurried by their ungovernable passions. In the confusion into which life was now thrown in the cities, human nature, always rebelling against the law and now its master, gladly showed itself ungoverned in passion, above respect for justice, and the enemy of all superiority, since revenge would not have been set above religion, and gain above justice, had it not been for the fatal power of envy. Indeed men too often take upon themselves in the prosecution of their revenge to set the example of doing away with those general laws to which all alike can look for salvation in adversity, instead of allowing them to subsist against the day of danger when their aid may be required.

4. The Statesman: Themistocles (1, 137)

As a citizen of Periclean Athens, Thucydides is fascinated by the problem of political leadership in a democracy. It is clear that he believes that democracy can work only when a man of great genius is at the helm. The first example of such a man is Themistocles, the hero of the Persian War.

Themistocles was a man who exhibited the most indubitable signs of genius; indeed, in this particular he has a claim on our admiration quite extraordinary and unparalleled. By his own native capacity, alike unformed and unsupplemented by study, he was at once the best judge in those sudden crises which admit of little or of no deliberation, and the best prophet of the future, even to its most distant possibilities. An able theoretical expositor of all that came within the sphere of his practice, he was not without the power of passing an adequate judgment in matters in which he had no experience. He could also excellently divine the good and evil which lay hid in the unseen future. In fine, whether we consider the extent of his natural powers, or the slightness of his application, this extraordinary man must be allowed to have surpassed all others in the faculty of intuitively meeting an emergency.

5. The Statesman: Pericles (2, 59-60)

The greatest statesman of his time, of course, was Pericles. In the second year of the war he was confronted with serious popular discontent and a challenge to his leadership. His response makes clear the qualities Thucydides admires in a popular leader.

After the second invasion of the Peloponnesians a change came over the spirit of the Athenians. Their land had now been twice laid waste; and war and pestilence at once pressed heavy upon them. They began to find fault with Pericles, as the author of the war and the cause of all their misfortunes, and became eager to come to terms with Lacedaemon, and actually sent ambassadors thither, who did not however succeed in their mission. Their despair was now complete and all vented itself upon Pericles. When he saw them exasperated at the present turn of affairs and acting exactly as he had anticipated, he called an assembly, being (it must be remembered) still general, with the double object of restoring confidence and of leading them from these angry feelings to a calmer and more hopeful state of mind. He accordingly came forward and spoke as follows:

"I was not unprepared for the indignation of which I have been the object, as I know its causes; and I have called an assembly for the purpose of reminding you upon certain points, and of protesting against your being unreasonably irritated with me, or cowed by your sufferings. I am of opinion that national greatness is more for the advantage of private citizens, than any individual well-being coupled with public humiliation. A man may be personally ever so well off, and yet if his country be ruined he must be ruined with it; whereas a flourishing commonwealth always affords chances of salvation to unfortunate individuals. Since then a state can support the misfortunes of private citizens, while they cannot support hers, it is surely the duty of every one to be forward in her defence, and not like you to be so confounded with your domestic afflictions as to give up all thoughts of the common safety, and to blame me for having counselled war and yourselves for having voted it. And yet if you are angry with me, it is with one who, as I believe, is second to no man either in knowledge of the proper policy, or in the ability to expound it, and who is moreover not only a patriot but an honest one. A man possessing that knowledge without that faculty of exposition might as well have no idea at all on the matter: if he had both these gifts, but no love for his country, he would be but a cold advocate for her interests; while were his patriotism not proof against bribery, everything would go for a price. So that if you thought that I was even moderately distinguished for these qualities when you took my advice and went to war, there is certainly no reason now why I should be charged with having done wrong.

"For those of course who have a free choice in the matter and whose fortunes are not at stake, war is the greatest of follies. But if the only choice was between submission with loss of independence, and danger with the hope of preserving that independence,—in such a case it is he who will not accept the risk that deserves blame, not he who will. I am the same man and do not alter, it is you who change, since in fact you took my advice while unhurt, and waited for misfortune to repent of it; and the apparent error of my policy lies in the infirmity of your resolution, since the suffering that it entails is being felt by every one among you, while its advantage is still remote and obscure to all, and a great and sudden reverse having befallen you, your mind is too much depressed to persevere in your resolves. For before what is sudden, unexpected, and least within calculation the spirit quails; and putting all else aside, the plague has certainly been an emergency of this kind. Born, however, as you are, citizens of a great state, and brought up, as you have been, with habits equal to your birth, you should be ready to face the greatest disasters and still to keep unimpaired the lustre of your name. For the judgment of mankind is as relentless to the weakness that falls short of a recognised renown, as it is jealous of the arrogance that aspires higher than its due. Cease then to grieve for your private afflictions, and address yourself instead to the safety of the commonwealth.

"If you shrink before the exertions which the war makes necessary, and fear that after all they may not have a happy result, you know the reasons by which I have often demon-

strated to you the groundlessness of your apprehension. If those
are not enough, I will now reveal an advantage arising from the
greatness of your dominion, which I think has never yet sug-
gested itself to you, which I never mentioned in my previous
speeches, and which has so bold a sound that I should scarce
adventure it now, were it not for the unnatural depression which
I see around me. You perhaps think that your empire extends
only over your allies; I will declare to you the truth. The visible
field of action has two parts, land and sea. In the whole of one
of these you are completely supreme, not merely as far as you
use it at present, but also to what further extent you may think
fit: in fine, your naval resources are such that your vessels may
go where they please, without the king or any other nation on
earth being able to stop them. So that although you may think
it a great privation to lose the use of your land and houses, still
you must see that this power is something widely different; and
instead of fretting on their account, you should really regard
them in the light of the gardens and other accessories that em-
bellish a great fortune, and as, in comparison, of little moment.
You should know too that liberty preserved by your efforts will
easily recover for us what we have lost, while, the knee once
bowed, even what you have will pass from you. Your fathers receiving these possessions not from others, but from themselves,
did not let slip what their labour had acquired, but delivered them
safe to you; and in this respect at least you must prove yourselves
their equals, remembering that to lose what one has got is more
disgraceful than to be baulked in getting, and you must confront
your enemies not merely with spirit but with disdain. Confidence
indeed a blissful ignorance can impart, ay, even to a coward's
breast, but disdain is the privilege of those who, like us, have
been assured by reflexion of their superiority to their adversary.
And where the chances are the same, knowledge fortifies courage
by the contempt which is its consequence, its trust being placed,
not in hope, which is the prop of the desperate, but in a judgment grounded upon existing resources, whose anticipations are
more to be depended upon.

"Again, your country has a right to your services in sustain-
ing the glories of her position. These are a common source of
pride to you all, and you cannot decline the burdens of empire
and still expect to share its honours. You should remember also
that what you are fighting against is not merely slavery as an

exchange for independence, but also loss of empire and danger from the animosities incurred in its exercise. Besides, to recede is no longer possible, if indeed any of you in the alarm of the moment has become enamoured of the honesty of such an un-ambitious part. For what you hold is, to speak somewhat plainly, a tyranny; to take it perhaps was wrong, but to let it go is unsafe. And men of these retiring views, making converts of others, would quickly ruin a state; indeed the result would be the same if they could live independent by themselves; for the retiring and unambitious are never secure without vigorous protectors at their side; in fine, such qualities are useless to an imperial city, though they may help a dependency to an unmolested servitude.

"But you must not be seduced by citizens like these nor be angry with me,—who, if I voted for war, only did as you did yourselves,—in spite of the enemy having invaded your country and done what you could be certain that he would do, if you refused to comply with his demands; and although besides what we counted for, the plague has come upon us—the only point indeed at which our calculation has been at fault. It is this, I know, that has had a large share in making me more unpopular than I should otherwise have been,—quite undeservedly, unless you are also prepared to give me the credit of any success with which chance may present you. Besides, the hand of Heaven must be borne with resignation, that of the enemy with fortitude; this was the old way at Athens, and do not you prevent it being so still. Remember, too, that if your country has the greatest name in all the world, it is because she never bent before disaster; because she has expended more life and effort in war than any other city, and has won for herself a power greater than any hitherto known, the memory of which will descend to the latest posterity; even if now, in obedience to the general law of decay, we should ever be forced to yield, still it will be remembered that we held rule over more Hellenes than any other Hellenic state, that we sustained the greatest wars against their united or separate powers, and inhabited a city unrivalled by any other in resources or magnitude. These glories may incur the censure of the slow and unambitious; but in the breast of energy they will awake emulation, and in those who must remain without them an envious regret. Hatred and unpopularity at the moment have fallen to the lot of all who have aspired to rule others; but where odium must be incurred, true wisdom incurs it for the highest objects. Hatred also is short-lived; but that which makes the splendour of the present and the glory of the future remains for ever unforgotten. Make your decision, therefore, for glory then and honour now, and attain both objects by instant and zealous effort: do not send heralds to Lacedaemon, and do not betray any sign of being oppressed by your present sufferings, since they whose minds are least sensitive to calamity, and whose hands are most quick to meet it, are the greatest men and the greatest communities."

Such were the arguments by which Pericles tried to cure the Athenians of their anger against him and to divert their thoughts from their immediate afflictions. As a community he succeeded in convincing them; they not only gave up all idea of sending to Lacedaemon, but applied themselves with increased energy to the war; still as private individuals they could not help smarting under their sufferings, the common people having been deprived of the little that they ever possessed, while the higher orders had lost fine properties with costly establishments and buildings in the country, and, worst of all, had war instead of peace. In fact, the public feeling against him did not subside until he had been fined. Not long afterwards, however, according to the way of the multitude, they again elected him general and committed all their affairs to his hands, having now become less sensitive to their private and domestic afflictions, and understanding that he was the best man of all for the public necessities. For as long as he was at the head of the state during the peace, he pursued a moderate and conservative policy; and in his time its greatness was at its height. When the war broke out, here also he seems to have rightly gauged the power of his country. He outlived its commencement two years and six months, and the correctness of his previsions respecting it became better known by his death. He told them to wait quietly, to pay attention to their marine, to attempt no new conquests, and to expose the city to no hazards during the war, and doing this, promised them a favourable result. What they did was the very contrary, allowing private ambitions and private interests, in matters apparently quite foreign to the war, to lead them into projects unjust both to themselves and to their allies—projects whose success would only conduce to the honour and advantage of private persons, and whose failure entailed certain disaster on the country in the war. The causes of this are not far to seek. Pericles indeed, by his rank, ability, and known integrity, was enabled to exercise an independent control over the multitude—in short, to lead them instead of being led by them; for as he never sought power by improper means, he was never compelled to flatter them, but, on the contrary, enjoyed so high an estimation that he could afford to anger them by contradiction. Whenever he saw them unseasonably and insolently elated, he would with a word reduce them to alarm; on the other hand, if they fell victims to a panic, he could at once restore them to confidence. In short, what was nominally a democracy became in his hands government by the first citizen. With his successors it was different. More on a level with one another, and each grasping at supremacy, they ended by committing even the conduct of state affairs to the whims of the multitude. This, as might have been expected in a great and sovereign state, produced a host of blunders, and amongst them the Sicilian expedition; though this failed not so much through a miscalculation of the power of those against whom it was sent, as through a fault in the senders in not taking the best measures afterwards to assist those who had gone out, but choosing rather to occupy themselves with private cabals for the leadership of the commons, by which they not only paralysed operations in the field, but also first introduced civil discord at home. Yet after losing most of their fleet besides other forces in Sicily, and with faction already dominant in the city, they could still for three years make head against their original adversaries, joined not only by the Sicilians, but also by their own allies nearly all in revolt, and at last by the king's son, Cyrus, who furnished the funds for the Peloponnesian navy. Nor did they finally succumb till they fell the victims of their own intestine disorders. So superfluously abundant were the resources from which the genius of Pericles foresaw an easy triumph in the war over the unaided forces of the Peloponnesians.

6. The Best Constitution (8, 97–98)

After the death of Pericles, Athens found no leader equal to him. The democracy suffered serious reversals, and in 411 the Athenians established a new, oligarchic, constitution. Thucydides' political position is made clear by his judgment on it.

... [T]he Athenians manned twenty ships and called immediately a first assembly in the Pnyx, where they had been used to meet formerly, and deposed the Four Hundred and voted to hand over the government to the Five Thousand, of which body all who furnished a suit of armour were to be members, decreeing also that no one should receive pay for the discharge of any office, or if he did should be held accursed. Many other assemblies were held afterwards, in which law-makers were elected and all other measures taken to form a constitution. It was during the first period of this constitution that the Athenians appear to have enjoyed the best government that they ever did, at least in my time. For the fusion of the high and the low was effected with judgment, and this was what first enabled the state to raise up her head after her manifold disasters.

7. *The Sophists and Socrates*

In the fifth century the traditions of the polis *came under heavy attack. Its institutions and ideas were subjected to pitiless scrutiny by a group of men collectively called Sophists. What they all had in common was the willingness to teach men and to accept pay for their teaching. Apart from that they appeared to hold very disparate views, some hewing close to the line of the orthodoxy of the* polis, *others attacking its very foundations. There was, however, an intellectual bond which connected the Sophists—all were sceptical of traditional values per se. Each required that traditional usages be tested by the rule of reason. In short, they introduced the purely intellectual element into Greek political thought.*

There is no doubt that Socrates was so close to the Sophists in the public mind as to persuade the Athenian people that he was a Sophist. It is clear that he was not, for he did not teach for pay and he consciously separated himself from and was critical of the Sophists. Yet the confusion was a natural one, for like them he examined all institutions and customs, demanding a rational justification for them. The following selections portray the views of some of the leading Sophists, those of Socrates, and some confrontations between them.

1. Protagoras and Socrates
(*Plato:* Protagoras, *316–320*)*

Protagoras has come to visit Athens, creating great excite-ment. The young aristocrats are eager to seek out his wisdom. Socrates accompanies one of them to the house of Callias where Protagoras is being entertained.

On entering we stopped a little, in order to look about us, and then walked up to Protagoras, and I said: Protagoras, my friend Hippocrates and I have come to see you.

Do you wish, he said, to speak with me alone, or in the presence of the company?

Whichever you please, I said; you shall determine when you have heard the purpose of our visit.

And what is your purpose? he said.

I must explain, I said, that my friend Hippocrates is a native Athenian; he is the son of Apollodorus, and of a great and pros-perous house, and he is himself in natural ability quite a match for anybody of his own age. I believe that he aspires to political eminence; and this he thinks that conversation with you is most likely to procure for him. And now you can determine whether you would wish to speak to him of your teaching alone or in the presence of the company.

Thank you, Socrates, for your consideration of me. For certainly a stranger finding his way into great cities, and per-suading the flower of the youth in them to leave the company of their kinsmen or any other acquaintances, old or young, and live with him, under the idea that they will be improved by his conversation, ought to be very cautious; great jealousies are aroused by his proceedings, and he is the subject of many en-mities and conspiracies. Now the art of the Sophist is, as I be-lieve, of great antiquity; but in ancient times those who prac-tised it, fearing this odium, veiled and disguised themselves under various names, some under that of poets, as Homer, Hesiod, and

* Translated by Benjamin Jowett.

Simonides, some, of hierophants and prophets, as Orpheus and Musaeus, and some, as I observe, even under the name of gymnastic-masters, like Iccus of Tarentum, or the more recently celebrated Herodicus, now of Selymbria and formerly of Megara, who is a first-rate Sophist. Your own Agathocles pretended to be a musician, but was really an eminent Sophist; also Pythocleides the Cean; and there were many others; and all of them, as I was saying, adopted these arts as veils or disguises because they were afraid of the odium which they would incur. But that is not my way, for I do not believe that they effected their purpose, which was to deceive the government, who were not blinded by them; and as to the people, they have no understanding, and only repeat what their rulers are pleased to tell them. Now to run away, and to be caught in running away, is the very height of folly, and also greatly increases the exasperation of mankind; for they regard him who runs away as a rogue, in addition to any other objections which they have to him; and therefore I take an entirely opposite course, and acknowledge myself to be a Sophist and instructor of mankind; such an open acknowledgment appears to me to be a better sort of caution than concealment. Nor do I neglect other precautions, and therefore I hope, as I may say, by the favour of heaven that no harm will come of the acknowledgment that I am a Sophist. And I have been now many years in the profession—for all my years when added up are many: there is no one here present of whom I might not be the father. Wherefore I should much prefer conversing with you, if you want to speak with me, in the presence of the company.

As I suspected that he would like to have a little display and glorification in the presence of Prodicus and Hippias, and would gladly show us to them in the light of his admirers, I said: But why should we not summon Prodicus and Hippias and their friends to hear us?

Very good, he said.

Suppose, said Callias, that we hold a council in which you may sit and discuss.—This was agreed upon, and great delight was felt at the prospect of hearing wise men talk; we ourselves took the chairs and benches, and arranged them by Hippias, where the other benches had been already placed. Meanwhile Callias and Alcibiades got Prodicus out of bed and brought in him and his companions.

When we were all seated, Protagoras said: Now that the

company are assembled, Socrates, tell me about the young man
of whom you were just now speaking.

I replied: I will begin again at the same point, Protagoras,
and tell you once more the purport of my visit: this is my
friend Hippocrates, who is desirous of making your acquaintance; he would like to know what will happen to him if he
associates with you. I have no more to say.

Protagoras answered: Young man, if you associate with me,
on the very first day you will return home a better man than you
came, and better on the second day than on the first, and better
every day than you were on the day before.

When I heard this, I said: Protagoras, I do not at all wonder
at hearing you say this; even at your age, and with all your
wisdom, if any one were to teach you what you did not know
before, you would become better no doubt: but please to answer
in a different way—I will explain how by an example. Let me
suppose that Hippocrates, instead of desiring your acquaintance,
wished to become acquainted with the young man Zeuxippus
of Heraclea, who has lately been in Athens, and he had come to
him as he has come to you, and had heard him say, as he has
heard you say, that every day he would grow and become better
if he associated with him: and then suppose that he were to ask
him, 'In what shall I become better, and in what shall I grow?'—
Zeuxippus would answer, 'In painting.' And suppose that he went
to Orthagoras the Theban, and heard him say the same thing,
and asked him, 'In what shall I become better day by day?' he
would reply, 'In flute-playing.' Now I want you to make the
same sort of answer to this young man and to me, who am asking questions on his account. When you say that on the first
day on which he associates with you he will return home a
better man, and on every day will grow in like manner,—in
what, Protagoras, will he be better? and about what?

When Protagoras heard me say this, he replied: You ask
questions fairly, and I like to answer a question which is fairly
put. If Hippocrates comes to me he will not experience the sort
of drudgery with which other Sophists are in the habit of insulting their pupils; who, when they have just escaped from the
arts, are taken and driven back into them by these teachers, and
made to learn calculation, and astronomy, and geometry, and
music (he gave a look at Hippias as he said this); but if he comes
to me, he will learn that which he comes to learn. And this is
prudence in affairs private as well as public; he will learn to

order his own house in the best manner, and he will be able to
speak and act for the best in the affairs of the state.

Do I understand you, I said; and is your meaning that you
teach the art of politics, and that you promise to make men good
citizens?

That, Socrates, is exactly the profession which I make.

Then, I said, you do indeed possess a noble art, if there is no
mistake about this; for I will freely confess to you, Protagoras,
that I have a doubt whether this art is capable of being taught,
and yet I know not how to disbelieve your assertion. And I
ought to tell you why I am of opinion that this art cannot be
taught or communicated by man to man. I say that the Athenians
are an understanding people, and indeed they are esteemed to be
such by the other Hellenes. Now I observe that when we are
met together in the assembly, and the matter in hand relates to
building, the builders are summoned as advisers; when the question is one of ship-building, then the ship-wrights; and the like
of other arts which they think capable of being taught and
learned. And if some person offers to give them advice who is
not supposed by them to have any skill in the art, even though
he be good-looking, and rich, and noble, they will not listen to
him, but laugh and hoot at him, until either he is clamoured
down and retires of himself; or if he persist, he is dragged away
or put out by the constables at the command of the prytanes.
This is their way of behaving about professors of the arts. But
when the question is an affair of state, then everybody is free to
have a say—carpenter, tinker, cobbler, sailor, passenger; rich
and poor, high and low—any one who likes gets up, and no one
reproaches him, as in the former case, with not having learned,
and having no teacher, and yet giving advice; evidently because
they are under the impression that this sort of knowledge cannot
be taught. And not only is this true of the state, but of individuals; the best and wisest of our citizens are unable to impart
their political wisdom to others: as for example, Pericles, the
father of these young men, who gave them excellent instruction
in all that could be learned from masters, in his own department
of politics neither taught them, nor gave them teachers; but
they were allowed to wander at their own free will in a sort
of hope that they would light upon virtue of their own accord.
Or take another example: there was Cleinias the younger brother
of our friend Alcibiades, of whom this very same Pericles was
the guardian; and he being in fact under the apprehension that

Cleinias would be corrupted by Alcibiades, took him away, and placed him in the house of Ariphron to be educated; but before six months had elapsed, Ariphron sent him back, not knowing what to do with him. And I could mention numberless other instances of persons who were good themselves, and never yet made any one else good, whether friend or stranger. Now I, Protagoras, having these examples before me, am inclined to think that virtue cannot be taught. But then again, when I listen to your words, I waver; and am disposed to think that there must be something in what you say, because I know that you have great experience, and learning, and invention. And I wish that you would, if possible, show me a little more clearly that virtue can be taught. Will you be so good?

The answer of Protagoras is the myth and argument included in Chapter 5.

2.   *Thrasymachus and Socrates*
(*Plato:* Republic, *336–354*)*

In the first book of the Republic *Socrates engages in a discussion of the meaning of justice. He is soon confronted by the views of Thrasymachus. The ensuing conversation sets forth one of the extreme positions of the Sophists and also illustrates the methods and attitudes of Socrates.*

I believe that Periander or Perdiccas or Xerxes or Ismenias the Theban, or some other rich and mighty man, who had a great opinion of his own power, was the first to say that justice is 'doing good to your friends and harm to your enemies.'

Most true, he said.

Yes, I said; but if this definition of justice also breaks down, what other can be offered?

Several times in the course of the discussion Thrasymachus had made an attempt to get the argument into his own hands,

* Translated by Benjamin Jowett.

and had been put down by the rest of the company, who wanted to hear the end. But when Polemarchus and I had done speaking and there was a pause, he could no longer hold his peace; and, gathering himself up, he came at us like a wild beast, seeking to devour us. We were quite panic-stricken at the sight of him.

He roared out to the whole company: What folly, Socrates, has taken possession of you all? And why, sillybillies, do you knock under to one another? I say that if you want really to know what justice is, you should not only ask but answer, and you should not seek honour to yourself from the refutation of an opponent, but have your own answer; for there is many a one who can ask and cannot answer. And now I will not have you say that justice is duty or advantage or profit or gain or interest, for this sort of nonsense will not do for me; I must have clearness and accuracy.

I was panic-stricken at his words, and could not look at him without trembling. Indeed I believe that if I had not fixed my eye upon him, I should have been struck dumb: but when I saw his fury rising, I looked at him first, and was therefore able to reply to him.

Thrasymachus, I said, with a quiver, don't be hard upon us. Polemarchus and I may have been guilty of a little mistake in the argument, but I can assure you that the error was not intentional. If we were seeking for a piece of gold, you would not imagine that we were 'knocking under to one another,' and so losing our chance of finding it. And why, when we are seeking for justice, a thing more precious than many pieces of gold, do you say that we are weakly yielding to one another and not doing our utmost to get at the truth? Nay, my good friend, we are most willing and anxious to do so, but the fact is that we cannot. And if so, you people who know all things should pity us and not be angry with us.

How characteristic of Socrates! he replied, with a bitter laugh;—that's your ironical style! Did I not foresee—have I not already told you, that whatever he was asked he would refuse to answer, and try irony or any other shuffle, in order that he might avoid answering?

You are a philosopher, Thrasymachus, I replied, and well know that if you ask a person what numbers make up twelve, taking care to prohibit him whom you ask from answering twice six, or three times four, or six times two, or four times three,

'for this sort of nonsense will not do for me,'—then obviously,
if that is your way of putting the question, no one can answer
you. But suppose that he were to retort, 'Thrasymachus, what
do you mean? If one of these numbers which you interdict be
the true answer to the question, am I falsely to say some other
number which is not the right one?—is that your meaning?—
How would you answer him?

Just as if the two cases were at all alike! he said.

Why should they not be? I replied; and even if they are not,
but only appear to be so to the person who is asked, ought he
not to say what he thinks, whether you and I forbid him or not?

I presume then that you are going to make one of the inter-
dicted answers?

I dare say that I may, notwithstanding the danger, if upon
reflection I approve of any of them.

But what if I give you an answer about justice other and
better, he said, than any of these? What do you deserve to have
done to you?

Done to me!—as becomes the ignorant, I must learn from
the wise—that is what I deserve to have done to me.

What, and no payment! a pleasant notion!

I will pay when I have the money, I replied.

But you have, Socrates, said Glaucon: and you, Thrasymachus, need be under no anxiety about money, for we will all
make a contribution for Socrates.

Yes, he replied, and then Socrates will do as he always does
—refuse to answer himself, but take and pull to pieces the answer
of some one else.

Why, my good friend, I said, how can any one answer who
knows, and says that he knows, just nothing; and who, even if
he has some faint notions of his own, is told by a man of authority not to utter them? The natural thing is, that the speaker
should be some one like yourself who professes to know and
can tell what he knows. Will you then kindly answer, for the
edification of the company and of myself?

Glaucon and the rest of the company joined in my request
and Thrasymachus, as any one might see, was in reality eager to
speak; for he thought that he had an excellent answer, and would
distinguish himself. But at first he affected to insist on my answering; at length he consented to begin. Behold, he said, the
wisdom of Socrates; he refuses to teach himself, and goes about
learning of others, to whom he never even says Thank you.

That I learn of others, I replied, is quite true; but that I am ungrateful I wholly deny. Money I have none, and therefore I pay in praise, which is all I have; and how ready I am to praise any one who appears to me to speak well you will very soon find out when you answer; for I expect that you will answer well.

Listen, then, he said; I proclaim that justice is nothing else than the interest of the stronger. And now why do you not praise me? But of course you won't.

Let me first understand you, I replied. Justice, as you say, is the interest of the stronger. What, Thrasymachus, is the meaning of this? You cannot mean to say that because Polydamas, the pancratiast, is stronger than we are, and finds the eating of beef conducive to his bodily strength, that to eat beef is therefore equally for our good who are weaker than he is, and right and just for us?

That's abominable of you, Socrates; you take the words in the sense which is most damaging to the argument.

Not at all, my good sir, I said; I am trying to understand them; and I wish that you would be a little clearer.

Well, he said, have you never heard that forms of government differ; there are tyrannies, and there are democracies, and there are aristocracies?

Yes, I know.

And the government is the ruling power in each state?

Certainly.

And the different forms of government make laws democratical, aristocratical, tyrannical, with a view to their several interests; and these laws, which are made by them for their own interests, are the justice which they deliver to their subjects, and him who transgresses them they punish as a breaker of the law, and unjust. And that is what I mean when I say that in all states there is the same principle of justice, which is the interest of the government; and as the government must be supposed to have power, the only reasonable conclusion is, that everywhere there is one principle of justice, which is the interest of the stronger.

Now I understand you, I said; and whether you are right or not I will try to discover. But let me remark, that in defining justice you have yourself used the word 'interest' which you forbade me to use. It is true, however, that in your definition the words 'of the stronger' are added.

A small addition, you must allow, he said.

Great or small, never mind about that: we must first enquire whether what you are saying is the truth. Now we are both agreed that justice is interest of some sort, but you go on to say 'of the stronger'; about this addition I am not so sure, and must therefore consider further.

Proceed.

I will; and first tell me, Do you admit that it is just for subjects to obey their rulers?

I do.

But are the rulers of states absolutely infallible, or are they sometimes liable to err?

To be sure, he replied, they are liable to err.

Then in making their laws they may sometimes make them rightly, and sometimes not?

True.

When they make them rightly, they make them agreeably to their interest; when they are mistaken, contrary to their interest; you admit that?

Yes.

And the laws which they make must be obeyed by their subjects,—and that is what you call justice?

Doubtless.

Then justice, according to your argument, is not only obedience to the interest of the stronger but the reverse?

What is that you are saying? he asked.

I am only repeating what you are saying, I believe. But let us consider: Have we not admitted that the rulers may be mistaken about their own interest in what they command, and also that to obey them is justice? Has not that been admitted?

Yes.

Then you must also have acknowledged justice not to be for the interest of the stronger, when the rulers unintentionally command things to be done which are to their own injury. For if, as you say, justice is the obedience which the subject renders to their commands, in that case, O wisest of men, is there any escape from the conclusion that the weaker are commanded to do, not what is for the interest, but what is for the injury of the stronger?

Nothing can be clearer, Socrates, said Polemarchus.

Yes, said Cleitophon, interposing, if you are allowed to be his witness.

But there is no need of any witness, said Polemarchus, for Thrasymachus himself acknowledges that rulers may sometimes command what is not for their own interest, and that for subjects to obey them is justice.

Yes, Polemarchus,—Thrasymachus said that for subjects to do what was commanded by their rulers is just.

Yes, Cleitophon, but he also said that justice is the interest of the stronger, and, while admitting both these propositions, he further acknowledged that the stronger may command the weaker who are his subjects to do what is not for his own interest; whence follows that justice is the injury quite as much as the interest of the stronger.

But, said Cleitophon, he meant by the interest of the stronger what the stronger thought to be his interest,—this was what the weaker had to do; and this was affirmed by him to be justice.

Those were not his words, rejoined Polemarchus.

Never mind, I replied, if he now says that they are, let us accept his statement. Tell me, Thrasymachus, I said, did you mean by justice what the stronger thought to be his interest, whether really so or not?

Certainly not, he said. Do you suppose that I call him who is mistaken the stronger at the time when he is mistaken?

Yes, I said, my impression was that you did so, when you admitted that the ruler was not infallible but might be sometimes mistaken.

You argue like an informer, Socrates. Do you mean, for example, that he who is mistaken about the sick is a physician in that he is mistaken? or that he who errs in arithmetic or grammar is an arithmetician or grammarian at the time when he is making the mistake, in respect of the mistake? True, we say that the physician or arithmetician or grammarian has made a mistake, but this is only a way of speaking; for the fact is that neither the grammarian nor any other person of skill ever makes a mistake in so far as he is what his name implies; they none of them err unless their skill fails them, and then they cease to be skilled artists. No artist or sage or ruler errs at the time when he is what his name implies; though he is commonly said to err, and I adopted the common mode of speaking. But to be perfectly accurate, since you are such a lover of accuracy, we should say that the ruler, in so far as he is a ruler, is unerring, and, being unerring, always commands that which is for his own interest;

and the subject is required to execute his commands; and therefore, as I said at first and now repeat, justice is the interest of
the stronger.

Indeed, Thrasymachus, and do I really appear to you to
argue like an informer?

Certainly, he replied.

And do you suppose that I ask these questions with any design of injuring you in the argument?

Nay, he replied, 'suppose' is not the word—I know it; but
you will be found out, and by sheer force of argument you will
never prevail.

I shall not make the attempt, my dear man; but to avoid
any misunderstanding occurring between us in future, let me
ask, in what sense do you speak of a ruler or stronger whose
interest, as you were saying, he being the superior, it is just that
the inferior should execute—is he a ruler in the popular or in the
strict sense of the term?

In the strictest of all senses, he said. And now cheat and play
the informer if you can; I ask no quarter at your hands. But you
never will be able, never.

And do you imagine, I said, that I am such a madman as to
try and cheat Thrasymachus? I might as well shave a lion.

Why, he said, you made the attempt a minute ago, and you
failed.

Enough, I said, of these civilities. It will be better that I
should ask you a question: Is the physician, taken in that strict
sense of which you are speaking, a healer of the sick or a maker
of money? And remember that I am now speaking of the true
physician.

A healer of the sick, he replied.

And the pilot—that is to say, the true pilot—is he a captain
of sailors or a mere sailor?

A captain of sailors.

The circumstance that he sails in the ship is not to be taken
into account; neither is he to be called a sailor; the name pilot
by which he is distinguished has nothing to do with sailing, but
is significant of his skill and of his authority over the sailors.

Very true, he said.

Now, I said, every art has an interest?

Certainly.

For which the art has to consider and provide?

Yes, that is the aim of art.

And the interest of any art is the perfection of it—this and nothing else?

What do you mean?

I mean what I may illustrate negatively by the example of the body. Suppose you were to ask me whether the body is self-sufficing or has wants, I should reply: Certainly the body has wants; for the body may be ill and require to be cured, and has therefore interests to which the art of medicine ministers; and this is the origin and intention of medicine, as you will acknowledge. Am I not right?

Quite right, he replied.

But is the art of medicine or any other art faulty or deficient in any quality in the same way that the eye may be deficient in sight or the ear fail of hearing, and therefore requires another art to provide for the interests of seeing and hearing—has art in itself, I say, any similar liability to fault or defect, and does every art require another supplementary art to provide for its interests, and that another and another without end? Or have the arts to look only after their own interests? Or have they no need either of themselves or of another?—having no faults or defects, they have no need to correct them, either by the exercise of their own art or of any other; they have only to consider the interest of their subject-matter. For every art remains pure and faultless while remaining true—that is to say, while perfect and unimpaired. Take the words in your precise sense, and tell me whether I am not right.

Yes, clearly.

Then medicine does not consider the interest of medicine, but the interest of the body?

True, he said.

Nor does the art of horsemanship consider the interests of the art of horsemanship, but the interests of the horse; neither do any other arts care for themselves, for they have no needs; they care only for that which is the subject of their art?

True, he said.

But surely, Thrasymachus, the arts are the superiors and rulers of their own subjects?

To this he assented with a good deal of reluctance.

Then, I said, no science or art considers or enjoins the interest of the stronger or superior, but only the interest of the subject and weaker?

He made an attempt to contest this proposition also, but finally acquiesced.

Then, I continued, no physician, in so far as he is a physician, considers his own good in what he prescribes, but the good of his patient; for the true physician is also a ruler having the human body as a subject, and is not a mere money-maker; that has been admitted?

Yes.

And the pilot likewise, in the strict sense of the term, is a ruler of sailors and not a mere sailor?

That has been admitted.

And such a pilot and ruler will provide and prescribe for the interest of the sailor who is under him, and not for his own or the ruler's interest?

He gave a reluctant 'Yes.'

Then, I said, Thrasymachus, there is no one in any rule who, in so far as he is a ruler, considers or enjoins what is for his own interest, but always what is for the interest of his subject or suitable to his art; to that he looks, and that alone he considers in everything which he says and does.

When we had got to this point in the argument, and every one saw that the definition of justice had been completely upset, Thrasymachus, instead of replying to me, said: Tell me, Socrates, have you got a nurse?

Why do you ask such a question, I said, when you ought rather to be answering?

Because she leaves you to snivel, and never wipes your nose: she has not even taught you to know the shepherd from the sheep.

What makes you say that? I replied.

Because you fancy that the shepherd or neathered fattens or tends the sheep or oxen with a view to their own good and not to the good of himself or his master; and you further imagine that the rulers of states, if they are true rulers, never think of their subjects as sheep, and that they are not studying their own advantage day and night. Oh, no; and so entirely astray are you in your ideas about the just and unjust as not even to know that justice and the just are in reality another's good; that is to say, the interest of the ruler and stronger, and the loss of the subject and servant; and injustice the opposite; for the unjust is lord over the truly simple and just: he is the stronger, and his subjects do what is for his interest, and minister to his happiness, which

is very far from being their own. Consider further, most foolish
Socrates, that the just is always a loser in comparison with the
unjust. First of all, in private contracts: wherever the unjust is
the partner of the just you will find that, when the partnership
is dissolved, the unjust man has always more and the just less.
Secondly, in their dealings with the State: when there is an in-
come-tax, the man will pay more and the unjust less on the same
amount of income; and when there is anything to be received the
one gains nothing and the other much. Observe also what happens when they take an office; there is the just man neglecting
his affairs and perhaps suffering other losses, and getting nothing
out of the public, because he is just; moreover he is hated by his
friends and acquaintance for refusing to serve them in unlawful
ways. But all this is reversed in the case of the unjust man. I am
speaking, as before, of injustice on a large scale in which the
advantage of the unjust is more apparent; and my meaning will
be most clearly seen if we turn to that highest form of injustice
in which the criminal is the happiest of men, and the sufferers
or those who refuse to do injustice are the most miserable—that
is to say tyranny, which by fraud and force takes away the property of others, not little by little but wholesale; comprehending
in one, things sacred as well as profane, private and public; for
which acts of wrong, if he were detected perpetrating any one
of them singly, he would be punished and incur great disgrace
—they who do such wrong in particular cases are called robbers
of temples, and man-stealers and burglars and swindlers and
thieves. But when a man besides taking away the money of the
citizens has made slaves of them, then, instead of these names of
reproach, he is termed happy and blessed, not only by the citizens
but by all who hear of his having achieved the consummation of
injustice. For mankind censure injustice, fearing that they may
be the victims of it and not because they shrink from committing
it. And thus, as I have shown, Socrates, injustice, when on a sufficient scale, has more strength and freedom and mastery than
justice; and, as I said at first, justice is the interest of the stronger,
whereas injustice is a man's own profit and interest.

Thrasymachus, when he had thus spoken, having, like a bath-
man, deluged our ears with his words, had a mind to go away.
But the company would not let him; they insisted that he should
remain and defend his position; and I myself added my own
humble request that he would not leave us. Thrasymachus, I said
to him, excellent man, how suggestive are your remarks! And are

you going to run away before you have fairly taught or learned
whether they are true or not? Is the attempt to determine the
way of man's life so small a matter in your eyes—to determine
how life may be passed by each one of us to the greatest advantage?

And do I differ from you, he said, as to the importance of the
enquiry?

You appear rather, I replied, to have no care or thought about
us, Thrasymachus—whether we live better or worse from not
knowing what you say you know, is to you a matter of indifference. Prithee, friend, do not keep your knowledge to yourself; we are a large party; and any benefit which you confer
upon us will be amply rewarded. For my own part I openly declare that I am not convinced, and that I do not believe injustice
to be more gainful than justice, even if uncontrolled and allowed
to have free play. For, granting that there may be an unjust man
who is able to commit injustice either by fraud or force, still
this does not convince me of the superior advantage of injustice,
and there may be others who are in the same predicament with
myself. Perhaps we may be wrong; if so, you in your wisdom
should convince us that we are mistaken in preferring justice to
injustice.

And how am I to convince you, he said, if you are not already
convinced by what I have just said; what more can I do for
you? Would you have me put the proof bodily into your souls?

Heaven forbid! I said; I would only ask you to be consistent;
or, if you change, change openly and let there be no deception.
For I must remark, Thrasymachus, if you will recall what was
previously said, that although you began by defining the true
physician in an exact sense, you did not observe a like exactness
when speaking of the shepherd; you thought that the shepherd
as a shepherd tends the sheep not with a view to their own good,
but like a mere diner or banquetter with a view to the pleasures
of the table; or, again, as a trader for sale in the market, and not
as a shepherd. Yet surely the art of the shepherd is concerned
only with the good of his subjects; he has only to provide the
best for them, since the perfection of the art is already ensured
whenever all the requirements of it are satisfied. And that was
what I was saying just now about the ruler. I conceived that the
art of the ruler, considered as ruler, whether in a state or in
private life, could only regard the good of his flock or subjects;

whereas you seem to think that the rulers in states, that is to say, the true rulers, like being in authority.

Think! Nay, I am sure of it.

Then why in the case of lesser offices do men never take them willingly without payment, unless under the idea that they govern for the advantage not of themselves but of others? Let me ask you a question: Are not the several arts different, by reason of their each having a separate function? And, my dear illustrious friend, do say what you think, that we may make a little progress.

Yes, that is the difference, he replied.

And each art gives us a particular good and not merely a general one—medicine, for example, gives us health; navigation, safety at sea, and so on?

Yes, he said.

And the art of payment has the special function of giving pay: but we do not confuse this with other arts, any more than the art of the pilot is to be confused with the art of medicine, because the health of the pilot may be improved by a sea voyage. You would not be inclined to say, would you, that navigation is the art of medicine, at least if we are to adopt your exact use of language?

Certainly not.

Or because a man is in good health when he receives pay you would not say that the art of payment is medicine?

I should say not.

Nor would you say that medicine is the art of receiving pay because a man takes fees when he is engaged in healing?

Certainly not.

And we have admitted, I said, that the good of each art is specially confined to the art?

Yes.

Then, if there be any good which all artists have in common, that is to be attributed to something of which they all have the common use?

True, he replied.

And when the artist is benefited by receiving pay the advantage is gained by an additional use of the art of pay, which is not the art professed by him?

He gave a reluctant assent to this.

Then the pay is not derived by the several artists from their respective arts. But the truth is, that while the art of medicine gives health, and the art of the builder builds a house, another art attends them which is the art of pay. The various arts may be doing their own business and benefiting that over which they preside, but would the artist receive any benefit from his art unless he were paid as well?

I suppose not.

But does he therefore confer no benefit when he works for nothing?

Certainly, he confers a benefit.

Then now, Thrasymachus, there is no longer any doubt that neither arts nor governments provide for their own interests; but, as we were before saying, they rule and provide for the interests of their subjects who are the weaker and not the stronger —to their good they attend and not to the good of the superior. And this is the reason, my dear Thrasymachus, why, as I was just saying, no one is willing to govern; because no one likes to take in hand the reformation of evils which are not his concern without remuneration. For, in the execution of his work, and in giving his orders to another, the true artist does not regard his own interest, but always that of his subjects; and therefore in order that rulers may be willing to rule, they must be paid in one of three modes of payment, money, or honour, or a penalty for refusing.

What do you mean, Socrates? said Glaucon. The first two modes of payment are intelligible enough, but what the penalty is I do not understand, or how a penalty can be a payment.

You mean that you do not understand the nature of this payment which to the best men is the great inducement to rule? Of course you know that ambition and avarice are held to be, as indeed they are, a disgrace?

Very true.

And for this reason, I said, money and honour have no attraction for them; good men do not wish to be openly demanding payment for governing and so to get the name of hirelings, nor by secretly helping themselves out of the public revenues to get the name of thieves. And not being ambitious they do not care about honour. Wherefore necessity must be laid upon them, and they must be induced to serve from the fear of punishment. And this, as I imagine, is the reason why the forwardness to take office, instead of waiting to be compelled, has been deemed dishonourable. Now the worst part of the punishment is that he who refuses to rule is liable to be ruled by one who is worse than himself. And the fear of this, as I conceive, induces the good to take office, not because they would, but because they cannot help —not under the idea that they are going to have any benefit or enjoyment themselves, but as a necessity, and because they are not able to commit the task of ruling to any one who is better than themselves, or indeed as good. For there is reason to think that if a city were composed entirely of good men, then to avoid office would be as much an object of contention as to obtain office is at present; then we should have plain proof that the true ruler is not meant by nature to regard his own interest, but that of his subjects; and every one who knew this would choose rather to receive a benefit from another than to have the trouble of conferring one. So far am I from agreeing with Thrasymachus that justice is the interest of the stronger. This latter question need not be further discussed at present; but when Thrasymachus says that the life of the unjust is more advantageous than that of the just, his new statement appears to me to be of a far more serious character. Which of us has spoken truly? And which sort of life, Glaucon, do you prefer?

I for my part deem the life of the just to be the more advantageous, he answered.

Did you hear all the advantages of the unjust which Thrasymachus was rehearsing?

Yes, I heard him, he replied, but he has not convinced me.

Then shall we try to find some way of convincing him, if we can, that he is saying what is not true?

Most certainly, he replied.

If, I said, he makes a set speech and we make another recounting all the advantages of being just, and he answers and we rejoin, there must be a numbering and measuring of the goods which are claimed on either side, and in the end we shall want judges to decide; but if we proceed in our enquiry as we lately did, by making admissions to one another, we shall unite the offices of judge and advocate in our own persons.

Very good, he said.

And which method do I understand you to prefer? I said.

That which you propose.

Well, then, Thrasymachus, I said, suppose you begin at the beginning and answer me. You say that perfect injustice is more gainful than perfect justice?

Yes, that is what I say, and I have given you my reasons.

And what is your view about them? Would you call one of them virtue and the other vice?

Certainly.

I suppose that you would call justice virtue and injustice vice?

What a charming notion! So likely too, seeing that I affirm injustice to be profitable and justice not.

What else then would you say?

The opposite, he replied.

And would you call justice vice?

No, I would rather say sublime simplicity.

Then would you call injustice malignity?

No; I would rather say discretion.

And do the unjust appear to you to be wise and good?

Yes, he said; at any rate those of them who are able to be perfectly unjust, and who have the power of subduing states and nations; but perhaps you imagine me to be talking of cutpurses. Even this profession if undetected has advantages, though they are not to be compared with those of which I was just now speaking.

I do not think that I misapprehend your meaning, Thrasymachus, I replied; but still I cannot hear without amazement that you class injustice with wisdom and virtue, and justice with the opposite.

Certainly I do so class them.

Now, I said, you are on more substantial and almost unanswerable ground; for if the injustice which you were maintaining to be profitable had been admitted by you as by others to be vice and deformity, an answer might have been given to you on received principles; but now I perceive that you will call injustice honourable and strong, and to the unjust you will attribute all the qualities which were attributed by us to the just, seeing that you do not hesitate to rank injustice with wisdom and virtue.

You have guessed most infallibly, he replied.

Then I certainly ought not to shrink from going through with the argument so long as I have reason to think that you, Thrasymachus, are speaking your real mind; for I do believe that you are now in earnest and are not amusing yourself at our expense.

I may be in earnest or not, but what is that to you?—to refute the argument is your business.

Very true; I said; that is what I have to do: But will you be so good as answer yet one more question? Does the just man try to gain any advantage over the just?

Far otherwise; if he did he would not be the simple amusing creature which he is.

And would he try to go beyond just action?

He would not.

And how would he regard the attempt to gain an advantage over the unjust; would that be considered by him as just or unjust?

He would think it just, and would try to gain the advantage; but he would not be able.

Whether he would or would not be able, I said, is not to the point. My question is only whether the just man, while refusing to have more than another just man, would wish and claim to have more than the unjust?

Yes, he would.

And what of the unjust—does he claim to have more than the just man and to do more than is just?

Of course, he said, for he claims to have more than all men.

And the unjust man will strive and struggle to obtain more than the unjust man or action, in order that he may have more than all?

True.

We may put the matter thus, I said—the just does not desire more than his like but more than his unlike, whereas the unjust desires more than both his like and his unlike?

Nothing, he said, can be better than that statement.

And the unjust is good and wise, and the just is neither?

Good again, he said.

And is not the unjust like the wise and good and the just unlike them?

Of course, he said, he who is of a certain nature, is like those who are of a certain nature; he who is not, not.

Each of them, I said, is such as his like is?

Certainly, he replied.

Very good, Thrasymachus, I said; and now to take the case of the arts: you would admit that one man is a musician and another not a musician?

Yes.

And which is wise and which is foolish?

Clearly the musician is wise, and he who is not a musician is foolish.

And he is good in as far as he is wise, and bad in as far as he is foolish?

Yes.

And you would say the same sort of thing of the physician?

Yes.

And do you think, my excellent friend, that a musician when he adjusts the lyre would desire or claim to exceed or go beyond a musician in the tightening and loosening the strings?

I do not think that he would.

But he would claim to exceed the non-musician?

Of course.

And what would you say of the physician? In prescribing meats and drinks would he wish to go beyond another physician or beyond the practice of medicine?

He would not.

But he would wish to go beyond the non-physician?

Yes.

And about knowledge and ignorance in general; see whether you think that any man who has knowledge ever would wish to have the choice of saying or doing more than another man who has knowledge. Would he not rather say or do the same as his like in the same case?

That, I suppose, can hardly be denied.

And what of the ignorant? would he not desire to have more than either the knowing or the ignorant?

I dare say.

And the knowing is wise?

Yes.

And the wise is good?

True.

Then the wise and good will not desire to gain more than his like, but more than his unlike and opposite?

I suppose so.

Whereas the bad and ignorant will desire to gain more than both?

Yes.

But did we not say, Thrasymachus, that the unjust goes beyond both his like and unlike? Were not these your words?

They were.

And you also said that the just will not go beyond his like but his unlike?

Yes.

Then the just is like the wise and good, and the unjust like the evil and ignorant?

That is the inference.

And each of them is such as his like is?

That was admitted.

Then the just has turned out to be wise and good and the unjust evil and ignorant.

Thrasymachus made all these admissions, not fluently, as I repeat them, but with extreme reluctance; it was a hot summer's day, and the perspiration poured from him in torrents; and then I saw what I had never seen before, Thrasymachus blushing. As we were now agreed that justice was virtue and wisdom, and injustice vice and ignorance, I proceeded to another point:

Well, I said, Thrasymachus, that matter is now settled; but were we not also saying that injustice had strength; do you remember?

Yes, I remember, he said, but do not suppose that I approve of what you are saying or have no answer; if however I were to answer, you would be quite certain to accuse me of haranguing; therefore either permit me to have my say out, or if you would rather ask, do so, and I will answer 'Very good,' as they say to storytelling old women, and will nod 'Yes' and 'No.'

Certainly not, I said, if contrary to your real opinion.

Yes, he said, I will, to please you, since you will not let me speak. What else would you have?

Nothing in the world, I said; and if you are so disposed I will ask and you shall answer.

Proceed.

Then I will repeat the question which I asked before, in order that our examination of the relative nature of justice and injustice may be carried on regularly. A statement was made that injustice is stronger and more powerful than justice, but now justice, having been identified with wisdom and virtue, is easily shown to be stronger than injustice, if injustice is ignorance; this can no longer be questioned by any one. But I want to view the matter, Thrasymachus, in a different way: You would not deny that a state may be unjust and may be unjustly attempting to enslave other states, or may have already enslaved them, and may be holding many of them in subjection?

True, he replied; and I will add that the best and most perfectly unjust state will be most likely to do so.

I know, I said, that such was your position; but what I would further consider is, whether this power which is possessed by the superior state can exist or be exercised without justice or only with justice.

If you are right in your view, and justice is wisdom, then only with justice; but if I am right, then without justice.

I am delighted, Thrasymachus, to see you not only nodding assent and dissent, but making answers which are quite excellent.

That is out of civility to you, he replied.

You are very kind, I said; and would you have the goodness also to inform me, whether you think that a state, or an army, or a band of robbers and thieves, or any other gang of evil-doers could act at all if they injured one another?

No, indeed, he said, they could not.

But if they abstained from injuring one another, then they might act together better?

Yes.

And this is because injustice creates divisions and hatreds and fighting, and justice imparts harmony and friendship; is not that true, Thrasymachus?

I agree, he said, because I do not wish to quarrel with you.

How good of you, I said; but I should like to know also whether injustice, having this tendency to arouse hatred, wherever existing, among slaves or among freemen, will not make them hate one another and set them at variance and render them incapable of common action?

Certainly.

And even if injustice be found in two only, will they not quarrel and fight, and become enemies to one another and to the just?

They will.

And suppose injustice abiding in a single person, would your wisdom say that she loses or that she retains her natural power?

Let us assume that she retains her power.

Yet is not the power which injustice exercises of such a nature that wherever she takes up her abode, whether in a city, in an army, in a family, or in any other body, that body is, to begin with, rendered incapable of united action by reason of sedition and distraction: and does it not become its own enemy and at variance with all that opposes it, and with the just? Is not this the case?

Yes, certainly.

And is not injustice equally fatal when existing in a single person; in the first place rendering him incapable of action because he is not at unity with himself, and in the second place making him an enemy to himself and the just? Is not that true, Thrasymachus?

Yes.

And O my friend, I said, surely the gods are just?

Granted that they are.

But if so, the unjust will be the enemy of the gods, and the just will be their friend?

Feast away in triumph, and take your fill of the argument; I will not oppose you, lest I should displease the company.

Well then, proceed with your answers, and let me have the remainder of my repast. For we have already shown that the just are clearly wiser and better and abler than the unjust, and that the unjust are incapable of common action; nay more, that to speak as we did of men who are evil acting at any time vigorously together, is not strictly true, for if they had been perfectly evil, they would have laid hands upon one another; but it is evident that there must have been some remnant of justice in them, which enabled them to combine; if there had not been they would have injured one another as well as their victims; they were but half-villains in their enterprises; for had they been whole villains, and utterly unjust, they would have been utterly incapable of action. That, as I believe, is the truth of the matter, and not what you said at first. But whether the just have a better and happier life than the unjust is a further question which we also proposed to consider. I think that they have, and for the reasons which I have given; but still I should like to examine further, for no light matter is at stake, nothing less than the rule of human life.

Proceed.

I will proceed by asking a question: Would you not say that a horse has some end?

I should.

And the end or use of a horse or of anything would be that which could not be accomplished, or not so well accomplished, by any other thing?

I do not understand, he said.

Let me explain: Can you see, except with the eye?

Certainly not.

Or hear, except with the ear?

No.

These then may be truly said to be the ends of these organs?

They may.

But you can cut off a vine-branch with a dagger or with a chisel, and in many other ways?

Of course.

And yet not so well as with a pruning-hook made for the purpose?

True.

May we not say that this is the end of a pruning-hook?

We may.

Then now I think you will have no difficulty in understanding my meaning when I asked the question whether the end of anything would be that which could not be accomplished, or not so well accomplished, by any other thing?

I understand your meaning, he said, and assent.

And that to which an end is appointed has also an excellence? Need I ask again whether the eye has an end?

It has.

And has not the eye an excellence?

Yes.

And the ear has an end and an excellence also?

True.

And the same is true of all other things; they have each of them an end and a special excellence?

That is so.

Well, and can the eyes fulfil their end if they are wanting in their own proper excellence and have a defect instead?

How can they, he said, if they are blind and cannot see?

You mean to say, if they have lost their proper excellence, which is sight; but I have not arrived at that point yet. I would rather ask the question more generally, and only enquire whether the things which fulfil their ends fulfil them by their own proper excellence, and fail of fulfilling them by their own defect?

Certainly, he replied.

I might say the same of the ears; when deprived of their own proper excellence they cannot fulfil their end?

True.

And the same observation will apply to all other things?

I agree.

Well; and has not the soul an end which nothing else can fulfil? for example, to superintend and command and deliberate and the like. Are not these functions proper to the soul, and can they rightly be assigned to any other?

To no other.

And is not life to be reckoned among the ends of the soul?

Assuredly, he said.

And has not the soul an excellence also?

Yes.

And can she or can she not fulfil her own ends when deprived of that excellence?

She cannot.

Then an evil soul must necessarily be an evil ruler and super-intendent, and the good soul a good ruler?

Yes, necessarily.

And we have admitted that justice is the excellence of the soul, and injustice the defect of the soul?

That has been admitted.

Then the just soul and the just man will live well, and the unjust man will live ill?

That is what your argument proves.

And he who lives well is blessed and happy, and he who lives ill the reverse of happy?

Certainly.

Then the just is happy, and the unjust miserable?

So be it.

But happiness and not misery is profitable.

Of course.

Then, my blessed Thrasymachus, injustice can never be more profitable than justice.

3. Callicles and Socrates
(Plato: Gorgias, 482–492)*

In the Gorgias, *Socrates is confronted by the ideas of Callicles, a young Athenian aristocrat. He is not himself a
Sophist but his views are those of some of the Sophists. In
the following selection he presents an intensified and somewhat different form of the views of Thrasymachus.*

Cal. O Socrates, you are a regular declaimer, and seem to be
running riot in the argument. And now you are declaiming in
this way because Polus has fallen into the same error himself of
which he accused Gorgias:—for he said that when Gorgias was
asked by you whether, if some one came to him who wanted to
learn rhetoric, and did not know justice, he would teach him
justice, Gorgias in his modesty replied that he would, because
he thought that mankind in general would be displeased if he
answered "No"; and then in consequence of this admission,
Gorgias was compelled to contradict himself, that being just the
sort of thing in which you delight. Whereupon Polus laughed
at you deservedly, as I think; but now he has himself fallen into
the same trap. I cannot say very much for his wit when he con-
ceded to you that to do is more dishonourable than to suffer
injustice, for this was the admission which led to his being en-
tangled by you; and because he was too modest to say what he
thought, he had his mouth stopped. For the truth is, Socrates,
that you, who pretend to be engaged in the pursuit of truth, are
appealing now to the popular and vulgar notions of right, which
are not natural, but only conventional. Convention and nature
are generally at variance with one another: and hence, if a
person is too modest to say what he thinks, he is compelled to
contradict himself; and you, in your ingenuity perceiving the
advantage to be thereby gained, slyly ask of him who is arguing
conventionally a question which is to be determined by the rule
of nature; and if he is talking of the rule of nature, you slip away

* Translated by Benjamin Jowett.

to custom: as, for instance, you did in this very discussion about doing and suffering injustice. When Polus was speaking of the conventionally dishonourable, you assailed him from the point of view of nature; for by the rule of nature, to suffer injustice is the greater disgrace because the greater evil; but conventionally, to do evil is the more disgraceful. For the suffering of injustice is not the part of a man, but of a slave, who indeed had better die than live; since when he is wronged and trampled upon, he is unable to help himself, or any other about whom he cares. The reason, as I conceive, is that the makers of laws are the majority who are weak; and they make laws and distribute praises and censures with a view to themselves and to their own interests; and they terrify the stronger sort of men, and those who are able to get the better of them, in order that they may not get the better of them; and they say, that dishonesty is shameful and unjust; meaning, by the word injustice, the desire of a man to have more than his neighbours; for knowing their own inferiority, I suspect that they are too glad of equality. And therefore the endeavour to have more than the many, is conventionally said to be shameful and unjust, and is called injustice, whereas nature herself intimates that it is just for the better to have more than the worse, the more powerful than the weaker; and in many ways she shows, among men as well as among animals, and indeed among whole cities and races, that justice consists in the superior ruling over and having more than the inferior. For on what principle of justice did Xerxes invade Hellas, or his father the Scythians? (not to speak of numberless other examples). Nay, but these are the men who act according to nature; yes, by Heaven, and according to the law of nature: not, perhaps, according to that artificial law, which we invent and impose upon our fellows, of whom we take the best and strongest from their youth upwards, and tame them like young lions,—charming them with the sound of the voice and saying to them, that with equality they must be content, and that the equal is the honourable and the just. But if there were a man who had sufficient force, he would shake off and break through and escape from all this; he would trample under foot all our formulas and spells and charms, and all our laws which are against nature: the slave would rise in rebellion and be lord over us, and the light of natural justice would shine forth. And this I take to be the sentiment of Pindar, when he says in his poem, that

Law is the king of all, of mortals as well as of immortals;

this, as he says,

Makes might to be right, doing violence with highest hand; as
I infer from the deeds of Heracles for without buying them—

—I do not remember the exact words, but the meaning is, that
without buying them, and without their being given to him, he
carried off the oxen of Geryon, according to the law of natural
right, and that the oxen and other possessions of the weaker and
inferior properly belong to the stronger and superior. And this
is true, as you may ascertain, if you will leave philosophy and go
on to higher things: for philosophy, Socrates, if pursued in moderation and at the proper age, is an elegant accomplishment, but
too much philosophy is the ruin of human life. Even if a man has
good parts, still, if he carries philosophy into later life, he is
necessarily ignorant of all those things which a gentleman and a
person of honour ought to know; he is inexperienced in the laws
of the State, and in the language which ought to be used in the
dealings of man with man, whether private or public, and utterly
ignorant of the pleasures and desires of mankind and of human
character in general. And people of this sort, when they betake
themselves to politics or business, are as ridiculous as I imagine
the politicians to be, when they make their appearance in the
arena of philosophy. For, as Euripides says,

Every man shines in that and pursues that, and devotes the
greatest portion of the day to that in which he most excels,

but anything in which he is inferior, he avoids and depreciates,
and praises the opposite from partiality to himself, and because
he thinks that he will thus praise himself. The true principle is to
unite them. Philosophy, as a part of education, is an excellent
thing, and there is no disgrace to a man while he is young in pursuing such a study; but when he is more advanced in years, the
thing becomes ridiculous, and I feel towards philosophers as I
do towards those who lisp and imitate children. For I love to see
a little child, who is not of an age to speak plainly, lisping at his
play; there is an appearance of grace and freedom in his utterance,
which is natural to his childish years. But when I hear some small
creature carefully articulating its words, I am offended; the sound

is disagreeable, and has to my ears the twang of slavery. So when I hear a man lisping, or see him playing like a child, his behaviour appears to me ridiculous and unmanly and worthy of stripes. And I have the same feeling about students of philosophy; when I see a youth thus engaged,—the study appears to me to be in character, and becoming a man of liberal education, and him who neglects philosophy I regard as an inferior man, who will never aspire to anything great or noble. But if I see him continuing the study in later life, and not leaving off, I should like to beat him, Socrates; for, as I was saying, such a one, even though he have good natural parts, becomes effeminate. He flies from the busy centre and the market-place, in which, as the poet says, men become distinguished; he creeps into a corner for the rest of his life, and talks in a whisper with three or four admiring youths, but never speaks out like a freeman in a satisfactory manner. Now I, Socrates, am very well inclined towards you, and my feeling may be compared with that of Zethus towards Amphion, in the play of Euripides, whom I was mentioning just now: for I am disposed to say to you much what Zethus said to his brother, that you, Socrates, are careless about the things of which you ought to be careful; and that you

> Who have a soul so noble, are remarkable for a puerile exterior;
> Neither in a court of justice could you state a case, or give any
>   reason or proof.
> Or offer valiant counsel on another's behalf.

And you must not be offended, my dear Socrates, for I am speaking out of good-will towards you, if I ask whether you are not ashamed of being thus defenceless; which I affirm to be the condition not of you only but of all those who will carry the study of philosophy too far. For suppose that some one were to take you, or any of your sort, off to prison, declaring that you had done wrong when you had done no wrong, you must allow that you would not know what to do:—there you would stand giddy and gaping, and not having a word to say; and when you went up before the Court, even if the accuser were a poor creature and not good for much, you would die if he were disposed to claim the penalty of death. And yet, Socrates, what is the value of

> An art which converts a man of sense into a fool,

who is helpless, and has no power to save either himself or others,

when he is in the greatest danger and is going to be despoiled by
his enemies of all his goods, and has to live, simply deprived of
his rights of citizenship?—he being a man who, if I may use the
expression, may be boxed on the ears with impunity. Then, my
good friend, take my advice, and refute no more:

> Learn the philosophy of business, and acquire the reputation of
> wisdom. But leave to others these niceties,

whether they are to be described as follies or absurdities:

> For they will only
> Give you poverty for the inmate of your dwelling.

Cease, then, emulating these paltry splitters of words, and
emulate only the man of substance and honour, who is well to do.

Soc. If my soul, Callicles, were made of gold, should I not
rejoice to discover one of those stones with which they test gold,
and the very best possible one to which I might bring my soul;
and if the stone and I agreed in approving of her training, then
I should know that I was in a satisfactory state, and that no other
test was needed by me.

Cal. What is your meaning, Socrates?

Soc. I will tell you; I think that I have found in you the
desired touchstone.

Cal. Why?

Soc. Because I am sure that if you agree with me in any of
the opinions which my soul forms, I have at last found the truth
indeed. For I consider that if a man is to make a complete trial
of the good or evil of the soul, he ought to have three qualities—
knowledge, good-will, outspokenness, which are all possessed by
you. Many whom I meet are unable to make trial of me, because
they are not wise as you are; others are wise, but they will not
tell me the truth, because they have not the same interest in me
which you have; and these two strangers, Gorgias and Polus, are
undoubtedly wise men and my very good friends, but they are
not outspoken enough, and they are too modest. Why, their
modesty is so great that they are driven to contradict themselves,
first one and then the other of them, in the face of a large company, on matters of the highest moment. But you have all the
qualities in which these others are deficient, having received an
excellent education; to this many Athenians can testify. And you
are my friend. Shall I tell you why I think so? I know that you,

Callicles, and Tisander of Aphidnae, and Andron the son of Androtion, and Nausicydes of the deme of Cholarges, studied together: there were four of you, and I once heard you advising with one another as to the extent to which the pursuit of philosophy should be carried, and, as I know, you came to the conclusion that the study should not be pushed too much into detail. You were cautioning one another not to be overwise; you were afraid that too much wisdom might unconsciously to yourselves be the ruin of you. And now when I hear you giving the same advice to me which you then gave to your most intimate friends, I have a sufficient evidence of your real good-will to me. And of the frankness of your nature and freedom from modesty I am assured by yourself, and the assurance is confirmed by your last speech. Well then, the inference in the present case clearly is, that if you agree with me in an argument about any point, that point will have been sufficiently tested by us, and will not require to be submitted to any further test. For you could not have agreed with me, either from lack of knowledge or from superfluity of modesty, nor yet from a desire to deceive me, for you are my friend, as you tell me yourself. And therefore when you and I are agreed, the result will be the attainment of perfect truth. Now there is no nobler enquiry, Callicles, than that which you censure me for making,—What ought the character of a man to be, and what his pursuits, and how far is he to go, both in maturer years and in youth? For be assured that if I err in my own conduct I do not err intentionally, but from ignorance. Do not then desist from advising me, now that you have begun, until I have learned clearly what this is which I am to practise, and how I may acquire it. And if you find me assenting to your words, and hereafter not doing that to which I assented, call me 'dolt,' and deem me unworthy of receiving further instruction. Once more, then, tell me what you and Pindar mean by natural justice: Do you not mean that the superior should take the property of the inferior by force; that the better should rule the worse, the noble have more than the mean? Am I not right in my recollection?

Cal. Yes; that is what I was saying, and so I still aver.

Soc. And do you mean by the better the same as the superior? for I could not make out what you were saying at the time— whether you meant by the superior the stronger, and that the weaker must obey the stronger, as you seemed to imply when you said that great cities attack small ones in accordance with natural right, because they are superior and stronger, as though the superior and stronger and better were the same; or whether the better may be also the inferior and weaker, and the superior the worse, or whether better is to be defined in the same way as superior: this is the point which I want to have cleared up. Are the superior and better and stronger the same or different?

Cal. I say unequivocally that they are the same.

Soc. Then the many are by nature superior to the one against whom, as you were saying, they make the laws?

Cal. Certainly.

Soc. Then the laws of the many are the laws of the superior?

Cal. Very true.

Soc. Then they are the laws of the better; for the superior class are far better, as you were saying?

Cal. Yes.

Soc. And since they are superior, the laws which are made by them are by nature good?

Cal. Yes.

Soc. And are not the many of opinion, as you were lately saying, that justice is equality, and that to do is more disgraceful than to suffer injustice?—is that so or not? Answer, Callicles, and let no modesty be found to come in the way; do the many think, or do they not think thus?—I must beg of you to answer, in order that if you agree with me I may fortify myself by the assent of so competent an authority.

Cal. Yes; the opinion of the many is what you say.

Soc. Then not only custom but nature also affirms that to do is more disgraceful than to suffer injustice, and that justice is equality; so that you seem to have been wrong in your former assertion, when accusing me you said that nature and custom are opposed, and that I, knowing this, was dishonestly playing between them, appealing to custom when the argument is about nature, and to nature when the argument is about custom?

Cal. This man will never cease talking nonsense. At your age, Socrates, are you not ashamed to be catching at words and chuckling over some verbal slip? do you not see—have I not told you already, that by superior I mean better: do you imagine me to say, that if a rabble of slaves and nondescripts, who are of no use except perhaps for their physical strength, get together, their ipsissima verba are laws?

Soc. Ho! my philosopher, is that your line?

Cal. Certainly.

Soc. I was thinking, Callicles, that something of the kind must
have been in your mind, and that is why I repeated the question,
—What is the superior? I wanted to know clearly what you
meant; for you surely do not think that two men are better than
one, or that your slaves are better than you because they are
stronger? Then please to begin again, and tell me who the better
are, if they are not the stronger; and I will ask you, great Sir,
to be a little milder in your instructions, or I shall have to run
away from you.

Cal. You are ironical.

Soc. No, by the hero Zethus, Callicles, by whose aid you were
just now saying many ironical things against me, I am not:—tell
me, then, whom you mean by the better?

Cal. I mean the more excellent.

Soc. Do you not see that you are yourself using words which
have no meaning and that you are explaining nothing?—will you
tell me whether you mean by the better and superior the wiser,
or if not, whom?

Cal. Most assuredly, I do mean the wiser.

Soc. Then according to you, one wise man may often be
superior to ten thousand fools, and he ought to rule them, and
they ought to be his subjects, and he ought to have more than
they should. This is what I believe that you mean (and you must
not suppose that I am word-catching), if you allow that the one
is superior to the ten thousand?

Cal. Yes; that is what I mean, and that is what I conceive to be
natural justice—that the better and wiser should rule and have
more than the inferior.

Soc. Stop there, and let me ask you what you would say in
this case: Let us suppose that we are all together as we are now;
there are several of us, and we have a large common store of
meats and drinks, and there are all sorts of persons in our company having various degrees of strength and weakness, and one
of us, being physician, is wiser in the matter of food than all the
rest, and he is probably stronger than some and not so strong as
others of us—will he not, being wiser, be also better than we are,
and our superior in this matter of food?

Cal. Certainly.

Soc. Either, then, he will have a larger share of the meats and
drinks, because he is better, or he will have the distribution of all
of them by reason of his authority, but he will not expend or
make use of a larger share of them on his own person, or if he

does, he will be punished;—his share will exceed that of some, and be less than that of others, and if he be the weakest of all, he being the best of all will have the smallest share of all, Callicles: —am I not right, my friend?

Cal. You talk about meats and drinks and physicians and other nonsense; I am not speaking of them.

Soc. Well, but do you admit that the wiser is the better? Answer "Yes" or "No."

Cal. Yes.

Soc. And ought not the better to have a larger share?

Cal. Not of meats and drinks.

Soc. I understand: then, perhaps, of coats—the skillfullest weaver ought to have the largest coat, and the greatest number of them, and go about clothed in the best and finest of them?

Cal. Fudge about coats!

Soc. Then the skilfullest and best in making shoes ought to have the advantage in shoes; the shoemaker, clearly, should walk about in the largest shoes, and have the greatest number of them?

Cal. Fudge about shoes! What nonsense are you talking?

Soc. Or, if this is not your meaning, perhaps you would say that the wise and good and true husbandman should actually have a larger share of seeds, and have as much seed as possible for his own land?

Cal. How you go on, always talking in the same way, Socrates!

Soc. Yes, Callicles, and also about the same things.

Cal. Yes, by the Gods, you are literally always talking of cobblers and fullers and cooks and doctors, as if this had to do with our argument.

Soc. But why will you not tell me in what a man must be superior and wiser in order to claim a larger share; will you neither accept a suggestion, nor offer one?

Cal. I have already told you. In the first place, I mean by superiors not cobblers or cooks, but wise politicians who understand the administration of a state, and who are not only wise, but also valiant and able to carry out their designs, and not the men to faint from want of soul.

Soc. See now, most excellent Callicles, how different my charge against you is from that which you bring against me, for you reproach me with always saying the same; but I reproach you with never saying the same about the same things, for at one time you were defining the better and the superior to be the

stronger, then again as the wiser, and now you bring forward
a new notion; the superior and the better are now declared by
you to be the more courageous: I wish, my good friend, that
you would tell me, once for all, whom you affirm to be the
better and superior, and in what they are better?

Cal. I have already told you that I mean those who are wise
and courageous in the administration of a state—they ought to
be the rulers of their states, and justice consists in their having
more than their subjects.

Soc. But whether rulers or subjects will they or will they not
have more than themselves, my friend?

Cal. What do you mean?

Soc. I mean that every man is his own ruler; but perhaps you
think that there is no necessity for him to rule himself; he is only
required to rule others?

Cal. What do you mean by his "ruling over himself"?

Soc. A simple thing enough; just what is commonly said, that
a man should be temperate and master of himself, and ruler of
his own pleasures and passions.

Cal. What innocence! you mean those fools,—the temperate?

Soc. Certainly:—any one may know that to be my meaning.

Cal. Quite so, Socrates; and they are really fools, for how can
a man be happy who is the servant of anything? On the contrary,
I plainly assert, that he who would truly live ought to allow his
desires to wax to the uttermost, and not to chastise them; but
when they have grown to their greatest he should have courage
and intelligence to minister to them and to satisfy all his long-
ings. And this I affirm to be natural justice and nobility. To this
however the many cannot attain; and they blame the strong man
because they are ashamed of their own weakness, which they
desire to conceal, and hence they say that intemperance is base.
As I have remarked already, they enslave the nobler natures, and
being unable to satisfy their pleasures, they praise temperance
and justice out of their own cowardice. For if a man had been
originally the son of a king, or had a nature capable of acquiring
an empire or a tyranny or sovereignty, what could be more truly
base or evil than temperance—to a man like him, I say, who might
freely be enjoying every good, and has no one to stand in his
way, and yet his admitted custom and reason and the opinion of
other men to be lords over him?—must not he be in a miserable
plight whom the reputation of justice and temperance hinders
from giving more to his friends than to his enemies, even though

he be a ruler in his city? Nay, Socrates, for you profess to be a
votary of the truth, and the truth is this:—that luxury and intemperance and license, if they be provided with means, are
virtue and happiness—all the rest is a mere bauble, agreements
contrary to nature, foolish talk of men, nothing worth.

4. Socrates and Politicians
(Plato: Gorgias, 515–522)*

Soc. And now, my friend, as you are already beginning to be
a public character, and are admonishing and reproaching me for
not being one, suppose that we ask a few questions of one another.
Tell me, then, Callicles, how about making any of the citizens
better? Was there ever a man who was once vicious, or unjust,
or intemperate, or foolish, and became by the help of Callicles
good and noble? Was there ever such a man, whether citizen
or stranger, slave or freeman? Tell me, Callicles, if a person were
to ask these questions of you, what would you answer? Whom
would you say that you had improved by your conversation?
There may have been good deeds of this sort which were done
by you as a private person, before you came forward in public.
Why will you not answer?

Cal. You are contentious, Socrates.

Soc. Nay, I ask you, not from a love of contention, but because I really want to know in what way you think that affairs
should be administered among us—whether, when you come to
the administration of them, you have any other aim but the
improvement of the citizens? Have we not already admitted
many times over that such is the duty of a public man? Nay, we
have surely said so; for if you will not answer for yourself I
must answer for you. But if this is what the good man ought to
effect for the benefit of his own state, allow me to recall to you
the names of those whom you were just now mentioning, Pericles,
and Cimon, and Miltiades, and Themistocles, and ask whether
you still think that they were good citizens.

Cal. I do.

Soc. But if they were good, then clearly each of them must
have made the citizens better instead of worse?

* Translated by Benjamin Jowett.

Cal. Yes.

Soc. And, therefore, when Pericles first began to speak in the assembly, the Athenians were not so good as when he spoke last?

Cal. Very likely.

Soc. Nay, my friend, "likely" is not the word; for if he was a good citizen, the inference is certain.

Cal. And what difference does that make?

Soc. None; only I should like further to know whether the Athenians are supposed to have been made better by Pericles, or, on the contrary, to have been corrupted by him; for I hear that he was the first who gave the people pay, and made them idle and cowardly, and encouraged them in the love of talk and of money.

Cal. You heard that, Socrates, from the laconising set who bruise their ears.

Soc. But what I am going to tell you now is not mere hearsay, but well known both to you and me: that at first, Pericles was glorious and his character unimpeached by any verdict of the Athenians—this was during the time when they were not so good —yet afterwards, when they had been made good and gentle by him, at the very end of his life they convicted him of theft, and almost put him to death, clearly under the notion that he was a malefactor.

Cal. Well, but how does that prove Pericles' badness?

Soc. Why, surely you would say that he was a bad manager of asses or horses or oxen, who had received them originally neither kicking nor butting nor biting him, and implanted in them all these savage tricks? Would he not be a bad manager of any animals who received them gentle, and made them fiercer than they were when he received them? What do you say?

Cal. I will do you the favour of saying "yes."

Soc. And will you also do me the favour of saying whether man is an animal?

Cal. Certainly he is.

Soc. And was not Pericles a shepherd of men?

Cal. Yes.

Soc. And if he was a good political shepherd, ought not the animals who were his subjects, as we were just now acknowledging, to have become more just, and not more unjust?

Cal. Quite true.

Soc. And are not just men gentle, as Homer says?—or are you of another mind?

Cal. I agree.

Soc. And yet he really did make them more savage than he received them, and their savageness was shown towards himself; which he must have been very far from desiring.

Cal. Do you want me to agree with you?

Soc. Yes, if I seem to you to speak the truth.

Cal. Granted then.

Soc. And if they were more savage, must they not have been more unjust and inferior?

Cal. Granted again.

Soc. Then upon this view, Pericles was not a good statesman?

Cal. That is, upon your view.

Soc. Nay, the view is yours, after what you have admitted. Take the case of Cimon again. Did not the very persons whom he was serving ostracize him, in order that they might not hear his voice for ten years? and they did just the same to Themistocles, adding the penalty of exile; and they voted that Miltiades, the hero of Marathon, should be thrown into the pit of death, and he was only saved by the Prytanis. And yet, if they had been really good men, as you say, these things would never have happened to them. For the good charioteers are not those who at first keep their place, and then, when they have broken-in their horses, and themselves become better charioteers, are thrown out—that is not the way either in charioteering or in any profession.—What do you think?

Cal. I should think not.

Soc. Well, but if so, the truth is as I have said already, that in the Athenian State no one has ever shown himself to be a good statesman—you admitted that this was true of our present statesmen, but not true of former ones, and you preferred them to the others; yet they have turned out to be no better than our present ones; and therefore, if they were rhetoricians, they did not use the true art of rhetoric or of flattery, or they would not have fallen out of favour.

Cal. But surely, Socrates, no living man ever came near any one of them in his performances.

Soc. O, my dear friend, I say nothing against them regarded as the serving-men of the State; and I do think that they were certainly more serviceable than those who are living now, and better able to gratify the wishes of the State; but as to transforming those desires and not allowing them to have their way, and using the powers which they had, whether of persuasion or of force, in the improvement of their fellow-citizens, which is the prime object of the truly good citizen, I do not see that in these respects they were a whit superior to our present statesmen, although I do admit that they were more clever at providing ships and walls and docks, and all that. You and I have a ridiculous way, for during the whole time that we are arguing, we are always going round and round to the same point, and constantly misunderstanding one another. If I am not mistaken, you have admitted and acknowledged more than once, that there are two kinds of operations which have to do with the body, and two which have to do with the soul: one of the two is ministerial, and if our bodies are hungry provides food for them, and if they are thirsty gives them drink, or if they are cold supplies them with garments, blankets, shoes, and all that they crave. I use the same images as before intentionally, in order that you may understand me the better. The purveyor of the articles may provide them either wholesale or retail, or he may be the maker of any of them,—the baker, or the cook, or the weaver, or the shoemaker, or the currier; and in so doing, being such as he is, he is naturally supposed by himself and every one to minister to the body. For none of them know that there is another art—an art of gymnastic and medicine which is the true minister of the body, and ought to be the mistress of all the rest, and to use their results according to the knowledge which she has and they have not, of the real good or bad effects of meats and drinks on the body. All other arts which have to do with the body are servile and menial and illiberal; and gymnastic and medicine are, as they ought to be, their mistresses. Now, when I say that all this is equally true of the soul, you seem at first to know and understand and assent to my words, and then a little while afterwards you come repeating, Has not the State had good and noble citizens? and when I ask you who they are, you reply, seemingly quite in earnest, as if I had asked, Who are or have been good trainers?—and you replied, Thearion, the baker, Mithoecus, who wrote the Sicilian cookery-book, Sarambus, the vintner: these are ministers of the body, first-rate in their art; for the first makes admirable loaves, the second excellent dishes, and the third capital wine;—to me these appear to be the exact parallel of the statesmen whom you mention. Now you would not be altogether pleased if I said to you, My friend, you know nothing of gymnastics; those of whom you are speaking to me are only the ministers and purveyors of luxury, who have no good or noble notions of their art, and may very likely be filling and fattening men's bodies and gaining their approval, although the result is that they lose their original flesh in the long run, and become thinner than they were before; and yet they, in their simplicity, will not attribute their diseases and loss of flesh to their entertainers; but when in after years the unhealthy surfeit brings the attendant penalty of disease, he who happens to be near them at the time, and offers them advice, is accused and blamed by them, and if they could they would do him some harm; while they proceed to eulogize the men who have been the real authors of the mischief. And that, Callicles, is just what you are now doing. You praise the men who feasted the citizens and satisfied their desires, and people say that they have made the city great, not seeing that the swollen and ulcerated condition of the State is to be attributed to these elder statesmen; for they have filled the city full of harbours and docks and walls and revenues and all that, and have left no room for justice and temperance. And when the crisis of the disorder comes, the people will blame the advisers of the hour, and applaud Themistocles and Cimon and Pericles, who are the real authors of their calamities; and if you are not careful they may assail you and my friend Alcibiades, when they are losing not only their new acquisitions, but also their original possessions; not that you are the authors of these misfortunes of theirs, although you may perhaps be accessories to them. A great piece of work is always being made, as I see and am told, now as of old, about our statesmen. When the State treats any of them as malefactors, I observe that there is a great uproar and indignation at the supposed wrong which is done to them; "after all their many services to the State, that they should unjustly perish,"—so the tale runs. But the cry is all a lie; for no statesman ever could be unjustly put to death by the city of which he is the head. The case of the professed statesman is, I believe, very much like that of the professed sophist; for the sophists, although they are wise men, are nevertheless guilty of a strange piece of folly; professing to be teachers of virtue, they will often accuse their disciples of wronging them, and defrauding them of their pay, and showing no gratitude for their services. Yet what can be more absurd than that men who have become just and good, and whose injustice has been taken away from them, and who have had justice implanted in them by their teachers, should act unjustly by reason of the injustice which is not in them? Can anything be more irrational, my friends, than this? You, Callicles, compel me to be a mob-orator, because you will not answer.

Cal. And you are the man who cannot speak unless there is some one to answer?

Soc. I suppose that I can; just now, at any rate, the speeches which I am making are long enough because you refuse to answer me. But I adjure you by the god of friendship, my good sir, do tell me whether there does not appear to you to be a great inconsistency in saying that you have made a man good, and then blaming him for being bad?

Cal. Yes, it appears so to me.

Soc. Do you never hear our professors of education speaking in this inconsistent manner?

Cal. Yes, but why talk of men who are good for nothing?

Soc. I would rather say, why talk of men who profess to be rulers, and declare that they are devoted to the improvement of the city, and nevertheless upon occasion declaim against the utter vileness of the city:—do you think that there is any difference between one and the other? My good friend, the sophist and the rhetorician, as I was saying to Polus, are the same, or nearly the same; but you ignorantly fancy that rhetoric is a perfect thing, and sophistry a thing to be despised; whereas the truth is, that sophistry is as much superior to rhetoric as legislation is to the practice of law, or gymnastic to medicine. The orators and sophists, as I am inclined to think, are the only class who cannot complain of the mischief ensuing to themselves from that which they teach others, without in the same breath accusing themselves of having done no good to those whom they profess to benefit. Is not this a fact?

Cal. Certainly it is.

Soc. If they were right in saying that they make men better, then they are the only class who can afford to leave their remuneration to those who have been benefited by them. Whereas if a man has been benefited in any other way, if, for example, he has been taught to run by a trainer, he might possibly defraud him of his pay, if the trainer left the matter to him, and made no agreement with him that he should receive money as soon as he had given him the utmost speed; for not because of any deficiency of speed do men act unjustly, but by reason of injustice.

Cal. Very true.

Soc. And he who removes injustice can be in no danger of

being treated unjustly: he alone can safely leave the honorarium to his pupils, if he be really able to make them good—am I not right?

Cal. Yes.

Soc. Then we have found the reason why there is no dishonour in a man receiving pay who is called in to advise about building or any other art?

Cal. Yes, we have found the reason.

Soc. But when the point is, how a man may become best himself, and best govern his family and state, then to say that you will give no advice gratis is held to be dishonourable?

Cal. True.

Soc. And why? Because only such benefits call forth a desire to requite them, and there is evidence that a benefit has been conferred when the benefactor receives a return; otherwise not. Is this true?

Cal. It is.

Soc. Then to which service of the State do you invite me? determine for me. Am I to be the physician of the State who will strive and struggle to make the Athenians as good as possible; or am I to be the servant and flatterer of the State? Speak out, my good friend, freely and fairly as you did at first and ought to do again, and tell me your entire mind.

Cal. I say then that you should be the servant of the State.

Soc. The flatterer? Well, sir, that is a noble invitation.

Cal. The Mysian, Socrates, or what you please. For if you refuse, the consequences will be—

Soc. Do not repeat the old story—that he who likes will kill me and get my money; for then I shall have to repeat the old answer, that he will be a bad man and will kill the good, and that the money will be of no use to him, but that he will wrongly use that which he wrongly took, and if wrongly, basely, and if basely, hurtfully.

Cal. How confident you are, Socrates, that you will never come to harm! you seem to think that you are living in another country, and can never be brought into a court of justice, as you very likely may be brought by some miserable and mean person.

Soc. Then I must indeed be a fool, Callicles, if I do not know that in the Athenian State any man may suffer anything. And if I am brought to trial and incur the dangers of which you speak, he will be a villain who brings me to trial—of that I am very sure, for no good man would accuse the innocent. Nor shall I be surprised if I am put to death. Shall I tell you why I anticipate this?

Cal. By all means.

Soc. I think that I am the only or almost the only Athenian living who practises the true art of politics: I am the only politician of my time. Now, seeing that when I speak my words are not uttered with any view of gaining favour and that I look to what is best and not to what is most pleasant, having no mind to use those arts and graces which you recommend, I shall have nothing to say in the justice court. And you might argue with me, as I was arguing with Polus:—I shall be tried just as a physician would be tried in a court of little boys at the indictment of the cook. What would he reply under such circumstances, if some one were to accuse him, saying, "Oh my boys, many evil things has this man done to you: he is the death of you, especially of the younger ones among you, cutting and burning and starving and suffocating you, until you know not what to do; he gives you the bitterest potions, and compels you to hunger and thirst. How unlike the variety of meats and sweets on which I feasted you!" What do you suppose that the physician would be able to reply when he found himself in such a predicament? If he told the truth he could only say, "All these evil things, my boys, I did for your health," and then would there not just be a clamour among a jury like that? How they would cry out!

Cal. I dare say.

Soc. Would he not be utterly at a loss for a reply?

Cal. He certainly would.

Soc. And I too shall be treated in the same way, as I well know, if I am brought before the court. For I shall not be able to rehearse to the people the pleasures which I have procured for them, and which, although I am not disposed to envy either the procedures or enjoyers of them, are deemed by them to be benefits and advantages. And if any one says that I corrupt young men, and perplex their minds, or that I speak evil of old men, and use bitter words towards them, whether in private or public, it is useless for me to reply, as I truly might:—"All this I do for the sake of justice, and with a view to your interest, my judges, and to nothing else." And therefore there is no saying what may happen to me.

Cal. And do you think, Socrates, that a man who is thus defenceless is in a good position?

Soc. Yes, Callicles, if he have that defence, which as you have often acknowledged he should have—if he be his own defence, and have never said or done anything wrong, either in respect of gods or men; and this has been repeatedly acknowledged by us to be the best sort of defence. And if any one could convict me of inability to defend myself or others after this sort, I should blush for shame, whether I was convicted before many, or before a few, or by myself alone; and if I died from want of ability to do so, that would indeed grieve me. But if I died because I have no powers of flattery or rhetoric, I am very sure that you would not find me repining at death. For no man who is not an utter fool and coward is afraid of death itself, but he is afraid of doing wrong. For to go to the world below having one's soul full of injustice is the last and worst of all evils.

5. Hippias and Socrates
(*Xenophon:* Memorabilia, *4, 4, 5–25*)*

Such views frequently found expression in his conversations with different persons; I recollect the substance of one that he had with Hippias of Elis concerning Justice. Hippias, who had not been in Athens for a considerable time, found Socrates talking: he was saying that if you want to have a man taught cobbling or building or smithing or riding, you know where to send him to learn the craft: some indeed declare that if you want to train up a horse or an ox in the way he should go, teachers abound. And yet, strangely enough, if you want to learn Justice yourself, or to have your son or servant taught it, you know not where to go for a teacher.

When Hippias heard this, "How now?" he cried in a tone of raillery, "still the same old sentiments, Socrates, that I heard from you so long ago?"

"Yes, Hippias," he replied, "always the same, and—what is more astonishing—on the same topics too! You are so learned that I daresay you never say the same thing on the same subjects."

"I certainly try to say something fresh every time."

"Do you mean, about what you know? For example, in

* Translated by E. C. Marchant in *The Loeb Classical Library* by permission of William Heinemann, Ltd.

answer to the question, 'How many letters are there in "Socrates" and how do you spell it?' do you try to say something different now from what you said before? Or take figures: suppose you are asked if twice five are ten, don't you give the same answer now as you gave before?"

"About letters and figures, Socrates, I always say the same thing, just like you. As for Justice, I feel confident that I can now say that which neither you nor anyone else can contradict."

"Upon my word, you mean to say that you have made a great discovery, if jurymen are to cease from voting different ways, citizens from disputing and litigation, and wrangling about the justice of their claims, cities from quarrelling about their rights and making war; and for my part, I don't see how to tear myself away from you till I have heard about your great discovery."

"But I vow you shall not hear unless you first declare your own opinion about the nature of Justice; for it's enough that you mock at others, questioning and examining everybody, and never willing to render an account yourself or to state an opinion about anything."

"Indeed, Hippias! Haven't you noticed that I never cease to declare my notions of what is just?"

"And how can you call that an account?"

"I declare them by my deeds, anyhow, if not by my words. Don't you think that deeds are better evidence than words?"

"Yes, much better, of course; for many say what is just and do what is unjust; but no one who does what is just can be unjust."

"Then have you ever found me dealing in perjury or calumny, or stirring up strife between friends or fellow-citizens, or doing any other unjust act?

"I have not."

"To abstain from what is unjust is just, don't you think?"

"Even now, Socrates, you are clearly endeavouring to avoid stating what you think Justice to be. You are saying not what the just do, but what they don't do."

"Well, I thought that unwillingness to do injustice was sufficient proof of Justice. But, if you don't think so, see whether you like this better: I say that what is lawful is just."

"Do you mean, Socrates, that lawful and just are the same thing?"

"I do."

"Because I don't see what you mean by lawful or what you mean by just."

"Does the expression 'laws of a state' convey a meaning to you?"

"It does."

"And what do you think they are?"

"Covenants made by the citizens whereby they have enacted what ought to be done and what ought to be avoided."

"Then would not that citizen who acts in accordance with these acts lawfully, and he who transgresses them act unlawfully?"

"Yes, certainly."

"And would not he who obeys them do what is just, and he who disobeys them do what is unjust?"

"Certainly."

"Then would not he who does what is just be just, and he who does what is unjust be unjust?"

"Of course."

"Consequently he who acts lawfully is just, and he who acts unlawfully is unjust."

"Laws," said Hippias, "can hardly be thought of much account, Socrates, or observance of them, seeing that the very men who passed them often reject and amend them."

"Yes," said Socrates, "and after going to war, cities often make peace again."

"To be sure."

"Then is there any difference, do you think, between belittling those who obey the laws on the ground that the laws may be annulled, and blaming those who behave well in the wars on the ground that peace may be made? Or do you really censure those who are eager to help their fatherland in the wars?"

"No, of course not."

"Lycurgus the Lacedaemonian now—have you realised that he would not have made Sparta to differ from other cities in any respect, had he not established obedience to the laws most securely in her? Among rulers in cities, are you not aware that those who do most to make the citizens obey the laws are the best, and that the city in which the citizens are most obedient to the laws has the best time in peace and is irresistible in war? And again, agreement is deemed the greatest blessing for cities: their senates and their best men constantly exhort the citizens to agree, and everywhere in Greece there is a law that the citi-

zens shall promise under oath to agree, and everywhere they
take this oath. The object of this, in my opinion, is not that the
citizens may vote for the same choirs, not that they may praise
the same flute-players, not that they may select the same poets,
not that they may like the same things, but that they may obey
the laws. For those cities whose citizens abide by them prove
strongest and enjoy most happiness; but without agreement no
city can be made a good city, no house can be made a prosperous house. And how is the individual citizen less likely to incur
penalties from the state, and more certain to gain honour than
by obeying the laws? How less likely to be defeated in the
courts or more certain to win? Whom would anyone rather trust
as guardian of his money or sons or daughters? Whom would
the whole city think more trustworthy than the man of lawful
conduct? From whom would parents or kinsfolk or servants or
friends or fellow-citizens or strangers more surely get their just
rights? Whom would enemies rather trust in the matter of a
truce or treaty or terms of peace? Whom would men rather
choose for an ally? And to whom would allies rather entrust
leadership or command of a garrison, or cities? Whom would
anyone more confidently expect to show gratitude for benefits
received? Or whom would one rather benefit than him from
whom he thinks he will receive due gratitude? Whose friendship would anyone desire, or whose enmity would he avoid
more earnestly? Whom would anyone less willingly make war
on than him whose friendship he covets and whose enmity he
is fain to avoid, who attracts the most friends and allies, and
the fewest opponents and enemies?

"So, Hippias, I declare lawful and just to be the same thing.
If you are of the contrary opinion, tell me."

"Upon my word, Socrates," answered Hippias, "I don't
think my opinion is contrary to what you have said about
Justice."

"Do you know what is meant by 'unwritten laws,' Hippias?"

"Yes, those that are uniformly observed in every country."

"Could you say that men made them?"

"Nay, how could that be, seeing that they cannot all meet
together and do not speak the same language?"

"Then by whom have these laws been made, do you suppose?"

"I think that the gods made these laws for men. For among
all men the first law is to fear the gods."

"Is not the duty of honouring parents another universal law?"

"Yes, that is another."

"And that parents shall not have sexual intercourse with their children nor children with their parents?"

"No, I don't think that is a law of God."

"Why so?"

"Because I notice that some transgress it."

"Yes, and they do many other things contrary to the laws. But surely the transgressors of the laws ordained by the gods pay a penalty that a man can in no wise escape, as some, when they transgress the laws ordained by man, escape punishment, either by concealment or by violence."

"And pray what sort of penalty is it, Socrates, that may not be avoided by parents and children who have intercourse with one another?"

"The greatest, of course. For what greater penalty can men incur when they beget children than begetting them badly?"

"How do they beget children badly then, if, as may well happen, the fathers are good men and the mothers good women?"

"Surely because it is not enough that the two parents should be good. They must also be in full bodily vigour: unless you suppose that those who are in full vigour are no more efficient as parents than those who have not yet reached that condition or have passed it."

"Of course that is unlikely."

"Which are the better then?"

"Those who are in full vigour, clearly."

"Consequently those who are not in full vigour are not competent to become parents?"

"It is improbable, of course."

"In that case then, they ought not to have children?"

"Certainly not."

"Therefore those who produce children in such circumstances produce them wrongly?"

"I think so."

"Who then will be bad fathers and mothers, if not they?"

"I agree with you there too."

"Again, is not the duty of requiting benefits universally recognised by law?"

"Yes, but this law too is broken."

"Then does not a man pay forfeit for the breach of that law too, in the gradual loss of good friends and the necessity of hunting those who hate him? Or is it not true that, whereas those who benefit an acquaintance are good friends to him, he is hated by them for his ingratitude, if he makes no return, and then, because it is most profitable to enjoy the acquaintance of such men, he hunts them most assiduously?"

"Assuredly, Socrates, all this does suggest the work of the gods. For laws that involve in themselves punishment meet for those who break them, must, I think, be framed by a better legislator than man."

"Then, Hippias, do you think that the gods ordain what is just or what is otherwise?"

"Not what is otherwise—of course not; for if a god ordains not that which is just, surely no other legislator can do so."

"Consequently, Hippias, the gods too accept the identification of just and lawful."

By such words and actions he encouraged Justice in those who resorted to his company.

6. Antiphon: On Truth*

Justice [in the ordinary view] consists in not transgressing [or rather, is not being known to transgress] any of the legal rules (νόμιμα) of the State in which one lives as a citizen. A man, therefore, would practise justice in the way most advantageous to himself if, in the presence of witnesses, he held the laws in high esteem, but, in the absence of witnesses, and when he was by himself, he held in high esteem the rules of nature (τὰ τῆς φύσεως). The reason is that the rules of the laws (τὰ τῶν νόμων) are adventitious, while the rules of nature are inevitable [and innate]; and again that the rules of the laws are created by covenant (ὁμολογηθέντα) and not produced by nature (φύντα), while the rules of nature are exactly the reverse. A man, therefore, who transgresses legal rules, is free from shame and punishment whenever he is unobserved by those who made the covenant, and is subject to shame and punishment only when he is observed. It is otherwise with transgression of the rules which are innate in nature. If a man strains any of these rules beyond what it can bear, the evil consequences are none the less, if he

* Translated by Sir Ernest Barker in *Greek Political Theory* (London, 1918), pp. 95–99. By permission of Methuen and Co., Ltd. The bracketed inserts are those of the translator.

is entirely unobserved, and none the greater, if he is seen of all men; and this is because the injury which he incurs is not due to men's opinion (διὰ δόξαν), but to the facts of the case (δἰ ἀλήθειαν).

The question with which we are here concerned arises from every point of view (πάντων ἕνεκα). Most of the things which are legally just are [none the less] in the position of being inimical to nature. By law it has been laid down for the eyes what they should see and what they should not see; for the ears what they should hear, and what they should not hear; for the tongue what it should speak, and what it should not speak; for the hands what they should do, and what they should not do; for the feet whither they should go, and whither they should not go; and for the mind what it should desire, and what it should not desire. Now the things from which the laws seek to turn men away are no more [? less] agreeable or akin to nature than the things which the laws seek to turn men towards. [This may be proved as follows.] To nature belong both life and death. Men draw life from the things that are advantageous to them: they incur death from the things that are disadvantageous to them. But the things which are established as advantageous in the view of the law are restraints on nature [i.e., they prevent men from drawing life, which belongs to nature from the things that are really advantageous to them], whereas the things established by nature as advantageous are free [i.e., they leave men free to draw life from the things that are really advantageous to them; for they are identical with those things]. Therefore things which cause pain [and so are akin to death] do not, on a right view, benefit nature more [on the contrary, they benefit nature less] than things which cause pleasure [and so are akin to life]; and therefore, again, things which cause suffering would not be more advantageous [on the contrary, they would be less advantageous] than things which cause happiness— for things which are really (τῷ ἀληθεῖ) advantageous ought not to cause detriment, but gain. . . . [Take the case of those] who retaliate only after suffering injury, and are never themselves the aggressors; or those who behave well to their parents, though their parents behave badly to them; or those, again, who allow others to prefer charges [against them] on oath, and bring no such charges themselves. Of the actions here mentioned one would find many to be inimical to nature. They involve more suffering when less is possible, less pleasure when more is possible, and injury when freedom from injury is possible.

[The writer now attacks legal justice from another point of view. Hitherto he has attacked law and its presumptions; now he attacks law-courts and their operation. Hitherto he has argued that law makes wrong what is right; now he argues that the machinery of the law cannot carry its own false presumptions into effect.] Now if those who adopted such courses received any help from the laws, or those who did not adopt such courses, but took the opposite line, suffered any loss from the laws, there would be some use in paying obedience to the laws. But, as a matter of fact, it is obvious that legal justice is inadequate to help those who adopt such courses. In the beginning [i.e., before any legal cognisance can be taken of the facts] it permits the injured party to be injured and the offending party to commit his offence. But it is not only that legal justice is in no position, at this point, to prevent the injured party from being injured, or the offending party from committing his offence. There is more. If we consider the action of legal justice in reference to retribution [which at any rate it professes to give] we find that such justice is no more favourable to the injured than it is to the offending party. [The remaining lines of the fragment are mutilated; but they seem to mean that, when a case comes before a court for trial, the injured party is in no better a position, and may be in a worse position, than the offending. He can only affirm the fact of injury, and endeavour to persuade the court of the fact. The injured party can deny the fact, and seek to persuade the court of the truth of his denial. What finally determines the court is the greater ability of one or other of the parties; and there is no guarantee that the greater ability will be found on the side of the injured party.]

[Those who are born of a great house] we revere and venerate: those who are born of a humble house we neither revere nor venerate. On this point we are [not civilized, but] barbarized in our behaviour to one another. Our natural endowment is the same for us all, on all points, whether we are Greeks or barbarians. We may observe the characteristics of any of the powers which by nature are necessary to all men. . . . None of us is set apart [by any peculiarity of such natural powers] either as a Greek or as a barbarian. We all breathe the air through our mouth and nostrils.

7. *Socrates and the Law* (*Plato:* Crito)*

Crito]

PERSONS OF THE DIALOGUE: SOCRATES, CRITO
SCENE: The Prison of Socrates

Socrates. Why have you come at this hour, Crito? it must be quite early?

Crito. Yes, certainly.

Soc. What is the exact time?

Cr. The dawn is breaking.

Soc. I wonder that the keeper of the prison would let you in.

Cr. He knows me, because I often come, Socrates; moreover, I have done him a kindness.

Soc. And are you only just arrived?

Cr. No, I came some time ago.

Soc. Then why did you sit and say nothing, instead of at once awakening me?

Cr. I should not have liked myself, Socrates, to be in such great trouble and unrest as you are—indeed I should not: I have been watching with amazement your peaceful slumbers; and for that reason I did not awake you, because I wished to minimize the pain. I have always thought you to be of a happy disposition; but never did I see anything like the easy, tranquil manner in which you bear this calamity.

Soc. Why, Crito, when a man has reached my age he ought not to be repining at the approach of death.

Cr. And yet other old men find themselves in similar misfortunes, and age does not prevent them from repining.

Soc. That is true. But you have not told me why you come at this early hour.

Cr. I come to bring you a message which is sad and painful;

* Translated by Benjamin Jowett.

not, as I believe, to yourself, but to all of us who are your friends, and saddest of all to me.

Soc. What? Has the ship come from Delos, on the arrival of which I am to die?

Cr. No, the ship has not actually arrived, but she will probably be here to-day, as persons who have come from Sunium tell me that they left her there; and therefore to-morrow, Socrates, will be the last day of your life.

Soc. Very well, Crito; if such is the will of God, I am willing: but my belief is that there will be a delay of a day.

Cr. Why do you think so?

Soc. I will tell you. I am to die on the day after the arrival of the ship.

Cr. Yes; that is what the authorities say.

Soc. But I do not think that the ship will be here until to-morrow; this I infer from a vision which I had last night, or rather only just now, when you fortunately allowed me to sleep.

Cr. And what was the nature of the vision?

Soc. There appeared to me the likeness of a woman, fair and comely, clothed in bright raiment, who called to me and said: O Socrates,

The third day hence to fertile Phthia shalt thou go.

Cr. What a singular dream, Socrates!

Soc. There can be no doubt about the meaning, Crito, I think.

Cr. Yes; the meaning is only too clear. But, oh! my beloved Socrates, let me entreat you once more to take my advice and escape. For if you die I shall not only lose a friend who can never be replaced, but there is another evil: people who do not know you and me will believe that I might have saved you if I had been willing to give money, but that I did not care. Now, can there be a worse disgrace than this—that I should be thought to value money more than the life of a friend? For the many will not be persuaded that I wanted you to escape, and that you refused.

Soc. But why, my dear Crito, should we care about the opinion of the many? Good men, and they are the only persons who are worth considering, will think of these things truly as they occurred.

Cr. But you see, Socrates, that the opinion of the many must be regarded, for what is now happening shows that they can do the greatest evil to any one who has lost their good opinion.

Soc. I only wish it were so, Crito; and that the many could do the greatest evil; for then they would also be able to do the greatest good—and what a fine thing this would be! But in reality they can do neither; for they cannot make a man either wise or foolish; and whatever they do is the result of chance.

Cr. Well, I will not dispute with you; but please to tell me, Socrates, whether you are not acting out of regard to me and your other friends: are you not afraid that if you escape from prison we may get into trouble with the informers for having stolen you away, and lost either the whole or a great part of our property; or that even a worse evil may happen to us? Now, if you fear on our account, be at ease; for in order to save you, we ought surely to run this, or even a greater risk; be persuaded, then, and do as I say.

Soc. Yes, Crito, that is one fear which you mention, but by no means the only one.

Cr. Fear not—there are persons who are willing to get you out of prison at no great cost; and as for the informers, they are far from being exorbitant in their demands—a little money will satisfy them. My means, which are certainly ample, are at your service, and if you have a scruple about spending all mine, here are strangers who will give you the use of theirs; and one of them, Simmias the Theban, has brought a large sum of money for this very purpose; and Cebes and many others are prepared to spend their money in helping you to escape. I say, therefore, do not hesitate on our account, and do not say, as you did in the court, that you will have a difficulty in knowing what to do with yourself anywhere else. For men will love you in other places to which you may go, and not in Athens only; there are friends of mine in Thessaly, if you like to go to them, who will value and protect you, and no Thessalian will give you any trouble. Nor can I think that you are at all justified, Socrates, in betraying your own life when you might be saved; in acting thus you are playing into the hands of your enemies, who are hurrying on your destruction. And further I should say that you are deserting your own children; for you might bring them up and educate them; instead of which you go away and leave them, and they will have to take their chance; and if they do not meet with the usual fate of orphans, there will be small thanks to you. No man should bring children into the world who is unwilling to persevere to the end of their nurture and education. But you appear to be choosing the easier part, not the better and manlier, which would have been more becoming in one who professes to care for virtue in all his actions, like yourself. And indeed, I am ashamed not only of you, but of us who are your friends, when I reflect that the whole business will be attributed entirely to our want of courage. The trial need never have come on, or might have been managed differently; and this last act, or crowning folly, will seem to have occurred through our negligence and cowardice, who might have saved you, if we had been good for anything; and you might have saved yourself, for there was no difficulty at all. See now, Socrates, how sad and discreditable are the consequences, both to us and you. Make up your mind then, or rather have your mind already made up, for the time of deliberation is over, and there is only one thing to be done, which must be done this very night, and if we delay at all will be no longer practicable or possible; I beseech you therefore, Socrates, be persuaded by me, and do as I say.

Soc. Dear Crito, your zeal is invaluable, if a right one; but if wrong, the greater the zeal the greater the danger; and therefore we ought to consider whether I shall or shall not do as you say. For I am and always have been one of those natures who must be guided by reason, whatever the reason may be which upon reflection appears to me to be the best; and now that this chance has befallen me, I cannot repudiate my own words: the principles which I have hitherto honoured and revered I still honour, and unless we can at once find other and better principles, I am certain not to agree with you; no, not even if the power of the multitude could inflict many more imprisonments, confiscations, deaths, frightening us like children with hobgoblin terrors. What will be the fairest way of considering the question? Shall I return to your old argument about the opinions of men?—we were saying that some of them are to be regarded, and others not. Now were we right in maintaining this before I was condemned? And has the argument which was once good now proved to be talk for the sake of talking—mere childish nonsense? That is what I want to consider with your help, Crito:—whether, under my present circumstances, the argument appears to be in any way different or not; and is to be allowed by me or disallowed. That argument, which, as I believe, is maintained by many persons of authority, was to the effect, as I was saying, that the opinions of some men are to be regarded, and of other men not to be regarded. Now you, Crito, are not going to die to-morrow—at least, there is no human probability of this—and therefore you are disinterested and not liable to be deceived by the circumstances in which you are placed. Tell me then, whether I am right in saying that some opinions, and the opinions of some men only, are to be valued, and that other opinions, and the opinions of other men, are not to be valued. I ask you whether I was right in maintaining this?

Cr. Certainly.

Soc. The good are to be regarded, and not the bad?

Cr. Yes.

Soc. And the opinions of the wise are good, and the opinions of the unwise are evil?

Cr. Certainly.

Soc. And what was said about another matter? Is the pupil who devotes himself to the practice of gymnastics supposed to attend to the praise and blame and opinion of every man, or of one man only—his physician or trainer, whoever he may be?

Cr. Of one man only.

Soc. And he ought to fear the censure and welcome the praise of that one only, and not of the many?

Cr. Clearly so.

Soc. And he ought to act and train, and eat and drink in the way which seems good to his single master who has understanding, rather than according to the opinion of all other men put together?

Cr. True.

Soc. And if he disobeys and disregards the opinion and approval of the one, and regards the opinion of the many who have no understanding, will he not suffer evil?

Cr. Certainly he will.

Soc. And what will the evil be, whither tending and what affecting, in the disobedient person?

Cr. Clearly, affecting the body; that is what is destroyed by the evil.

Soc. Very good; and is not this true, Crito, of other things which we need not separately enumerate? In questions of just and unjust, fair and foul, good and evil, which are the subjects of our present consultation, ought we to follow the opinion of the many and to fear them; or the opinion of the one man who has understanding? ought we not to fear and reverence him more than all the rest of the world: and if we desert him shall we not destroy and injure that principle in us which may be assumed to be improved by justice and deteriorated by injustice;—there is such a principle?

Cr. Certainly there is, Socrates.

Soc. Take a parallel instance:—if, acting under the advice of those who have no understanding, we destroy that which is improved by health and is deteriorated by disease, would life be worth having? And that which has been destroyed is—the body?

Cr. Yes.

Soc. Could we live, having an evil and corrupted body?

Cr. Certainly not.

Soc. And will life be worth having, if that higher part of man be destroyed, which is improved by justice and depraved by injustice? Do we suppose that principle, whatever it may be in man, which has to do with justice and injustice, to be inferior to the body?

Cr. Certainly not.

Soc. More honourable than the body?

Cr. Far more.

Soc. Then, my friend, we must not regard what the many say of us: but what he, the one man who has understanding of just and unjust, will say, and what the truth will say. And therefore you begin in error when you advise that we should regard the opinion of the many about just and unjust, good and evil, honourable and dishonourable.—'Well,' some one will say, 'but the many can kill us.'

Cr. Yes, Socrates; that will clearly be the answer.

Soc. And it is true: but still I find with surprise that the old argument is unshaken as ever. And I should like to know whether I may say the same of another proposition—that not life, but a good life, is to be chiefly valued?

Cr. Yes, that also remains unshaken.

Soc. And a good life is equivalent to a just and honourable one—that holds also?

Cr. Yes, it does.

Soc. From these premisses I proceed to argue the question whether I ought or ought not to try and escape without the consent of the Athenians: and if I am clearly right in escaping, then I will make the attempt; but if not, I will abstain. The other considerations which you mention, of money and loss of character and the duty of educating one's children, are, I fear, only the doctrines of the multitude, who would be as ready to restore

people to life, if they were able, as they are to put them to death
—and with as little reason. But now, since the argument has thus
far prevailed, the only question which remains to be considered
is, whether we shall do rightly either in escaping or in suffering
others to aid in our escape and paying them in money and thanks,
or whether in reality we shall not do rightly; and if the latter,
then death or any other calamity which may ensue on my remaining here must not be allowed to enter into the calculation.

Cr. I think that you are right, Socrates; how then shall we
proceed?

Soc. Let us consider the matter together, and do you either
refute me if you can, and I will be convinced; or else cease, my
dear friend, from repeating to me that I ought to escape against
the wishes of the Athenians: for I highly value your attempts
to persuade me to do so, but I may not be persuaded against my
own better judgment. And now please to consider my first position, and try how you can best answer me.

Cr. I will.

Soc. Are we to say that we are never intentionally to do
wrong, or that in one way we ought and in another we ought not
to do wrong, or is doing wrong always evil and dishonourable,
as I was just now saying, and as has been already acknowledged
by us? Are all our former admissions which were made within
a few days to be thrown away? And have we, at our age, been
earnestly discoursing with one another all our life long only to
discover that we are no better than children? Or, in spite of the
opinion of the many, and in spite of consequences whether better
or worse, shall we insist on the truth of what was then said, that
injustice is always an evil and dishonour to him who acts unjustly? Shall we say so or not?

Cr. Yes.

Soc. Then we must do no wrong?

Cr. Certainly not.

Soc. Nor when injured injure in return, as the many imagine;
for we must injure no one at all?

Cr. Clearly not.

Soc. Again, Crito, may we do evil?

Cr. Surely not, Socrates.

Soc. And what of doing evil in return for evil, which is the
morality of the many—is that just or not?

Cr. Not just.

Soc. For doing evil to another is the same as injuring him?

Cr. Very true.

Soc. Then we ought not to retaliate or render evil for evil to any one, whatever evil we may have suffered from him. But I would have you consider, Crito, whether you really mean what you are saying. For this opinion has never been held, and never will be held, by any considerable number of persons; and those who are agreed and those who are not agreed upon this point have no common ground, and can only despise one another when they see how widely they differ. Tell me, then, whether you agree with and assent to my first principle, that neither injury nor retaliation nor warding off evil by evil is ever right. And shall that be the premiss of our argument? Or do you decline and dissent from this? For so I have ever thought, and continue to think; but, if you are of another opinion, let me hear what you have to say. If, however, you remain of the same mind as formerly, I will proceed to the next step.

Cr. You may proceed, for I have not changed my mind.

Soc. Then I will go on to the next point, which may be put in the form of a question:—Ought a man to do what he admits to be right, or ought he to betray the right?

Cr. He ought to do what he thinks right.

Soc. But if this is true, what is the application? In leaving the prison against the will of the Athenians, do I wrong any? or rather do I not wrong those whom I ought least to wrong? Do I not desert the principles which were acknowledged by us to be just—what do you say?

Cr. I cannot tell, Socrates; for I do not know.

Soc. Then consider the matter in this way:—Imagine that I am about to play truant (you may call the proceeding by any name which you like), and the laws and the government come and interrogate me: "Tell us, Socrates," they say; "what are you about? are you not going by an act of yours to overturn us—the laws, and the whole state, as far as in you lies? Do you imagine that a state can subsist and not be overthrown, in which the decisions of law have no power, but are set aside and trampled upon by individuals?" What will be our answer, Crito, to these and the like words? Any one, and especially a rhetorician, will have a good deal to say on behalf of the law which requires a sentence to be carried out. He will argue that this law should not be set aside; and shall we reply, "Yes; but the state has injured us and given an unjust sentence." Suppose I say that?

Cr. Very good, Socrates.

Soc. "And was that our agreement with you?" the law would answer; "or were you to abide by the sentence of the state?" And if I were to express my astonishment at their words, the law would probably add: "Answer, Socrates, instead of opening your eyes—you are in the habit of asking and answering questions. Tell us,—What complaint have you to make against us which justifies you in attempting to destroy us and the state? In the first place did we not bring you into existence? Your father married your mother by our aid and begat you. Say whether you have any objection to urge against those of us who regulate marriage?" None, I should reply. "Or against those of us who after birth regulate the nurture and education of children, in which you also were trained? Were not the laws, which have the charge of education, right in commanding your father to train you in music and gymnastic?" Right, I should reply. "Well then, since you were brought into the world and nurtured and educated by us, can you deny in the first place that you are our child and slave, as your fathers were before you? And if this is true you are not on equal terms with us; nor can you think that you have a right to do to us what we are doing to you. Would you have any right to strike or revile or do any other evil to your father or your master, if you had one, because you have been struck or reviled by him, or received some other evil at his hands?—you would not say this? And because we think right to destroy you, do you think that you have any right to destroy us in return, and your country as far as in you lies? Will you, O professor of true virtue, pretend that you are justified in this? Has a philosopher like you failed to discover that our country is more to be valued and higher and holier far than mother or father or any ancestor, and more to be regarded in the eyes of the gods and of men of understanding? also to be soothed, and gently and reverently entreated when angry, even more than a father, and either to be persuaded, or if not persuaded, to be obeyed? And when we are punished by her, whether with imprisonment or stripes, the punishment is to be endured in silence; and if she leads us to wounds or death in battle, thither we follow as is right; neither may any one yield or retreat or leave his rank, but whether in battle or in a court of law, or in any other place, he must do what his city and his country order him; or he must change their view of what is just: and if he may do no violence to his father or mother, much less may he do violence to his country." What answer shall we make to this, Crito? Do the laws speak truly, or do they not?

Cr. I think that they do.

Soc. Then the laws will say, "Consider, Socrates, if we are speaking truly that in your present attempt you are going to do us an injury. For, having brought you into the world, and nurtured and educated you, and given you and every other citizen a share in every good which we had to give, we further proclaim to any Athenian by the liberty which we allow him, that if he does not like us when he has become of age and has seen the ways of the city, and made our acquaintance, he may go where he pleases and take his goods with him. None of us laws will forbid him or interfere with him. Any one who does not like us and the city, and who wants to emigrate to a colony or to any other city, may go where he likes, retaining his property. But he who has experience of the manner in which we order justice and administer the state, and still remains, has entered into an implied contract that he will do as we command him. And he who disobeys us is, as we maintain, thrice wrong; first, because in disobeying us he is disobeying his parents; secondly, because we are the authors of his education; thirdly, because he has made an agreement with us that he will duly obey our commands; and he neither obeys them nor convinces us that our commands are unjust; and we do not rudely impose them, but give him the alternative of obeying or convincing us;—that is what we offer, and he does neither.

"These are the sort of accusations to which, as we were saying, you, Socrates, will be exposed if you accomplish your intentions; you, above all other Athenians." Suppose now I ask, why I rather than anybody else? they will justly retort upon me that I above all other men have acknowledged the agreement. "There is clear proof," they will say, "Socrates, that we and the city were not displeasing to you. Of all Athenians you have been the most constant resident in the city, which, as you never leave, you may be supposed to love. For you never went out of the city either to see the games, except once when you went to the Isthmus, or to any other place unless when you were on military service; nor did you travel as other men do. Nor had you any curiosity to know other states or their laws: your affections did not go beyond us and our state; we were your special favourites, and you acquiesced in our government of you; and here in this city you begat your children, which is a proof of your satisfaction. Moreover, you might in the course of the trial, if you had liked, have fixed the penalty at banishment; the state which refuses to let you go now would have let you go then. But you pretended that you preferred death to exile, and that you were not unwilling to die. And now you have forgotten these fine sentiments, and pay no respect to us the laws, of whom you are the destroyer; and are doing what only a miserable slave would do, running away and turning your back upon the compacts and agreements which you made as a citizen. And first of all answer this very question: Are we right in saying that you agreed to be governed according to us in deed, and not in word only? Is that true or not?' How shall we answer, Crito? Must we not assent?

Cr. We cannot help it, Socrates.

Soc. Then will they not say: 'You, Socrates, are breaking the covenants and agreements which you made with us at your leisure, not in any haste or under any compulsion or deception, but after you have had seventy years to think of them, during which time you were at liberty to leave the city, if we were not to your mind, or if our covenants appeared to you to be unfair. You had your choice, and might have gone either to Lacedaemon or Crete, both which states are often praised by you for their good government, or to some other Hellenic or foreign state. Whereas you, above all other Athenians, seemed to be so fond of the state, or, in other words, of us her laws (and who would care about a state which has no laws?), that you never stirred out of her; the halt, the blind, the maimed were not more stationary in her than you were. And now you run away and forsake your agreements. Not so, Socrates, if you will take our advice; do not make yourself ridiculous by escaping out of the city.

"For just consider, if you transgress and err in this sort of way, what good will you do either to yourself or to your friends? That your friends will be driven into exile and deprived of citizenship, or will lose their property, is tolerably certain; and you yourself, if you fly to one of the neighbouring cities, as, for example, Thebes or Megara, both of which are well governed, will come to them as an enemy, Socrates, and their government will be against you, and all patriotic citizens will cast an evil eye upon you as a subverter of the laws, and you will confirm in the minds of the judges the justice of their own condemnation

of you. For he who is a corrupter of the laws is more than likely
to be a corrupter of the young and foolish portion of mankind.
Will you then flee from well-ordered cities and virtuous men?
and is existence worth having on these terms? Or will you go
to them without shame, and talk to them, Socrates? And what
will you say to them? What you say here about virtue and justice
and institutions and laws being the best things among men?
Would that be decent of you? Surely not. But if you go away
from well-governed states to Crito's friends in Thessaly, where
there is great disorder and licence, they will be charmed to hear
the tale of your escape from prison, set off with ludicrous particulars of the manner in which you were wrapped in a goatskin
or some other disguise, and metamorphosed as the manner is of
runaways; but will there be no one to remind you that in your
old age you were not ashamed to violate the most sacred laws
from a miserable desire of a little more life? Perhaps not, if you
keep them in a good temper; but if they are out of temper you
will hear many degrading things; you will live, but how?—as the
flatterer of all men, and the servant of all men; and doing what?
—eating and drinking in Thessaly, having gone abroad in order
that you may get a dinner. And where will be your fine sentiments about justice and virtue? Say that you wish to live for the
sake of your children—you want to bring them up and educate
them—will you take them into Thessaly and deprive them of
Athenian citizenship? Is this the benefit which you will confer
upon them? Or are you under the impression that they will be
better cared for and educated here if you are still alive, although
absent from them; for your friends will take care of them? Do
you fancy that if you are an inhabitant of Thessaly they will
take care of them, and if you are an inhabitant of the other
world that they will not take care of them? Nay; but if they who
call themselves friends are good for anything, they will—to be
sure they will.

"Listen, then, Socrates, to us who have brought you up.
Think not of life and children first, and of justice afterwards,
but of justice first, that you may be justified before the princes
of the world below. For neither will you nor any that belong
to you be happier or holier or juster in this life, or happier in
another, if you do as Crito bids. Now you depart in innocence,
a sufferer and not a doer of evil; a victim, not of the laws but of
men. But if you go forth, returning evil for evil, and injury for

injury, breaking the covenants and agreements which you have made with us, and wronging those whom you ought least of all to wrong, that is to say, yourself, your friends, your country, and us, we shall be angry with you while you live, and our brethren, the laws in the world below, will receive you as an enemy; for they will know that you have done your best to destroy us. Listen, then, to us and not to Crito."

This, dear Crito, is the voice which I seem to hear murmuring in my ears, like the sound of the flute in the ears of the mystic; that voice, I say, is humming in my ears, and prevents me from hearing any other. And I know that anything more which you may say will be vain. Yet speak, if you have anything to say.

Cr. I have nothing to say, Socrates.

Soc. Leave me then, Crito, to fulfil the will of God, and to follow whither he leads.

8. Xenophon and Isocrates

The devastation of the long Peloponnesian War shook the confidence of the polis. The homelessness and poverty which resulted from it created and intensified internal dissensions which threatened each city with endemic civil war. At the same time, the inability of the city-states to end their squabbling and to live in peace severally or to unite into a larger governmental unit led many to despair of the continuation of the free and independent polis. Xenophon (ca. 430– 354 B.C.) was an Athenian aristocrat who lived through these troubled times. Like many aristocrats he admired the Spartan constitution for its balance and stability and for its essentially oligarchic character.

1. *Xenophon on the Spartan Constitution* (The Constitution of the Spartans *1, 2, 3, 4, 6, 7, 8, 9, 10, 14, 15*)*

I recall the astonishment with which I first noted the unique position of Sparta among the states of Hellas, the relatively sparse population, and at the same time the extraordinary power and prestige of the community. I was puzzled to account for the fact. It was only when I came to consider the peculiar institutions of the Spartans that my wonderment ceased. Or rather, it is transferred to the legislator who gave them those laws, obedience to which has been the secret of their prosperity. This legislator, Lycurgus, I admire, and hold him to have been one of the wisest of mankind. Certainly he was no servile imitator of other states. It was by a stroke of invention rather, and on a pattern much in opposition to the commonly-accepted one, that he brought his fatherland to this pinnacle of prosperity. . . .

With this exposition of the customs in connection with the birth of children, I wish now to explain the systems of education in fashion here and elsewhere. Throughout the rest of Hellas the custom on the part of those who claim to educate their sons in the best way is as follows. As soon as the children are of an age to understand what is said to them they are immediately placed under the charge of Paidagogoi (or tutors), who are also attendants, and sent off to the school of some teacher to be taught grammar, music, and the concerns of the palaestra. Besides this they are given shoes to wear which tend to make their feet tender, and their bodies are enervated by various changes of clothing. And as for food, the only measure recognized is that which is fixed by appetite.

But when we turn to Lycurgus, instead of leaving it to each member of the state privately to appoint a slave to be his son's tutor, he set over the young Spartans a public guardian, the Paidonomos, to give him his proper title, with complete authority over them. This guardian was selected from those who filled the highest magistracies. He had authority to hold musters of the boys, and as their overseer, in case of any misbehaviour, to chas-

* Translated by Henry G. Dakyns.

tise severely. The legislator further provided the pastor with a body of youths in the prime of life, and bearing whips, to inflict punishment when necessary, with this happy result that in Sparta modesty and obedience ever go hand in hand, nor is there lack of either. . . .

Furthermore, and in order that the boys should not want a ruler, even in case the guardian himself were absent, he gave to any citizen who chanced to be present authority to lay upon them injunctions for their good, and to chastise them for any trespass committed. By so doing he created in the boys of Sparta a most rare modesty and reverence. And indeed there is nothing which, whether as boys or men, they respect more highly than the ruler. Lastly, and with the same intention, that the boys must never be reft of a ruler, even if by chance there were no grown man present, he laid down the rule that in such a case the most active of the Leaders or Prefects was to become ruler each of his own division. The conclusion being that under no circumstances whatever are the boys of Sparta destitute of one to rule them. . . .

Coming to the critical period at which a boy ceases to be a boy and becomes a youth, we find that it is just then that the rest of the world proceed to emancipate their children from the private tutor and the schoolmaster, and, without substituting any further ruler, are content to launch them into absolute independence.

Here, again, Lycurgus took an entirely opposite view of the matter. This, if observation might be trusted, was the season when the tide of animal spirits flows fast, and the froth of insolence rises to the surface; when, too, the most violent appetites for pleasures invade the mind. This, then, was the right moment at which to impose constant labours upon the growing youth, and to devise for him a subtle system of absorbing occupation. And by a crowning enactment, which said that he who shrank from the duties imposed on him would forfeit henceforth all claim to the glorious honours of the state, he caused, not only the public authorities, but those personally interested in the youths to take serious pains so that no single individual of them should by an act of cowardice find himself utterly despised within the body politic. . . .

But if he was thus careful in the education of the stripling, the Spartan lawgiver showed a still greater anxiety in dealing with those who had reached the prime of opening manhood; considering their immense importance to the city in the scale of good, if only they proved themselves the men they should be. He had only to look around to see that wherever the spirit of emulation is most deeply seated, there, too, their choruses and gymnastic contests will present alike a far higher charm to eye and ear. And on the same principle he persuaded himself that he needed only to confront his youthful warriors in the strife of valour, and with like result. They also, in their degree, might be expected to attain to some unknown height of manly virtue. . . .

With regard to those who have already passed the vigour of early manhood, and on whom the highest magistracies henceforth devolve, there is a like contrast. In Hellas generally we find that at this age the need of further attention to physical strength is removed, although the imposition of military service continues. But Lycurgus made it customary for that section of his citizens to regard hunting as the highest honour suited to their age; but not to the exclusion of any public duty. And his aim was that they might be equally able to undergo the fatigues of war with those in the prime of early manhood. . . .

There are other points in which this legislator's views run counter to those commonly accepted. Thus: in other states the individual citizen is master over his own children, servants and belongings generally; but Lycurgus, whose aim was to secure to all the citizens a considerable share in one another's goods without mutual injury, enacted that each one should have an equal power over his neighbour's children as over his own. The principle is this. When a man knows that this, that, and the other person are fathers of children subject to his own authority, he must perforce deal by them even as he desires his own children to be dealt by. And, if a boy chance to have received a whipping, not from his own father but some other, and goes and complains to his own father, it would be thought wrong on the part of that father if he did not inflict a second whipping on his son. A striking proof, in its way, how completely they trust each other not to impose dishonourable commands upon their children.

In the same way he empowered them to use their neighbour's servants in case of need. This communism he applied also to dogs used for the chase; in so far that a party in need of dogs will invite the owner to the chase, and if he is not at leisure to attend himself, at any rate he is happy to let his dogs go. The same applies to the use of horses. Some one has fallen sick perhaps, or is in want of a carriage, or is anxious to reach some point or other quickly —in any case he has a right, if he sees a horse anywhere, to take and use it, and restores it safe and sound when he has done with it. . . .

There are yet other customs in Sparta which Lycurgus instituted in opposition to those of the rest of Hellas, and the following among them. We all know that in the generality of states every one devotes his full energy to the business of making money: one man as a tiller of the soil, another as a mariner, a third as a merchant, whilst others depend on various arts to earn a living. But at Sparta Lycurgus forbade his freeborn citizens to have anything whatsoever to do with the concerns of money-making. As freemen, he enjoined upon them to regard as their concern exclusively those activities upon which the foundations of civic liberty are based.

And indeed, one may well ask, for what reason should wealth be regarded as a matter for serious pursuit in a community where, partly by a system of equal contributions to the necessaries of life, and partly by the maintenance of a common standard of living, the lawgiver placed so effectual a check upon the desire for riches for the sake of luxury? What inducement, for instance, would there be to make money, even for the sake of wearing apparel, in a state where personal adornment is held to lie not in the costliness of the clothes they wear, but in the healthy condition of the body to be clothed? Nor again could there be much inducement to amass wealth, in order to be able to expend it on the members of a common mess, where the legislator had made it seem far more glorious that a man should help his fellows by the labour of his body than by costly outlay. The latter being, as he finely phrased it, the function of wealth, the former an activity of the soul.

He went a step farther, and set up a strong barrier (even in a society such as I have described) against the pursuance of money-making by wrongful means. In the first place, he established a coinage of so extraordinary a sort, that even a single sum of ten minas could not come into a house without attracting the notice, either of the master himself, or of some member of his household. In fact, it would occupy a considerable space, and need a waggon to carry it. Gold and silver themselves, moreover, are liable to search, and in case of detection, the possessor subjected to a penalty. In fact, to repeat the question asked above, for what reason should money-making become an earnest pursuit in a community where the possession of wealth entails more pain than its employment brings satisfaction?

But to proceed. We are all aware that there is no state in the world in which greater obedience is shown to magistrates, and to the laws themselves, than Sparta. But, for my part, I am disposed to think that Lycurgus could never have attempted to establish this healthy condition, until he had first secured the unanimity of the most powerful members of the state. I infer this for the following reasons. In other states the leaders in rank and influence do not even desire to be thought to fear the magistrates. Such a thing they would regard as in itself a symbol of servility. In Sparta, on the contrary, the stronger a man is the more readily does he bow before constituted authority. And indeed, they pride themselves on their humility, and on a prompt obedience, running, or at any rate not crawling with laggard step, at the word of command. Such an example of eager discipline, they are persuaded, set by themselves, will not fail to be followed by the rest. And this is precisely what has taken place. It is reasonable to suppose that it was these same noblest members of the state who combined to lay the foundation of the ephorate, after they had come to the conclusion themselves that of all the blessings which a state, or an army, or a household can enjoy, obedience is the greatest. Since, as they could not but reason, the greater the power with which men fence about authority, the greater the fascination it will exercise upon the mind of the citizen, to the enforcement of obedience.

Accordingly the ephors are competent to punish whomsoever they choose; they have power to exact fines on the spur of the moment; they have power to depose magistrates in mid career, nay, actually to imprison and bring them to trial on the capital charge. Entrusted with all these vast powers, they do not, as do the rest of states, allow the magistrates elected to exercise authority as they like, right through the year of office; but, in the style rather of despotic monarchs, or presidents of the games, at the first symptom of an offence against the law they inflict chastisement without warning and without hesitation.

But of all the many beautiful contrivances invented by Lycurgus to kindle a willing obedience to the laws in the hearts of the citizens, none, to my mind, was happier or more excellent than his unwillingness to deliver his code to the people at large, until, attended by the most powerful members of the state, he had betaken himself to Delphi, and there made inquiry of the god whether it were better for Sparta, and conducive to her interests, to obey the laws which he had framed. And not until the divine answer came, "Better will it be in every way," did he deliver them, laying it down as a last ordinance that to refuse obedience to a code which had the sanction of the Pythian god himself was a thing not illegal only, but impious.

The following too may well excite our admiration for Lycurgus. I speak of the consummate skill with which he induced the whole state of Sparta to regard an honourable death as preferable to an ignoble life. And indeed if any one will investigate the matter, he will find that by comparison with those who make it a principle to retreat in face of danger, actually fewer of these Spartans die in battle, since, to speak truth, salvation, it would seem, attends on virtue far more frequently than on cowardice —virtue, which is at once easier and sweeter, richer in resource and stronger of arm, than her opposite. And that virtue has another familiar attendant—to wit, glory—needs no showing, since all wish to ally themselves somehow with the good.

Yet the actual means by which he gave currency to these principles is a point which it were well not to overlook. It is clear that the lawgiver set himself deliberately to provide all the blessings of heaven for the good man, and a sorry and ill-starred existence for the coward.

In other states the man who shows himself base and cowardly wins to himself an evil reputation and the nickname of a coward, but that is all. For the rest he buys and sells in the same market-place with the good man; he sits beside him at the play; he exercises with him in the same gymnasium, and all as suits his humour. But at Lacedaemon there is not one man who would not feel ashamed to welcome the coward at the common mess-table, or to try conclusions with such an antagonist in a wrestling bout. Consider the day's round of his existence. The sides are being picked for a game of ball, but he is left out as the odd man: there is no place for him. During the choric dance he is driven away into ignominious quarters. Nay, in the very streets it is he who must step aside for others to pass, or, being seated, he must rise and make room, even for a younger man. At home he will have his maiden relatives to support in their isolation (and they will hold him to blame for their unwedded lives). A hearth with no wife to bless it—that is a condition he must face, and yet he will have to pay damages for incurring it. Let him not roam abroad with a smiling countenance; let him not imitate men whose fame is irreproachable, or he shall feel on his back the blows of his superiors. Such being the weight of infamy which is laid upon all cowards, I, for my part, am not surprised if in Sparta they deem death preferable to a life so steeped in dishonour and reproach.

That too was a happy enactment, in my opinion, by which Lycurgus provided for the continual cultivation of virtue, even to old age. By fixing the election to the council of elders as a last ordeal at the goal of life, he made it impossible for a high standard of virtuous living to be disregarded even in old age. (So, too, it is worthy of admiration in him that he lent his helping hand to virtuous old age. Thus, by making the elders sole arbiters in the trial for life, he contrived to charge old age with a greater weight of honour than that which is accorded to the strength of mature manhood.) And assuredly such a contest as this must appeal to the zeal of mortal man beyond all others in a supreme degree. Fair, doubtless, are contests of gymnastic skill, yet are they but trials of bodily excellence, but this contest for the seniory is of a higher sort—it is an ordeal of the soul itself. In proportion, therefore, as the soul is worthier than the body, so must these contests of the soul appeal to a stronger enthusiasm than their bodily antitypes.

And yet another point may well excite our admiration for Lycurgus largely. It had not escaped his observation that communities exist where those who are willing to make virtue their study and delight fail somehow in ability to add to the glory of their fatherland. That lesson the legislator laid to heart, and in Sparta he enforced, as a matter of public duty, the practice of every virtue by every citizen. And so it is that, just as man differs from man in some excellence, according as he cultivates or neglects to cultivate it, this city of Sparta, with good reason, outshines all other states in virtue, since she, and she alone, has made the attainment of a high standard of noble living a public duty.

And was not this a noble enactment, that whereas other states are content to inflict punishment only in cases where a man does wrong against his neighbour, Lycurgus imposed penalties no less severe on him who openly neglected to make himself as good as possible? For this, it seems, was his principle: in the one case, where a man is robbed, or defrauded, or kidnapped, and made a slave of, the injury of the misdeed, whatever it be, is personal to the individual so maltreated; but in the other case whole communities suffer foul treason at the hands of the base man and the coward. So that it was only reasonable, in my opinion, that he should visit the heaviest penalty upon these latter.

Moreover, he laid upon them, like some irresistible necessity, the obligation to cultivate the whole virtue of a citizen. Provided they duly performed the injunctions of the law, the city belonged to them, each and all, in absolute possession and on an equal footing. Weakness of limb or want of wealth was no drawback in his eyes. But as for him who, out of the cowardice of his heart, shrank from the performance of the law's injunction, the legislator pointed him out as disqualified to be regarded longer as a member of the brotherhood of peers.

It may be added that there is no doubt as to the great antiquity of this code of laws. The point is clear so far, that Lycurgus himself is said to have lived in the days of the Heracleidae. But being of so long standing, these laws, even at this day, still are stamped in the eyes of other men with all the novelty of youth. And the most marvellous thing of all is that, while everybody is agreed to praise these remarkable institutions, there is not a single state which cares to imitate them. . . .

Now, if the question be put to me whether the laws of Lycurgus remain still to this day unchanged, that indeed is an assertion which I should no longer venture to maintain; knowing, as I do, that in former times the Lacedaemonians preferred to live at home on moderate means, content to associate exclusively with themselves rather than to play the part of governor-general in foreign states and to be corrupted by flattery; knowing further, as I do, that formerly they dreaded to be detected in the possession of gold, whereas nowadays there are not a few who make it their glory and their boast to be possessed of it. I am very well aware that in former days alien acts were put in force for this very object. To live abroad was not allowed. And why? Simply in order that the citizens of Sparta might not take the infection of dishonesty and light-living from foreigners; whereas now I am very well aware that those who are reputed to be leading citizens have but one ambition, and that is to live to the end of their days as governors-general on a foreign soil. The days were when their sole anxiety was to fit themselves to lead the rest of Hellas. But nowadays they concern themselves much more to wield command than to be fit themselves to rule. And so it has come to pass that whereas in old days the states of

Hellas flocked to Lacedaemon seeking her leadership against the supposed wrongdoer, now numbers are inviting one another to prevent the Lacedaemonians again recovering their empire. Yet, if they have incurred all these reproaches, we need not wonder, seeing that they are so plainly disobedient to the god himself and to the laws of their own lawgiver Lycurgus.

I wish to explain with sufficient detail the nature of the covenant between king and state as instituted by Lycurgus; for this, I take it, is the sole type of rule which still preserves the original form in which it was first established; whereas other constitutions will be found either to have been already modified or else to be still undergoing modifications at this moment.

Lycurgus laid it down as law that the king shall offer in behalf of the state all public sacrifices, as being himself of divine descent, and whithersoever the state shall despatch her armies the king shall take the lead. He granted him to receive honorary gifts of the things offered in sacrifice, and he appointed him choice land in many of the provincial cities, enough to satisfy moderate needs without excess of wealth. And in order that the kings also might camp and mess in public he appointed them public quarters; and he honoured them with a double portion each at the evening meal, not in order that they might actually eat twice as much as others, but that the king might have wherewithal to honour whomsoever he desired. He also granted as a gift to each of the two kings to choose two mess-fellows, which same are called Pythii. He also granted them to receive out of every litter of swine one pig, so that the king might never be at a loss for victims if he wished to consult the gods.

Close by the palace a lake affords an unrestricted supply of water; and how useful that is for various purposes they best can tell who lack the luxury. Moreover, all rise from their seats to give place to the king, save only that the ephors rise not from their thrones of office. Monthly they exchange oaths, the ephors in behalf of the state, the king himself in his own behalf. And this is the oath on the king's part, "I will exercise my kingship in accordance with the established laws of the state." And on the part of the State the oath runs, "so long as he (who exercises kingship) shall abide by his oath we will not suffer his kingdom to be shaken."

These then are the honours bestowed upon the king during his lifetime at home, honours by no means much exceeding those of private citizens, since the lawgiver was minded neither to suggest to the kings the pride of the despotic monarch, nor, on the other hand, to engender in the heart of the citizen envy of their power. As to those other honours which are given to the king at his death, the laws of Lycurgus would seem plainly to signify hereby that these kings of Lacedaemon are not mere mortals but heroic beings, and that is why they are preferred in honour.

2. *Xenophon on the Tyrant* (Hiero, *8–11*)*

In the Hiero *Xenophon invented a dialogue between the Syracusan tyrant of that name and the poet Simonides. In the first part of the dialogue Hiero complains of the troubles and pains inherent in being a tyrant. Simonides argues for the great pleasure of absolute rule if it be moral and aim at virtue. The theme of the conversion of tyranny to virtuous monarchy may be found in Plato, Aristotle, and Isocrates as well. It is evidence of a growing disenchantment with the traditional* polis *and an interest in monarchy as a possible solution.*

Simonides took him up and said, "Well, Hiero, I do not wonder that you are for the moment out of heart with tyranny; since, desiring to be loved by human beings, you believe that tyranny is an obstacle in the way of your attaining this. However, I think myself able to teach you that ruling does not at all prevent your being loved, and that it even has the advantage of private life in this respect. While examining whether this is of itself the case, let us not yet inquire whether because of his greater potential the ruler also would be able to grant more favors; but rather, if the private man and the tyrant do similar things, consider which of the two wins more gratitude by means

* Translated by Marvin Kendrick in *On Tyranny*, by Leo Strauss (London, 1936), pp. 14–20. By permission of The Free Press of Glencoe. Bracketed inserts by translator.

of equal favors. I will begin with the simplest examples. First, suppose the ruler and the private man, when they see someone, address him in a friendly way. In this case, from which man do you believe the greeting gives the hearer more pleasure? Again, suppose both praise the same man; from which of them do you think the praise brings greater pleasure? Suppose each, when he offers sacrifice, honors the same man; from which of the two do you think the honor would obtain more gratitude? Suppose they alike attend a sick person; is it not obvious that attentions from the most powerful produce the greatest cheer? Suppose, then, they make equal gifts; is it not clear, in this case too, that favors of half the value from the most powerful are worth more than the whole of a grant from the private man? Indeed, I myself hold that even from gods a certain honor and grace attend a man who rules. For not only does ruling make a real man nobler, but this same man is also nobler to our view when he rules than when he lives privately; and we delight more in discoursing with those preeminent in honor than with those equal to us.

"As for boys, with regard to whom you found the most fault with tyranny, they are least offended at the old age of one who rules, and they pay least attention to the ugliness of whomever they happen to be intimate with. For his being honored itself helps most to dignify him, so that his offensiveness disappears, and what is noble appears more resplendent.

"Since, then, you [tyrants] obtain greater thanks by means of equal services, must it not be fitting, when you are able to confer benefits by accomplishing many times more things and are able to make many times more gifts, that you also be loved far more than the private men?"

Hiero answered at once, "No, by Zeus, Simonides," he said, "because we are compelled to do the things for which human beings are hated much more than private men. We must exact money if we are to have the means to spend on our needs; we must compel [men] to guard the things which need guarding; we must punish the unjust; we must restrain those who wish to be insolent; and when the moment comes to set out with all speed on an expedition by land or sea, we must not entrust the business to the sluggards. Moreover, the man who is a tyrant needs mercenaries. And no burden weighs heavier on the citizen than that. For the citizens believe that tyrants keep these mercenaries not to share equal honors with themselves, but to get the advantage by supporting them."

To this in its turn Simonides said, "Well, I do not deny that all these matters require attention, Hiero. Some cares seem to me, however, to lead to much hatred, whereas others seem to be mutually very gratifying. For to teach what is morally best, and to praise and honor the man who achieves this in the noblest way, is a concern which itself gives rise to mutual regard; whereas to rebuke the one who is slack in doing something, to coerce, to punish, to correct—these things necessarily give rise more to mutual enmity. Accordingly I say that the man who rules ought to command others to punish the one who requires coercion, but that he ought to award the prizes himself. What occurs at present confirms that this is a good arrangement. For whenever we wish our choruses to compete, the *Archon* offers the prizes, but he orders the managers of each chorus to assemble them, and others to instruct them and to apply coercion to those who are at all slack in performing. Accordingly, what gives rise to gratitude in these contests comes about at once through the *Archon*, and what is the contrary comes about through others. Now what prevents the other political things from also being managed in this way? For all the cities are apportioned up, some according to tribes, some according to divisions, others according to companies, and rulers are put in charge of each section. If someone should offer prizes to these sections, like choruses, for good arms, good discipline, horsemanship, bravery in war, and justice in contracts, it is likely that all these things, through emulation, would be practiced intently. Yes, and, by Zeus, they would set out on an expedition with more speed wherever required, striving for honor; they would contribute money more promptly when the moment for this came; and farming, certainly the most useful thing of all, but the least accustomed to being managed by emulation, would itself greatly improve, if someone should offer prizes by fields or villages to those who best cultivate the ground; and many good things would be accomplished by those among the citizens who turn to it vigorously. For the revenues would increase, and moderation would follow much more closely upon the absence of leisure. And as for evil doings, they arise less naturally in those who are busy.

"If imports are of any benefit to a city, the one honored the most for engaging in this would also bring together more importers. And if it should become apparent that the man who invents some painless revenue for the city will be honored, reflection itself would not be left uncultivated. To sum it up, if it should become clear with respect to all matters that the man who introduces something beneficial will not go unrewarded, he would stimulate many to engage in reflecting on something good. And whenever many are concerned with what is useful, this is necessarily discovered and perfected all the more.

"But if you are afraid, Hiero, that when prizes are offered among many, correspondingly many expenses will arise, keep in mind that no articles of commerce are cheaper than what human beings purchase by means of prizes. Do you see that in contests of horsemanship, gymnastic, and choruses small prizes bring forth great expenditures, much toil, and much care from human beings?"

And Hiero said, "Well, Simonides, you seem to me to speak well as far as these matters go; but have you anything to say regarding the mercenaries, so that I may not incur hatred because of them? Or do you mean that once a ruler wins friendship he will no longer need a bodyguard at all?"

"By Zeus, certainly he will need it," said Simonides. "For I know that it is inbred in some human beings, just as in horses, to be insolent in proportion as the needs they have are more fully satisfied. The fear inspired by the bodyguard would make such men more moderate. And as for the gentlemen, there is nothing, it seems to me, by means of which you would confer so great services on them as by the mercenaries. For surely you support them as guards for yourself; but before now many masters have died violently at the hands of their slaves. If, then, one—and this the first—of the mercenaries' orders should be, that as the bodyguard of all the citizens they were, whenever they perceived a thing of this kind, to go to the aid of all—and if they were ordered to guard against the evil-doers we all know arise in cities —the citizens would know they were helped by them. In addition to this, these [mercenaries] would probably best be able to provide confidence and safety for the husbandmen and property of herds and flocks in the country, alike for your own privately and for those throughout the country. They are capable, moreover, of providing the citizens with leisure to concern themselves with their private property, by guarding the positions of advantage.

Furthermore, as regards the secret and surprise attacks of enemies, who would be readier either to perceive them in advance or to prevent them than those who are always under arms and disciplined? Surely on a campaign, what is more useful to citizens than mercenaries? For [mercenaries] are likely to be readier to toil, run risks, and stand guard for the citizens. As for the neighboring cities, is there not a necessity, brought about by those who are constantly under arms, for them especially to desire peace? For being disciplined the mercenaries would best be able to preserve what belongs to their friends and to destroy what belongs to their enemies. Surely when the citizens realize that these mercenaries do no harm at all to one who commits no injustice; that they restrain those who wish to do evil; that they come to the aid of those who are unjustly wronged; and that they take counsel for and incur danger in behalf of the citizens —must they not necessarily spend very gladly for their upkeep? After all, men support guards privately, and for lesser objects than these."

"You must not, Hiero, shrink from spending from your private possessions for the common good. For it seems to me that what a man as tyrant lays out for the city is spent more on what is necessary than what he lays out for his private [estate]. Let us examine each detail point by point. First, which do you think would dignify you more, a house embellished at tremendous cost, or the whole city furnished with walls, temples, colonnades, market places, and harbors? As for arms, which of the two would appear more formidable to your enemies, you yourself fitted out in the most splendid arms, or your entire city well armed? Take revenues; in which way do you think they would become greater, if you should keep your private property alone productive, or if you should contrive to make the property of all the citizens so? And regarding the pursuit believed to be the most noble and magnificent of all, the raising of chariot horses, in which way do you think there would be greater dignity, if you yourself should raise the most teams among the Greeks and send them to the games, or if the most breeders, and the most in competition, should be from your city? And as for winning victories, which do you hold the nobler way, by the virtue of your team, or by the happiness of the city which you rule? I myself say that it is not fitting for a man who is a tyrant even to compete against private men. For, winning the victory, you would not be admired, but envied, as meeting the cost by means of many estates, and, losing, you would be ridiculed most of all.

"But I tell you, Hiero, that the contest is against others who rule cities; if you make the city you rule the happiest of these, know well that you are victorious in the most noble and magnificent contest among human beings. First, you would at once secure the love of your subjects, which is the very thing you happen to desire. Further, not one man would herald your victory, but all human beings would sing of your virtue. Being an object of attention you would be cherished not only by private men, but by many cities; marveled at not only in private, but in public among all as well; it would be possible for you, as far as safety is concerned, to travel wherever you wish, for the sake of viewing the sights; and it would be possible for you to do this remaining here. For there would be a continual festival by you of those wishing to display whatever wise, beautiful, or good thing they had, and of those desiring to serve you as well. Every man present would be your ally, and every man absent would desire to see you. Therefore, you would not only be liked, you would be loved by human beings; as for the fair, you would not need to test them, but to endure being tested by them; as for fear, you would have none, but you would cause fear in others that you might suffer some harm; you would have willing men obeying you, and you would see them willingly take thought for you; if there should be some danger, you would see not only allies, but also champions, and those eager; being deemed worthy of many gifts, you will not be at a loss for someone well disposed with whom to share them, with all men rejoicing at your good things and all fighting for those which are yours just as if they were their own. For treasuries, furthermore, you would have all the wealth of your friends.

"But enrich your friends with confidence, Hiero; for you will enrich yourself. Augment the city, for you will attach power to yourself. Acquire allies for it. Consider the fatherland to be your estate, the citizens your comrades, friends your own children, your sons the same as your life, and try to win victory by benefiting all these. For if you master your friends in beneficence, your enemies will be utterly unable to resist you. And if you do all these things, know well, of all the things among human beings you will acquire the noblest and most blessed possession; for being happy, you will not be envied."

3. Isocrates on Panhellenism
(Panegyrcus, *133-134, 167-174*)*

Isocrates (436-338 B.C.) was an Athenian orator who was deeply aware of the economic and social problems of his time. As a moderate bourgeois he sought prosperity, stability and a return to a less democratic constitution than that of contemporary Athens. Famous as an advocate of Hellenic unity, he makes clear in the following selection what the primary function of such unity was to be.

It is my opinion that if anyone should come here from another part of the world and behold the spectacle of the present state of our affairs, he would charge both the Athenians and the Lacedaemonians with utter madness, not only because we risk our lives fighting as we do over trifles when we might enjoy in security a wealth of possessions, but also because we continually impoverish our own territory while neglecting to exploit that of Asia. As for the barbarian, nothing is more to his purpose than to take measures to prevent us from ever ceasing to make war upon each other; while we, on the contrary, are so far from doing anything to embroil his interests or foment rebellion among his subjects that when, thanks to fortune, dissensions do break out in his empire we actually lend him a hand in putting them down. . . .

It were well to make the expedition in the present generation, in order that those who have shared in our misfortunes may also benefit by our advantages and not continue all their days in wretchedness. For sufficient is the time that is past, filled as it has been with every form of horror; for many as are the ills which are incident to the nature of man, we have ourselves invented more than those which necessity lays upon us, by engendering wars and factions among ourselves; and, in consequence, some are being put to death contrary to law in their own countries, others are wandering with their women and children in strange

* Translation from Isocrates are by George Norlin in *The Loeb Classical Library*. By permission of William Heinemann, Ltd.

lands, and many, compelled through lack of the necessities of life
to enlist in foreign armies, are being slain, fighting for their foes
against their friends.

Against these ills no one has ever protested; and people are not
ashamed to weep over the calamities which have been fabricated
by the poets, while they view complacently the real sufferings,
the many terrible sufferings, which result from our state of war;
and they are so far from feeling pity that they even rejoice more
in each other's sorrows than in their own blessings. But perhaps
many might even laugh at my simplicity if I should lament the
misfortunes of individual men, in times like these, when Italy has
been laid to waste, when Sicily has been enslaved, when such
mighty cities have been given over to the barbarians, and when
the remaining portions of the Hellenic race are in the gravest
peril.

I am amazed at those who hold power in our states, if they
think that they have occasion to be proud when they have never
been able either to propose or to conceive a remedy for a situation so momentous; for they ought, if they had been worthy of
their present reputation, to have dropped all else, and have proposed measures and given counsel about our war against the barbarians. Perhaps they might have helped us to get something
done; but even if they had given up before gaining their object,
they would, at any rate, have left to us their words as oracles for
the future. But as things are, those who are held in highest honour are intent on matters of little consequence, and have left it
to us, who stand aloof from public life, to advise on matters of
so great moment.

Nevertheless, the more faint-hearted our leading men happen
to be, the more vigorously must the rest of us look to the means
by which we shall deliver ourselves from our present discord.
For as matters now stand, it is in vain that we make our treaties
of peace; for we do not settle our wars, but only postpone them
and wait for the opportune moment when we shall have the
power to inflict some irreparable disaster upon each other.

We must clear from our path these treacherous designs and
pursue that course of action which will enable us to dwell in our
several cities with greater security and to feel greater confidence
in each other. What I have to say on these points is simple and
easy: It is not possible for us to cement an enduring peace unless
we join together in a war against the barbarians, nor for the
Hellenes to attain to concord until we wrest our material ad-

vantages from one and the same source and wage our wars against
one and the same enemy. When these conditions have been realized, and when we have been freed from the poverty which
afflicts our lives—a thing that breaks up friendships, perverts the
affections of kindred into enmity, and plunges the whole world
into war and strife—then surely we shall enjoy a spirit of concord, and the good will which we shall feel towards each other
will be genuine. For all these reasons, we must make it our para-
mount duty to transfer the war with all speed from our boundaries to the continent, since the only benefit which we can reap
from the wars which we have waged against each other is by
resolving that the experience which we have gained from them
shall be employed against the barbarians.

4. *Isocrates on the Ancestral Constitution* (Areopagiticus, *14–28, 39–45*)

*The rallying cry for opponents of the extreme democracy
of Athens was "The Ancestral Constitution," an almost mythical reconstruction composed of various elements: the laws
of Solon and Cleisthenes plus the fond wishes of the foes of
total democracy. The following selection paints a glowing
picture of the noble days before the time of Pericles.*

The soul of a state is nothing else than its polity, having as
much power over it as does the mind over the body; for it is this
which deliberates upon all questions, seeking to preserve what is
good and to ward off what is disastrous; and it is this which of
necessity assimilates to its own nature the laws, the public orators
and the private citizens; and all the members of the state must
fare well or ill according to the kind of polity under which they
live. And yet we are quite indifferent to the fact that our polity
has been corrupted, nor do we even consider how we may re-
deem it. It is true that we sit around in our shops denouncing the
present order and complaining that never under a democracy have

we been worse governed, but in our actions and in the sentiments which we hold regarding it we show that we are better satisfied with our present democracy than with that which was handed down to us by our forefathers.

It is in favour of the democracy of our forefathers that I intend to speak, and this is the subject on which I gave notice that I would address you. For I find that the one way—the only possible way—which can avert future perils from us and deliver us from our present ills is that we should be willing to restore that earlier democracy which was instituted by Solon, who proved himself above all others the friend of the people, and which was re-established by Cleisthenes, who drove out the tyrants and brought the people back into power—a government than which we could find none more favourable to the populace or more advantageous to the whole city. The strongest proof of this is that those who enjoyed this constitution wrought many noble deeds, won the admiration of all mankind, and took their place, by the common consent of the Hellenes, as the leading power of Hellas; whereas those who were enamoured of the present constitution made themselves hated of all men, suffered many indignities, and barely escaped falling into the worst of all disasters. And yet how can we praise or tolerate a government which has in the past been the cause of so many evils and which is now year by year ever drifting on from bad to worse? And how can we escape the fear that if we continue to progress after this fashion we may finally run aground on rocks more perilous than those which at that time loomed before us?

But in order that you may make a choice and come to a decision between the two constitutions, not from the summary statement you have just heard, but from exact knowledge, it behoves you, for your part, to render yourselves attentive to what I say, while I, for my part, shall try to explain them both to you as briefly as I can.

For those who directed the state in the time of Solon and Cleisthenes did not establish a polity which in name merely was hailed as the most impartial and the mildest of governments, while in practice showing itself the opposite to those who lived under it, nor one which trained the citizens in such fashion that they looked upon insolence as democracy, lawlessness as liberty, impudence of speech as equality, and licence to do what they pleased as happiness, but rather a polity which detested and punished such men and by so doing made all the citizens better and wiser.

But what contributed most to their good government of the state was that of the two recognized kinds of equality—that which makes the same award to all alike and that which gives to each man his due—they did not fail to grasp which was the more serviceable; but, rejecting as unjust that which holds that the good and the bad are worthy of the same honours, and preferring rather that which rewards and punishes every man according to his deserts, they governed the city on this principle, not filling the offices by lot from all the citizens, but selecting the best and the ablest for each function of the state; for they believed that the rest of the people would reflect the character of those who were placed in charge of their affairs.

Furthermore they considered that this way of appointing magistrates was also more democratic than the casting of lots, since under the plan of election by lot chance would decide the issue and the partizans of oligarchy would often get the offices; whereas under the plan of selecting the worthiest men, the people would have in their hands the power to choose those who were most attached to the existing constitution.

The reason why this plan was agreeable to the majority and why they did not fight over the offices was because they had been schooled to be industrious and frugal, and not to neglect their own possessions and conspire against the possessions of others, and not to repair their own fortunes out of the public funds, but rather to help out the commonwealth, should the need arise, from their private resources, and not to know more accurately the incomes derived from the public offices than those which accrued to them from their own estates. So severely did they abstain from what belonged to the state that it was harder in those days to find men who were willing to hold office than it is now to find men who are not begging for the privilege; for they did not regard a charge over public affairs as a chance for private gain but as a service to the state; neither did they from their first day in office seek to discover whether their predecessors had overlooked any source of profit, but much rather whether they had neglected any business of the state which pressed for settlement.

In a word, our forefathers had resolved that the people, as the supreme master of the state, should appoint the magistrates, call to account those who failed in their duty, and judge in cases of dispute; while those citizens who could afford the time and possessed sufficient means should devote themselves to the care of the commonwealth, as servants of the people, entitled to receive commendation if they proved faithful to their trust, and contenting themselves with this honour, but condemned, on the other hand, if they governed badly, to meet with no mercy, but to suffer the severest punishment. And how, pray, could one find a democracy more stable or more just than this, which appointed the most capable men to have charge of its affairs but gave to the people authority over their rulers?

Such was the constitution of their polity, and from this it is easy to see that also in their conduct day by day they never failed to act with propriety and justice; for when people have laid sound foundations for the conduct of the whole state it follows that in the details of their lives they must reflect the character of their government.

Such, then, as I have described, was the nature of the Council which our forefathers charged with the supervision of moral discipline—a council which considered that those who believed that the best citizens are produced in a state where the laws are prescribed with the greatest exactness were blind to the truth; for in that case there would be no reason why all of the Hellenes should not be on the same level, at any rate in so far as it is easy to borrow written codes from each other. But in fact, they thought, virtue is not advanced by written laws but by the habits of every-day life; for the majority of men tend to assimilate the manners and morals amid which they have been reared. Furthermore, they held that where there is a multitude of specific laws, it is a sign that the state is badly governed; for it is in the attempt to build up dikes against the spread of crime that men in such a state feel constrained to multiply the laws. Those who are rightly governed, on the other hand, do not need to fill their porticoes with written statutes, but only to cherish justice in their souls; for it is not by legislation, but by morals, that states are well directed, since men who are badly reared will venture to transgress even laws which are drawn up with minute exactness, whereas those who are well brought up will be willing to respect even a simple code. Therefore, being of this mind, our forefathers did not seek to discover first how they should penalize men who were lawless, but how they should produce citizens who would refrain from any punishable act; for they thought that this was their duty, while it was proper for private enemies alone to be zealous in the avenging of crime.

Now our forefathers exercised care over all the citizens, but most of all over the young. They saw that at this age men are most unruly of temper and filled with a multitude of desires, and that their spirits are most in need of being curbed by devotion to noble pursuits and by congenial labour; for only such occupations can attract and hold men who have been educated liberally and trained in high-minded ways.

However, since it was not possible to direct all into the same occupations, because of differences in their circumstances, they assigned to each one a vocation which was in keeping with his means; for they turned the needier towards farming and trade, knowing that poverty comes about through idleness, and evil-doing through poverty. Accordingly, they believed that by removing the root of evil they would deliver the young from the sins which spring from it. On the other hand, they compelled those who possessed sufficient means to devote themselves to horsemanship, athletics, hunting, and philosophy, observing that by these pursuits some are enabled to achieve excellence, others to abstain from many vices.

5. *Isocrates on Monarchy*
(Nicocles, *11–26*)

The following selection is from a speech Isocrates puts into the mouth of Nicocles, a king of Sypras and a friend of the orator.

On the former topic, how a ruler should act, you have heard Isocrates speak; on the following topic, what his subjects must do, I shall attempt to discourse, not with any thought of excelling him, but because this is the most fitting subject for me to discuss with you. For if I did not make clear what I desire you to do, I could not reasonably be angry with you if you were to mistake my purpose; but if, after I have announced my policy beforehand, none of my desires are carried out, then I should justly blame those who fail to obey me.

And I believe that I should most effectively exhort you and urge you to remember my words and heed them, not if I should confine myself to giving you advice and then, after counting out my precepts, make an end, but if, before doing this, I should prove to you, first, that you ought to be content with our present government, not only from necessity, nor because we have lived under it all our lives, but because it is the best of all governments; and, second, that I hold this office, not illegally nor as a usurper, but with the just sanction of gods and men, and by virtue of my earliest ancestors, and of my father and of myself. For, once these claims have been established, who will not condemn himself to the severest punishment if he fails to heed my counsels and commands?

Speaking, then, of forms of government (for this was the subject I set out to lay before you), I imagine that we all believe that it is altogether monstrous that the good and the bad should be thought worthy of the same privileges, and that it is of the very essence of justice that distinctions should be made between them, and that those who are unlike should not be treated alike but should fare and be rewarded in each case according to their deserts. Now oligarchies and democracies seek equality for those who share in the administration of them; and the doctrine is in high favour in those governments that one man should not have the power to get more than another—a principle which works in the interest of the worthless! Monarchies, on the other hand, make the highest award to the best man, the next highest to the next best, and in the same proportion to the third and the fourth and so on. Even if this practice does not obtain everywhere, such at least is the intention of the polity. And, mark you, monarchies more than other governments keep an appraising eye upon the characters and actions of men, as everyone will admit. Who, then, that is of sound mind would not prefer to share in a form of government under which his own worth shall not pass unnoticed, rather than be lost in the hurly-burly of the mob and not be recognized for what he is? Furthermore, we should be right in pronouncing monarchy also a milder government, in proportion as it is easier to give heed to the will of a single person than to seek to please many and manifold minds.

Now one might multiply arguments to prove that this form

of government is more agreeable and mild and just than others; yet, even from those I have advanced it is easy to see this at a glance. As for its other advantages, we can best appreciate how far monarchies excel other governments in planning and carrying out any course of action required of them if we place their most important practices side by side and try to review them. In the first place, then, men who enter upon office for an annual term are retired to private life before they have gained any insight into public affairs or any experience in handling them; while men who are permanently in charge of the same duties, even though they fall short of the others in natural ability, at any rate have a great advantage over them in experience. In the next place, the former neglect many things, because each looks to the others to do them; while the latter neglect nothing, knowing that whatever is done depends upon their own efforts. Then again, men who live in oligarchies or democracies are led by their mutual rivalries to injure the commonwealth; while those who live in monarchies, not having anyone to envy, do in all circumstances so far as possible what is best. Furthermore, the former are dilatory in action, for they spend most of their time over their private concerns; and when they do assemble in council, you will find them more often quarrelling with each other than deliberating together; while the latter, for whom no councils or times of meeting are prescribed, but who apply themselves to the state's business both day and night, do not let opportunities pass them by, but act in each case at the right moment. Again, the former are ill-disposed toward each other and would rather have their predecessors and their successors in office administer the state as badly as possible, in order that they may win for themselves as much credit as possible; while the latter, because they are in control of affairs throughout their lives, are at all times actuated by feelings of good will. But the greatest difference is this: men under other governments give attention to the affairs of state as if they were the concern of others; monarchs, as if they were their own concern; and the former employ as their advisers on state affairs the most self-assertive of their citizens; while the latter single out and employ the most sagacious; and the former honour those who are skilful in haranguing the crowd, while the latter honour those who understand how to deal with affairs.

And not only in matters of ordinary routine and of daily

occurrence do monarchies excel, but in war they have compassed every advantage; for in raising troops, and handling them so as to mislead and forestall the enemy, and in winning people over, now by persuasion, now by force, now by bribery, now by other means of conciliation, one-man rule is more efficient than the other forms of government. And of this one may be assured by facts no less than by words; for, in the first place, we all know that the empire of the Persians attained its great magnitude, not because of the intelligence of the population, but because they more than other peoples respect the royal office; secondly, that Dionysius, the tyrant, taking charge of Sicily when the rest of it had been devastated by war and when his own country, Syracuse, was in a state of siege, not only delivered it from the dangers which then threatened, but also made it the greatest of Hellenic states; and again, we know that while the Carthaginians and the Lacedaemonians, who are the best governed peoples of the world, are ruled by oligarchies at home, yet, when they take the field, they are ruled by kings. One might also point out that the state which more than any other abhors absolute rule meets with disaster when it sends out many generals, and with success when it wages war under a single leader.

And, indeed, how could any one show more convincingly than through these instances that monarchy is the most excellent of governments? For we see that those who are permanently ruled by kings have the greatest powers; that those who live in well-conducted oligarchies, when it comes to matters about which they are most concerned, appoint one man, in some cases a general, in others a king, to have full powers over their armies in the field; and that those who abhor absolute rule, whenever they send out many leaders, fail to accomplish a single one of their designs. And, if there is need to speak also of things old in story, it is said that even the gods are ruled by Zeus as king. If the saying is true, it is clear that the gods also prefer this regime; but if, on the other hand, no one knows the truth about this matter, and we by our own conjecture have simply supposed it to be so, it is a proof that we all hold monarchy in the highest esteem; for we should never have said that the gods live under it if we did not believe it to be far superior to all other governments.

9.   The Hellenistic Period

The conquest of Greece by Philip of Macedon brought an effective end to the life of the polis. His victory at Chaeronea in 338 over the combined forces of the Greeks meant the end of Greek independence. To be sure, independent cities continued to exist for centuries after, but these represented a mere shadow of the vital reality which had been the true polis. Deprived of control of foreign affairs, their really important internal arrangements determined by a foreign monarch, the postclassical cities had lost the kind of political freedom which was basic. They were cities, but they were not city-states; the passage of time marked their steady decline from sovereign states to municipal towns, merged in military empires.

The change in institutions produced a sweeping change in political ideas. New philosophies arose to compete with the established ones, Platonism and Aristoteleanism. In contrast to these earlier philosophies which were intensely political and rooted in the polis, the Cynics, Stoics, and Epicureans were cosmopolitan and almost apolitical. Their views paved the way for theorists who established a new theoretical foundation for Hellenistic monarchy.

1. Diogenes the Cynic
(Diogenes Laertius, 6, 72)*

Diogenes of Sinope (ca. 400–325 B.C.) was the founder of the Cynic school and in some ways a forerunner of Stoicism.

He maintained that all things are the property of the wise, and employed such arguments as those cited above. All things belong to the gods. The gods are friends to the wise, and friends share all property in common; therefore all things are the property of the wise. Again as to law: that it is impossible for society to exist without law; for without a city no benefit can be derived from that which is civilized. But the city is civilized, and there is no advantage in law without a city; therefore law is something civilized. He would ridicule good birth and fame and all such distinctions, calling them showy ornaments of vice. The only true commonwealth was, he said, that which is as wide as the universe. He advocated community of wives, recognizing no other marriage than a union of the man who persuades with the woman who consents. And for this reason he thought sons too should be held in common.

2. The Stoics (Diogenes Laertius, 7, 87–89, 121–123, 128–131)

A summary of the beliefs of the Stoics is presented by Diogenes Laertius in his life of Zeno (335–263 B.C.), a Phoenician who founded the Stoa at Athens.

This is why Zeno was the first (in his treatise *On the Nature of Man*) to designate as the end "life in agreement with nature" (or living agreeably to nature), which is the same as a virtuous

* Translated by R. D. Hicks in *The Loeb Classical Library*. By permission of William Heinemann, Ltd.

life, virtue being the goal towards which nature guides us. So too Cleanthes in his treatise *On Pleasure*, as also Posidonius, and Hecato in his work *On Ends*. Again, living virtuously is equivalent to living in accordance with experience of the actual course of nature, as Chrysippus says in the first book of his *De finibus;* for our individual natures are parts of the nature of the whole universe. And this is why the end may be defined as life in accordance with nature, or, in other words, in accordance with our own human nature as well as that of the universe, a life in which we refrain from every action forbidden by the law common to all things, that is to say, the right reason which pervades all things, and is identical with this Zeus, lord and ruler of all that is. And this very thing constitutes the virtue of the happy man and the smooth current of life, when all actions promote the harmony of the spirit dwelling in the individual man with the will of him who orders the universe. Diogenes then expressly declares the end to be to act with good reason in the selection of what is natural. Archedemus says the end is to live in the performance of all befitting actions.

By the nature with which our life ought to be in accord, Chrysippus understands both universal nature and more particularly the nature of man, whereas Cleanthes takes the nature of the universe alone as that which should be followed, without adding the nature of the individual.

And virtue, he holds, is a harmonious disposition, choiceworthy for its own sake and not from hope or fear or any external motive. Moreover, it is in virtue that happiness consists; for virtue is the state of mind which tends to make the whole of life harmonious. When a rational being is perverted, this is due to the deceptiveness of external pursuits or sometimes to the influence of associates. For the starting-points of nature are never perverse.

Again, the Stoics say that the wise man will take part in politics, if nothing hinders him—so, for instance, Chrysippus in the first book of his work *On Various Types of Life*—since thus he will restrain vice and promote virtue. Also (they maintain) he will marry, as Zeno says in his *Republic*, and beget children. Moreover, they say that the wise man will never form mere opinions, that is to say, he will never give assent to anything that is false; that he will also play the Cynic, Cynicism being a short cut to virtue, as Apollodorus calls it in his *Ethics;* that he will even turn cannibal under stress of circumstances. They declare that he alone is free and bad men are slaves, freedom being power of independent action, whereas slavery is privation of the same: though indeed there is also a second form of slavery consisting in subordination, and a third which implies possession of the slave as well as his subordination; the correlative of such servitude being lordship; and this too is evil. Moreover, according to them not only are the wise free, they are also kings; kingship being irresponsible rule, which none but the wise can maintain: so Chrysippus in his treatise vindicating Zeno's use of terminology. For he holds that knowledge of good and evil is a necessary attribute of the ruler, and that no bad man is acquainted with this science. Similarly the wise and good alone are fit to be magistrates, judges, or orators, whereas among the bad there is not one so qualified. Furthermore, the wise are infallible, not being liable to error. They are also without offence; for they do no hurt to others or to themselves. At the same time they are not pitiful and make no allowance for anyone; they never relax the penalties fixed by the laws, since indulgence and pity and even equitable consideration are marks of a weak mind, which affects kindness in place of chastizing. Nor do they deem punishments too severe. . . .

Another tenet of theirs is the perpetual exercise of virtue, as held by Cleanthes and his followers. For virtue can never be lost, and the good man is always exercising his mind, which is perfect. Again, they say that justice, as well as law and right reason, exists by nature and not by convention: so Chrysippus in his work *On the Morally Beautiful*. Neither do they think that the divergence of opinion between philosophers is any reason for abandoning the study of philosophy, since at that rate we should have to give up life altogether: so Posidonius in his *Exhortations*. Chrysippus allows that the ordinary Greek education is serviceable.

It is their doctrine that there can be no question of right as between man and the lower animals, because of their unlikeness. Thus Chrysippus in the first book of his treatise *On Justice*, and Posidonius in the first book of his *De officio*. Further, they say that the wise man will feel affection for the youths who by their countenance show a natural endowment for virtue. So Zeno in his *Republic*, Chrysippus in book i. of his work *On Modes of Life*, and Apollodorus in his *Ethics*.

Their definition of love is an effort toward friendliness due to visible beauty appearing, its sole end being friendship, not bodily enjoyment. At all events, they allege that Thrasonides, although he had his mistress in his power, abstained from her because she hated him. By which it is shown, they think, that love depends upon regard, as Chrysippus says in his treatise *Of Love*, and is not sent by the gods. And beauty they describe as the bloom or flower of virtue.

Of the three kinds of life, the contemplative, the practical, and the rational, they declare that we ought to choose the last, for that a rational being is expressly produced by nature for contemplation and for action. They tell us that the wise man will for reasonable cause make his own exit from life, on his country's behalf or for the sake of his friends, or if he suffer intolerable pain, mutilation, or incurable disease.

It is also their doctrine that amongst the wise there should be a community of wives with free choice of partners, as Zeno says in his *Republic* and Chrysippus in his treatise *On Government* [and not only they, but also Diogenes the Cynic and Plato]. Under such circumstances we shall feel paternal affection for all the children alike, and there will be an end of the jealousies arising from adultery. The best form of government they hold to be a mixture of democracy, kingship, and aristocracy (or the rule of the best).

3. *Epicurus* (Diogenes Laertius: Life of Epicurus *and* the Principal Doctrines)*

Epicurus (342–270 B.C.) was an Athenian who founded the second great school of Hellenistic philosophy in competition with the Stoics. In spite of their rivalry the political ideas of the Stoics and Epicureans appear remarkably similar in contrast to those of the classical thinkers.

Let us explain what he and his followers think about the wise man. Injuries are done by men either through hate or through

* Translated by Cyril Bailey in *Epicurus* (Oxford, 1926), pp. 117–121, 165, 167, 169; 95, 97, 99, 101, 103, 105. By permission of the Clarendon Press, Oxford.

envy or through contempt, all of which the wise man overcomes
by reasoning. When once a man has attained wisdom, he no
longer has any tendency contrary to it or willingly pretends
that he has. He will be more deeply moved by feelings, but this
will not prove an obstacle to wisdom. A man cannot become
wise with every kind of physical constitution, nor in every
nation. And even if the wise man be put on the rack, he is happy.
Only the wise man will show gratitude, and will constantly speak
well of his friends alike in their presence and their absence. Yet
when he is on the rack, then he will cry out and lament. The wise
man will not have intercourse with any woman with whom the
law forbids it, as Diogenes says in his summary of Epicurus' moral
teaching. Nor will he punish his slaves, but will rather pity them
and forgive any that are deserving. They do not think that the
wise man will fall in love, or care about his burial. They hold
that love is not sent from heaven, as Diogenes says in his . . . book,
nor should the wise man make elegant speeches. Sexual intercourse, they say, has never done a man good, and he is lucky if
it has not harmed him.

Moreover, the wise man will marry and have children, as
Epicurus says in the *Problems* and in the work *On Nature*. But
he will marry according to the circumstances of his life. He will
feel shame in the presence of some persons, and certainly will not
insult them in his cups, so Epicurus says in the *Symposium*. Nor
will he take part in public life, as he says in the first book *On
Lives*. Nor will he act the tyrant, or live like the Cynics, as he
writes in the second book *On Lives*. Nor will he beg. Moreover,
even if he is deprived of his eyesight, he will not end his whole
life, as he says in the same work. Also the wise man will feel
grief, as Diogenes says in the fifth book of the *Miscellanies*. He
will engage in lawsuits and will leave writings behind him, but
will not deliver speeches on public occasions. He will be careful
of his possessions and will provide for the future. He will be fond
of the country. He will face fortune and never desert a friend.
He will be careful of his reputation in so far as to prevent himself
from being despised. He will care more than other men for public
spectacles. He will erect statues of others, but whether he had
one himself or not, he would be indifferent. Only the wise man
could discourse rightly on music and poetry, but in practice he
would not compose poems. One wise man is not wiser than
another. He will be ready to make money, but only when he

is in straits and by means of his philosophy. He will pay court to a king, if occasion demands. He will rejoice at another's misfortunes, but only for his correction. And he will gather together a school, but never so as to become a popular leader. He will give lectures in public, but never unless asked; he will give definite teaching and not profess doubt. In his sleep he will be as he is awake, and on occasion he will even die for a friend.

They hold that faults are not all of equal gravity, that health is a blessing to some, but indifferent to others, that courage does not come by nature, but by a calculation of advantage. That friendship too has practical needs as its motive: one must indeed lay its foundations (for we sow the ground too for the sake of crops), but it is formed and maintained by means of community life among those who have reached the fullness of pleasure. They say also that there are two ideas of happiness, complete happiness, such as belongs to a god, which admits of no increase, and the happiness which is concerned with the addition and subtraction of pleasures.

Principal Doctrines]

I. The blessed and immortal nature knows no trouble itself nor causes trouble to any other, so that it is never constrained by anger or favour. For all such things exist only in the weak.

II. Death is nothing to us: for that which is dissolved is without sensation; and that which lacks sensation is nothing to us.

III. The limit of quantity in pleasures is the removal of all that is painful. Wherever pleasure is present, as long as it is there, there is neither pain of body nor of mind, nor of both at once.

IV. Pain does not last continuously in the flesh, but the acutest pain is there for a very short time, and even that which just exceeds the pleasure in the flesh does not continue for many days at once. But chronic illnesses permit a predominance of pleasure over pain in the flesh.

V. It is not possible to live pleasantly without living prudently and honourably and justly, nor again to live a life of prudence, honour, and justice without living pleasantly. And the man who does not possess the pleasant life, is not living prudently and honourably and justly, and the man who does not possess the virtuous life, cannot possibly live pleasantly.

VI. To secure protection from men anything is a natural good, by which you may be able to attain this end.

VII. Some men wished to become famous and conspicuous, thinking that they would thus win for themselves safety from other men. Wherefore if the life of such men is safe, they have obtained the good which nature craves; but if it is not safe, they do not possess that for which they strove at first by the instinct of nature.

VIII. No pleasure is a bad thing in itself: but the means which produce some pleasures bring with them disturbances many times greater than the pleasures.

IX. If every pleasure could be intensified so that it lasted and influenced the whole organism or the most essential parts of our nature, pleasures would never differ from one another.

X. If the things that produce the pleasures of profligates could dispel the fears of the mind about the phenomena of the sky and death and its pains, and also teach the limits of desires and of pains, we should never have cause to blame them: for they would be filling themselves full with pleasures from every source and never have pain of body or mind, which is the evil of life.

XI. If we were not troubled by our suspicions of the phenomena of the sky and about death, fearing that it concerns us, and also by our failure to grasp the limits of pains and desires, we should have no need of natural science.

XII. A man cannot dispel his fear about the most important matters if he does not know what is the nature of the universe but suspects the truth of some mythical story. So that without natural science it is not possible to attain our pleasures unalloyed.

XIII. There is no profit in securing protection in relation to men, if things above and things beneath the earth and indeed all in the boundless universe remain matters of suspicion.

XIV. The most unalloyed source of protection from men, which is secured to some extent by a certain force of expulsion, is in fact the immunity which results from a quiet life and the retirement from the world.

XV. The wealth demanded by nature is both limited and easily procured; that demanded by idle imaginings stretches on to infinity.

XVI. In but few things chance hinders a wise man, but the greatest and most important matters reason has ordained and throughout the whole period of life does and will ordain.

XVII. The just man is most free from trouble, the unjust most full of trouble.

XVIII. The pleasure in the flesh is not increased, when once the pain due to want is removed, but is only varied: and the limit as regards pleasure in the mind is begotten by the reasoned understanding of these very pleasures and of the emotions akin to them, which used to cause the greatest fear to the mind.

XIX. Infinite time contains no greater pleasure than limited time, if one measures by reason the limits of pleasure.

XX. The flesh perceives the limits of pleasure as unlimited and unlimited time is required to supply it. But the mind, having attained a reasoned understanding of the ultimate good of the flesh and its limits and having dissipated the fears concerning the time to come, supplies us with the complete life, and we have no further need of infinite time: but neither does the mind shun pleasure, nor, when circumstances begin to bring about the departure from life, does it approach its end as though it fell short in any way of the best life.

XXI. He who has learned the limits of life knows that that which removes the pain due to want and makes the whole of life complete is easy to obtain; so that there is no need of actions which involve competition.

XXII. We must consider both the real purpose and all the evidence of direct perception, to which we always refer the conclusions of opinion; otherwise, all will be full of doubt and confusion.

XXIII. If you fight against all sensations, you will have no standard by which to judge even those of them which you say are false.

XXIV. If you reject any single sensation and fail to distinguish between the conclusion of opinion as to the appearance awaiting confirmation and that which is actually given by the sensation or feeling, or each intuitive apprehension of the mind, you will confound all other sensations as well with the same groundless opinion, so that you will reject every standard of judgement. And if among the mental images created by your opinion you affirm both that which awaits confirmation and that which does not, you will not escape error, since you will have preserved the whole cause of doubt in every judgement between what is right and what is wrong.

XXV. If on each occasion instead of referring your actions

to the end of nature, you turn to some other nearer standard when you are making a choice or an avoidance, your actions will not be consistent with your principles.

xxvi. Of desires, all that do not lead to a sense of pain, if they are not satisfied, are not necessary, but involve a craving which is easily dispelled, when the object is hard to procure or they seem likely to produce harm.

xxvii. Of all the things which wisdom acquires to produce the blessedness of the complete life, far the greatest is the possession of friendship.

xxviii. The same conviction which has given us confidence that there is nothing terrible that lasts for ever or even for long, has also seen the protection of friendship most fully completed in the limited evils of this life.

xxix. Among desires some are natural and necessary, some natural but not necessary, and others neither natural nor necessary, but due to idle imagination.

xxx. Whenever in the case of desires which are physical, but do not lead to a sense of pain, if they are not fulfilled, the effort is intense, such pleasures are due to idle imagination, and it is not owing to their own nature that they fail to be dispelled, but owing to the empty imaginings of the man.

xxxi. The justice which arises from nature is a pledge of mutual advantage to restrain men from harming one another and save them from being harmed.

xxxii. For all living things which have not been able to make compacts not to harm one another or be harmed, nothing ever is either just or unjust; and likewise too for all tribes of men which have been unable or unwilling to make compacts not to harm or be harmed.

xxxiii. Justice never is anything in itself, but in the dealings of men with one another in any place whatever and at any time it is a kind of compact not to harm or be harmed.

xxxiv. Injustice is not an evil in itself, but only in consequence of the fear which attaches to the apprehension of being unable to escape those appointed to punish such actions.

xxxv. It is not possible for one who acts in secret contravention of the terms of the compact not to harm or be harmed, to be confident that he will escape detection, even if at present he escapes a thousand times. For up to the time of death it cannot be certain that he will indeed escape.

xxxvi. In its general aspect justice is the same for all, for it is a kind of mutual advantage in the dealings of men with one another: but with reference to the individual peculiarities of a country or any other circumstances the same thing does not turn out to be just for all.

xxxvii. Among actions which are sanctioned as just by law, that which is proved on examination to be of advantage in the requirements of men's dealings with one another, has the guarantee of justice, whether it is the same for all or not. But if a man makes a law and it does not turn out to lead to advantage in men's dealings with each other, then it no longer has the essential nature of justice. And even if the advantage in the matter of justice shifts from one side to the other, but for a while accords with the general concept, it is none the less just for that period in the eyes of those who do not confound themselves with empty sounds but look to the actual facts.

xxxviii. Where, provided the circumstances have not been altered, actions which were considered just, have been shown not to accord with the general concept in actual practice, then they are not just. But where, when circumstances have changed, the same actions which were sanctioned as just no longer lead to advantage, there they were just at the time when they were of advantage for the dealings of fellow-citizens with one another; but subsequently they are no longer just, when no longer of advantage.

xxxix. The man who has best ordered the element of disquiet arising from external circumstances has made those things that he could akin to himself and the rest at least not alien: but with all to which he could not do even this, he has refrained from mixing, and has expelled from his life all which it was of advantage to treat thus.

xl. As many as possess the power to procure complete immunity from their neighbours, these also live most pleasantly with one another, since they have the most certain pledge of security, and after they have enjoyed the fullest intimacy, they do not lament the previous departure of a dead friend, as though he were to be pitied.

4. Archytas, Diotogenes, Sthenidas, and Ecphantus on Kingship (Stobaeus: Anthologia, 4, 1, 132, 135, 136, 137, 138; 4, 5, 61; 4, 7, 61, 62, 64, 65, 66)*

The following quotations are fragments of the works of four Pythagorean philosophers preserved in an anthology composed by Stobaeus, a scholar of the fifth century A.D. Although there is no certainty of their date, it is highly likely that they are Hellenistic efforts to find a theoretical basis for the Oriental-type monarchies which had come into being after the death of Alexander the Great.

The unwritten laws of the gods which are opposed by the laws of wicked customs, inflict an evil lot and punishment upon those who do not obey them, and are the fathers and guides of the written laws and teachings which men enact. Law bears the same relation to the human soul and life as harmony to hearing and speech. For as law educates the soul and organizes the life, so harmony makes hearing intelligent and speech consistent. And I say that every community consists of the ruling element, the ruled, and a third element, the laws. Now laws are of two kinds, the animate [ἔμψυχος] law, which is the king, and the inanimate, the written law. So law is primary; for with reference to it the king is lawful [νόμιμος], the rulership is fitting [ἀκόλουθος], the ruled are free, and the whole community happy. But when the law is transgressed the king is a tyrant, the rulership unfit, the ruled are slaves, and the entire community wretched. For action is a combination of the elements of ruling, being ruled, and third, of efficiency [κρατέν]. So it is proper for the better to rule, for the worse to be ruled, but for both to have efficiency.

* Translated by Erwin R. Goodenough in "The Political Philosophy of Hellenistic Kingship," *Yale Classical Studies* I (1928, pp. 55–102.) By permission of the Yale University Press. The bracketed words or phrases are those of the translator.

For reason [τὸ λόγον ἔχον] should rule the soul, and the irrational should be ruled; but both should be efficient as over against the passions. For virtue arises out of a harmony of each of these, and virtue in turn leads the soul out of pleasure and pain into calmness and freedom from the passions [ἀπάθεια]. . . .

And the true ruler must not only be understanding and powerful in ruling well, but he must also be a lover of men, for it would be strange for a shepherd to be a hater of sheep and ill disposed toward his own flock. And he must be lawful as well, for so he will have understanding of rulership. For by his knowledge he will be able to judge correctly; by his power, to punish; by his excellence, to benefit; and by the laws, to do all these with reference to reason. And the best ruler would be the one who is closest to the law; but he would do nothing in his own interest, but only for the sake of his subjects, just as law exists not for its own sake but only for those subject to it. . . .

The most just man would be king, and the most lawful would be most just. For without justice no one would be king, and without law [there would be no] justice. For justice is in the law, and the law is the source [αἴτιος] of justice. But the king is Animate Law [νόμος ἔμψυχος], or is a legal ruler [νόμιμος ἄρχων]. So for this reason he is most just and most lawful. . . .

The duties of the king are threefold, military leadership, the dispensation of justice, and the cult of the gods. So then he will be able to lead well in arms if he thoroughly understands the art of war; and to dispense justice and to hear out his subjects if he has studied well the nature of justice and law; and to worship the gods in a pious and holy manner if he has reasoned out [ἐκλογισάμενος] the nature of deity and virtue. Accordingly the perfect king must be a good commander, judge, and priest; for these are fitting and proper to the king's supremacy and virtue alike. For the task of a pilot is to save [σῴζειν] the ship, of a charioteer to save the chariot, of a physician to save those who are ill, while the task of the king and captain is to save those who are in danger in war. For each of these is overseer and fashioner [δημιουργός] of the organization [σύστημα] of which he is the dictator. . . .

In judging and in distributing justice, whether as a whole in Public Law [ξυνᾷ], or to individuals in Private Law [ἰδίᾳ], it is right for the king to act as does God in his leadership and command of the universe. On the one hand, in public matters the king is to bring the whole kingdom into harmony with his single rule and leadership, while private matters of detail must be brought into accord with this same harmony and leadership. The king is also occupied in doing well to and benefiting [εὐεργετέν] his subjects, although in doing so he does not depart from justice and law. . . .

The third duty, that is, the worship of the gods, is no less fitting for a king. For the Best must be honored by the best man, and the Governing Principle by one who is governor. So just as God is the Best of those things which are most honorable by nature, likewise the king is best in the earthly and human realm. Now the king bears the same relation to the state [πόλιν] as God to the world; and the state is in the same ratio to the world as the king is to God. For the state, made as it is by a harmonizing together of many different elements, is an imitation of the order and harmony of the world, while the king who has an absolute rulership, and is himself Animate Law, has been metamorphosed into a deity among men. . . .

Wherefore the king must not be conquered by pleasure, but must himself conquer it. He must not resemble the multitude (indeed, he should be far different from them), and he must regard not pleasure but manly virtue [ἀνδραγαθία] as his proper objective. At the same time it is proper that one who desires to rule over others should first be able to rule over his own passions. . . .

Further, this is the rationale of his avarice. It is right for him to possess goods enough to benefit [εὐεργετέν] his friends and support the needy, and also to avenge himself upon his enemies with penalties. For the enjoyment of good fortune is most pleasant when joined with virtue. Similarly about his pre-eminence [ὑπεροχή]: for he must excel the rest in virtue and on that account be judged worthy to rule, but not on account of his wealth, or power, or military strength. For the first of these qualities he has in common with all sorts of people [τῶν τυχόντων], the second with irrational animals, the third with tyrants, while virtue alone is peculiar to good men. So that what king is self-controlled in pleasure, given to sharing his possessions, and is prudent and powerful in virtue, that man would be a king in very truth. And the people have the same proportion of goods and evils as the parts of the human soul. For avarice concerns the leading part of the soul, since desire [ἐπιθυμία] is a rational thing [λογική]; and love of honor and brutality have to do with the spirited element [θυμοειδές], for this is the living and dynamic part of the soul;

while love of pleasure concerns the desirous element, for this is the female and damp part of the soul. . . .

Injustice is the uttermost sin, and, by its compounded nature, involves the whole soul. Whence the king should harmonize together the well lawed city like a lyre. Knowing that the harmony of the multitude whose leadership God has given him ought to be attuned to himself, the king would begin by fixing in his own life the most just limitations and order of law. And besides issuing public decrees the good king should present to the state proper attitudes in body and mind. He should impersonate the statesman and have an appearance of practicality so as not to seem to the mob as either harsh or despicable, but at once pleasant and yet watchful from every angle. And he will succeed in this if first he makes an impression of majesty by his appearance and utterances, and by his looking the part of the ruler; if secondly, he be gracious both in conversation and in appearance, and in actual benefactions [εὐεργεσίας]; and third, if he inspire fear in his subjects by his hatred of evil and by his punishments, by his speed of action and in general by his skill and industry in kingly duties. For majesty, a godlike thing, can make him admired and honored by the multitude; graciousness will make him popular and beloved; while the ability to inspire fear will make him terrible and unconquerable in his dealings with enemies, but magnanimous and trustworthy toward his friends. And majesty must be one of his fixed attributes; he must do nothing base or worthy of the mob, but only things worthy of those who are admired, and to whom leadership and the power of the scepter belong; he must vie not with his inferiors or equals, but with his superiors. He must think, in the spirit of the greatness of his leadership, that the greatest pleasures are those which consist in good and great deeds rather than in enjoyment. He must separate himself from the human passions, and draw himself up close to the gods, not in arrogance, but in high-mindedness and in the exceeding greatness of his virtue. He must wrap himself about with such distinction and superiority in his appearance, in his thought life and reflections, and in the character of his soul, as well as in the actions, movements, and attitudes of his body. So will he succeed in putting into order those who look upon him, amazed at his majesty, at his self-control, and at his fitness for distinction. For to look upon the good king ought to affect the souls of those who see him no less than a flute or harmony.

Enough has been said about majesty; now I will try to dis-

cuss graciousness. Any king will be gracious who is generally
just, equitable and merciful. For justice is the binding and holding
together of the community [of the soul], and such a state of the
soul is the only basis for harmony with one's neighbors. For
justice bears the same relation to communion as rhythm to motion and harmony to the voice; for justice is a good shared in
common between the rulers and the ruled and is accordingly the
harmonizing principle in the political community. And equity
and mercy share the throne of justice, the one softening the
harshness of the injury, the other giving indulgence to those
suffering from some delinquency. And the good king must be
helpful to those who are in need, be grateful and not burdensome.
And he must give his aid not in some one way, but in any way
possible; and he must be grateful in proportion not to the size
of the present of honor which is made to him, but to the manner
and purpose of the one who is thus honoring him; and he must
not be burdensome to any man, particularly not to the lowly and
those in misfortune; for these, like men ill in body, are unable
to bear a heavy load. For the gods, and especially Zeus, the ruler
of all things, have such attributes. He also is majestic and awe-
inspiring both by his preëminence and by the greatness of his
virtue; and he is gracious in his benefactions and generosity, so
that he is called by the Ionic poet, "Father of gods and men";
and he inspires fear by the fact that he punishes evil doers, and
controls and rules all things, and has the thunderbolt in his hand
as a symbol of fearfulness. In all these respects, it must be borne
in mind, royalty is an imitation of divinity. . . .

The king must be a wise man, for so he will be a copy and
imitator of the first God. For God is the first king and ruler by
nature, while the other is so only by birth and imitation. The one
rules in the entire universe, the other upon earth; and the one
lives and rules all things forever and possesses wisdom [σοφία]
in himself, the other is temporal and has only understanding
[ἐπιστήμη]. And he would best imitate God by keeping himself
great-minded, merciful, and lacking in few things, and by evinc-
ing a fatherly disposition to those beneath him. For it is in this
way that the first God is recognized as father of gods and men,
by the fact that he is merciful to everything which is subject to
him, and never relinquishes his hold of the leadership; nor is he
satisfied at being the maker of all things alone, but he is the
supporter and teacher of all that is beautiful, and the lawgiver
equally to all. Such a leader upon earth and among men ought he

also to be who aspires to be king. And nothing which lacks a king or ruler is good; and without wisdom and understanding it is impossible to be either a king or ruler. Indeed he who is both king and wise will be a lawful imitator and servant of God. . . .

It seems to me to be clear from many bits of evidence that the nature of every animal is in harmony with the cosmos and the things in the cosmos. For inasmuch as it breathes along with the universe and is closely bound in that sequence which is at once the best and inevitable, it follows in the sweep of the universe, and is led about in accordance with the universal [κοινή] good order, and with the duration proper to each individual thing. Whence it has its name Cosmos, and is the most perfect of living beings. And in its parts, which are many and of diverse nature, some one living being rules which is most suitable in its origin, and in the fact that it has a greater share in divinity. And in the nature of the eternal God those things which have the first and highest conformity [ἀκολουθία] to divinity desire . . . and the planets. And in the region of the moon, beneath where bodies travel in a straight line, demonic nature achieves its development, but in our environment on the earth man has achieved the highest development, while it is the king who is most divine. . . .

He claims the lion's share of the better elements in our common nature. He is like the rest [of mankind] indeed in his earthly tabernacle [σκᾶνος], inasmuch as he is formed out of the same material; but he is fashioned by the supreme Artificer, who in making the king used himself as an Archetype. . . .

Accordingly the king, as a copy of the higher king, is a single and unique creation, for he is on the one hand always intimate with the one who made him, while to his subjects he appears as though he were in a light, the light of royalty. For he is judged and approved by this light, as is the mightiest of winged creatures, the eagle, set face to face with the sun. Thus royalty is explained in the fact that by its divine character and excessive brilliance it is hard to behold, except for those who have a legitimate claim. For bastard usurpers are confuted by complete bedazzlement, and by such vertigo as assails those who climb to a lofty height. But royalty is something with which people can live, if those who aspire to it are properly attuned to it, and are able to use it. Royalty is then a sure and incorruptible thing, very hard for a human being to achieve by reason of its exceeding divinity. And he who stands in it [*i.e.*, the king] must be pure and radiant in nature, so that he may not tarnish its exceeding brightness by his own blemishes, even as some people defile even the most sacred places, and some of those whom one meets are a pollution to those who meet them. And the one who thus lives in royalty ought to share in its immaculate nature, and to understand how much more divine he is than the rest, and how much more divine than he is are those others [the gods] by likening himself to whom he would do the best for himself and his subjects. And in the case of ordinary [ἄλλους] men, if they sin, their most holy purification is to make themselves like the rulers, whether it be law or king who orders affairs where they are. . . . For no one would ever doubt the existence of the world who was in it and part of it, nor would anyone be insensible of his own master who himself ruled over others.

The greatness of cosmic order consists in the fact that nothing unruled can be found, and that it is in a sense the teacher of rulership. For its beauty is revealed straightway if the one [the king] who imitates [God] in his virtue is beloved at once by him whom he is imitating and by his subjects. For no one who is beloved by God would be hated by men, since neither the stars nor the whole cosmos are at enmity with God, but rather if they hated the leader they would not obediently follow him. But it is the very fact that God rules well which causes good rulership to apply to both the king and his subjects. So then I suppose that the earthly king can fall short in no particular of the virtue of the heavenly king; but just as the king is an alien and foreign thing which has come down from heaven to man, so anyone would suppose that his virtues were the work of God, and have become the king's through God. . . .

On careful examination the foundation truth will appear to be as follows: For the first and most necessary of all things for the human race is that communion shared in by the king over men as well as by the master who rules all things in the universe. For apart from love and communion existence is impossible, as may be seen also in the case of bodies politic, leaving out of account what is ordinarily called communion. For such ordinary communion (mutual dependence) is beneath the nature of God and King, since they stand in no such need of each other as to be compelled to labor together to satisfy their wants and so render mutual assistance; for both God and King are perfect in virtue. But the love which shares in a common purpose in a city is a copy of the unanimity [ὁμόνοιαν] of the universe. Now without the regimentation which is affected by government no city would be habitable. For this laws are needed, as well as some sort of civil system, both by the ruling element and the ruled, if . . . Out of these things there is produced a common good, viz., a sort of fine harmony and tuning of the mass together which results from their concordant obedience. He who rules in accordance with virtue is called, and is, the king, for he has the same love and communion with his subjects as God has with the universe and the things in it. And there must exist complete good will [εὔνοια], first on the part of the king toward his subjects, and second on their part toward the king, such as is felt by a father toward his son, a shepherd toward his sheep, and by a law toward those who use it. . . .

In so far as he has a sacred and divine mentality he is truly a king; for by obeying this mentality he will cause all good things, but nothing that is evil. And he will clearly be just, one who has common relations with all. For communion [κοινωνία] consists in equality, and while in the distribution of equality justice plays the most important part, yet communion has its share. For it is impossible to be unjust while giving a share of equality, or to give a share of equality and not to be communal. And could one doubt that the self-sufficient man [ὁ αὐταρκής] is continent [ἐγκρατής]? For extravagance is the mother of incontinence who in turn is the mother of insurgency [ὕβρις], from whom most human ills arise. But self-sufficiency does not beget extravagance or her brood. Rather self-sufficiency, being a primal entity [ἀρχά], leads all things, but is itself led by nothing, and precisely this is a property alike of God and the king himself to be the ruler (whence he is called the "Self-Ruling"), but to be ruled by no one. Now that this could not occur apart from intelligence [φρόνησις] is clear, while it is obvious that God is the intelligence of the universe. For the universe is held together in arrangement and proper order, and this could not obtain without mind [νοῦς]. Nor could the king without intelligence have these virtues: I mean justice, continence, communion, and their sisters. . . .

In ruling over men and in controlling his own life he uses one and the same virtue, not massing acquisitions on account of any lack, for his personal service, but doing as one does in a life of action according to nature. For although this communion exists, yet each man lives sufficient unto himself. For in carrying out his life the self-sufficient man needs nothing outside of himself; and if he must live an active life, and so take other factors into account, still none the less will he keep his self-sufficiency. For

as he will have his friends as a result of his own virtue, so in
making use of them he acts in accordance with no other virtue
than what he uses also in his own life. This must follow since
there is no other virtue especially provided to this end. God,
who has neither ministers nor servants, makes no use of anyone
in giving His orders, nor does He crown or honor those who
obey Him, or disgrace those who disobey; not such are the means
he uses to extend his personal rule over a realm so vast. Rather,
it seems to me, by offering Himself as one worthy of imitation
God implants a desire [ζᾶλον] to imitate Him in every man who
has a nature like God's. God is Himself good, and to be so is His
sole and easy function [ἔργον], while those who imitate Him do
as a consequence all things better than other people. The resemblance which each man can achieve consists in self-sufficiency.
For there is not one group of virtues which do what is pleasing
to God, and another which imitate Him. Now the earthly king
would be just as self-sufficient as the rest of us (by imitating
God). For in making himself like God he would make himself
like the Most Powerful, and everyone who tried to be like him.
. . . Now when matters are put upon subjects by force and
necessity their individual zeal for imitation is sometimes diminished, for without good will [εὐνοίας] imitation is impossible, and
nothing diminishes good will like fear. Oh, that it were possible
to put from human nature all need for obedience! For the fact
that as mortal animals we are not exempt from it is the basest
trace of our earthiness, inasmuch as a deed of obedience is very
close to being one of necessity; for what just escapes being
brought about by the one is produced by the other. For whatever things can by their own nature use the Beautiful [τὸ καλόν],
have no occasion for obedience, as they have no fear of necessity.
The king alone is capable of putting this good into human nature
so that by imitation of him, their Better, they will follow in the
way they should go. But his logos, if it is accepted, strengthens
those who have been corrupted by evil nurture as if by drink,
and who have fallen into forgetfulness; it heals the sick, drives
out this forgetfulness which has settled upon them as a result of
their sin, and makes memory live in its place, from which so-
called obedience springs. Taking thus its beginning from seeds
of trifling import [φαῦλα σπέρματα] this grows up as something
excellent [σπουδαῖον], even in an earthly environment, in which
the logos, associating with man, restores what has been lost by sin.

10. *Polybius*

Polybius was a citizen of Megalopolis, capital of the Achaean League. As an officer of that League he was taken as a hostage to Rome where, as a member of the Scipionic circle, he had a unique opportunity to measure the history of Rome against Greek political theory.

1. The Purpose of the History (1, 1)*

Book 1]

Had the praise of History been passed over by former Chroniclers it would perhaps have been incumbent upon me to urge the choice and special study of records of this sort, as the readiest means men can have of correcting their knowledge of the past. But my predecessors have not been sparing in this respect. They have all begun and ended, so to speak, by enlarging on this theme: asserting again and again that the study of History is in the truest sense an education, and a training for political life; and that the most instructive, or rather the only, method of learning to bear with dignity the vicissitudes of fortune is to recall the catastrophes of others. It is evident, therefore, that no one need think it his duty to repeat what has been said by many, and said well. Least of all myself: for the surprising nature of the events which I have undertaken to relate is in itself sufficient to challenge and stimulate the attention of every one, old or young, to the study of my work. Can any one be so indifferent or idle as not to care to know by what means, and under what kind of polity, almost the whole inhabited world was conquered and brought under the dominion of the single city of Rome, and that too within a period of not quite fifty-three years? Or who again can be so completely absorbed in other subjects of contemplation or study, as to think any of them superior in importance to the accurate understanding of an event for which the past affords no precedent.

2. The Theory of Constitutional Development (6, 1–18, 43–57)

Preface]

I am aware that some will be at a loss to account for my interrupting the course of my narrative for the sake of entering upon the following disquisition on the Roman constitution. But

* Translations from Polybius are by E. S. Shuckburgh.

I think that I have already in many passages made it fully evident that this particular branch of my work was one of the necessities imposed on me by the nature of my original design; and I pointed this out with special clearness in the preface which explained the scope of my history. I there stated that the feature of my work which was at once the best in itself, and the most instructive to the students of it, was that it would enable them to know and fully realise in what manner, and under what kind of constitution, it came about that nearly the whole world fell under the power of Rome in somewhat less than fifty-three years,—an event certainly without precedent. This being my settled purpose, I could see no more fitting period than the present for making a pause, and examining the truth of the remarks about to be made on this constitution. In private life if you wish to satisfy yourself as to the badness or goodness of particular persons, you would not, if you wish to get a genuine test, examine their conduct at a time of uneventful repose, but in the hour of brilliant success or conspicuous reverse. For the true test of a perfect man is the power of bearing with spirit and dignity violent changes of fortune. An examination of a constitution should be conducted in the same way: and therefore being unable to find in our day a more rapid or more signal change than that which has happened to Rome, I reserved my disquisition on its constitution for this place. . . .

What is really educational and beneficial to students of history is the clear view of the causes of events, and the consequent power of choosing the better policy in a particular case. Now in every practical undertaking by a state we must regard as the most powerful agent for success or failure the form of its constitution; for from this as from a fountain-head all conceptions and plans of action not only proceed, but attain their consummation. . . .

Of the Greek republics, which have again and again risen to greatness and fallen into insignificance, it is not difficult to speak, whether we recount their past history or venture an opinion on their future. For to report what is already known is an easy task, nor is it hard to guess what is to come from our knowledge of what has been. But in regard to the Romans it is neither an easy matter to describe their present state, owing to the complexity of their constitution; nor to speak with confidence of their future, from our inadequate acquaintance with their peculiar institutions in the past whether affecting their public or their private life. It will require then no ordinary attention and study to get a clear and comprehensive conception of the distinctive features of this constitution.

Now, it is undoubtedly the case that most of those who profess to give us authoritative instruction on this subject distinguish three kinds of constitutions, which they designate *kingship*, *aristocracy*, *democracy*. But in my opinion the question might fairly be put to them, whether they name these as being the *only* ones, or as the *best*. In either case I think they are wrong. For it is plain that we must regard as the *best* constitution that which partakes of all these three elements. And this is no mere assertion, but has been proved by the example of Lycurgus, who was the first to construct a constitution—that of Sparta—on this principle. Nor can we admit that these are the *only* forms: for we have had before now examples of absolute and tyrannical forms of government, which, while differing as widely as possible from kingship, yet appear to have some points of resemblance to it; on which account all absolute rulers falsely assume and use, as far as they can, the title of king. Again there have been many instances of oligarchical governments having in appearance some analogy to aristocracies, which are, if I may say so, as different from them as it is possible to be. The same also holds good about democracy.

I will illustrate the truth of what I say. We cannot hold every absolute government to be a kingship, but only that which is accepted voluntarily, and is directed by an appeal to reason rather than to fear and force. Nor again is every oligarchy to be regarded as an aristocracy; the latter exists only where the power is wielded by the justest and wisest men selected on their merits. Similarly, it is not enough to constitute a democracy that the whole crowd of citizens should have the right to do whatever they wish or propose. But where reverence to the gods, succour of parents, respect to elders, obedience to laws, are traditional and habitual, in such communities, if the will of the majority prevail, we may speak of the form of government as a democracy. So then we enumerate six forms of government,—the three commonly spoken of which I have just mentioned, and three more allied forms, I mean *despotism, oligarchy* and *mob-rule*. The first of these arises without artificial aid and in the natural order of events. Next to this, and produced from it by the aid of art and adjustment, comes *kingship;* which degenerating into the evil form allied to it, by which I mean *tyranny*, both are once more destroyed and *aristocracy* produced. Again the latter being in the course of nature perverted to *oligarchy*, and the people passionately avenging the unjust acts of their rulers, *democracy* comes into existence; which again by its violence and contempt of law becomes sheer *mob-rule*. No clearer proof of the truth of what I say could be obtained than by a careful observation of the natural origin, genesis, and decadence of these several forms of government. For it is only by seeing distinctly how each of them is produced that a distinct view can also be obtained of its growth, zenith, and decadence, and the time, circumstance, and place in which each of these may be expected to recur. This method I have assumed to be especially applicable to the Roman constitution, because its origin and growth have from the first followed natural causes.

Now the natural laws which regulate the merging of one form of government into another are perhaps discussed with greater accuracy by Plato and some other philosophers. But their treatment, from its intricacy and exhaustiveness, is only within the capacity of a few. I will therefore endeavour to give a summary of the subject, just so far as I suppose it to fall within the scope of a practical history and the intelligence of ordinary people. For if my exposition appear in any way inadequate, owing to the general terms in which it is expressed, the details contained in what is immediately to follow will amply atone for what is left for the present unsolved.

What is the origin then of a constitution, and whence is it produced? Suppose that from floods, pestilences, failure of crops, or some such causes the race of man is reduced almost to extinction. Such things we are told have happened, and it is reasonable to think will happen again. Suppose accordingly all knowledge of social habits and arts to have been lost. Suppose that from the survivors, as from seeds, the race of man to have again multiplied. In that case I presume they would, like the animals, herd together; for it is but reasonable to suppose that bodily weakness would induce them to seek those of their own kind to herd with. And in that case too, as with the animals, he who was superior to the rest in strength of body or courage of soul would lead and rule them. For what we see happen in the case of animals that are without the faculty of reason, such as bulls, goats, and cocks,— among whom there can be no dispute that the strongest take the lead,—that we must regard as in the truest sense the teaching of nature. Originally, then it is probable that the condition of life among men was this,—herding together like animals and following the strongest and bravest as leaders. The limit of this authority would be physical strength, and the name we should give it would be despotism. But as soon as the idea of family ties and social relation has arisen amongst such agglomerations of men, then is born also the idea of kingship, and then for the first time mankind conceives the notion of goodness and justice and their reverse.

The way in which such conceptions originate and come into existence is this. The intercourse of the sexes is an instinct of nature, and the result is the birth of children. Now, if any one of these children who have been brought up, when arrived at maturity, is ungrateful and makes no return to those by whom he was nurtured, but on the contrary presumes to injure them by word and deed, it is plain that he will probably offend and annoy such as are present, and have seen the care and trouble bestowed by the parents on the nurture and bringing up of their children. For seeing that men differ from the other animals in being the only creatures possessed of reasoning powers, it is clear that such a difference of conduct is not likely to escape their observation; but that they will remark it when it occurs, and express their displeasure on the spot: because they will have an eye to the future, and will reason on the likelihood of the same occurring to each of themselves. Again, if a man has been rescued or helped in an hour of danger, and, instead of showing gratitude to his preserver, seeks to do him harm, it is clearly probable that the rest will be displeased and offended with him, when they know it: sympathising with their neighbour and imagining themselves in his case. Hence arises a notion in every breast of the meaning and theory of duty, which is in fact the beginning and end of justice. Similarly, again, when any one man stands out as the champion of all in a time of danger, and braves with firm courage the onslaught of the most powerful wild beasts, it is probable that such a man would meet with marks of favour and pre-eminence from the common people; while he who acted in a contrary way would fall under their contempt and dislike. From this, once more, it is reasonable to suppose that there would arise in the minds of the multitude a theory of the disgraceful and the honourable, and of the difference between them; and that one should be sought and imitated for its advantages, the other shunned. When, therefore, the leading and most powerful man among his people ever encourages such persons in accordance with the popular sentiment, and thereby assumes in the eyes of his subject the appearance of being the distributor to each man according to his deserts, they no longer obey him and support his rule from fear of violence, but rather from conviction of its utility, however old he may be, rallying round him with one heart and soul, and fighting against all who form designs against his government. In this way he becomes a *king* instead of a *despot* by imperceptible degrees, reason having ousted brute courage and bodily strength from their supremacy.

This then is the natural process of formation among mankind of the notion of goodness and justice, and their opposites; and this is the origin and genesis of genuine kingship: for people do not only keep up the government of such men personally, but for their descendants also for many generations; from the conviction that those who are born from and educated by men of this kind will have principles also like theirs. But if they subsequently become displeased with their descendants, they do not any longer decide their choice of rulers and kings by their physical strength or brute courage; but by the differences of their intellectual and reasoning faculties, from practical experience of the decisive importance of such a distinction. In old times, then, those who were once thus selected, and obtained this office, grew old in their royal functions, making magnificent strongholds and surrounding them with walls and extending their frontiers, partly for the security of their subjects, and partly to provide them with abundance of the necessaries of life; and while engaged in these works they were exempt from all vituperation or jealousy; because they did not make their distinctive dress, food, or drink, at all conspicuous, but lived very much like the rest, and joined in the everyday employments of the common people. But when their royal power became hereditary in their family, and they found every necessary for security ready to their hands, as well as more than was necessary for their personal support, then they gave the rein to their appetites; imagined that rulers must needs wear different clothes from those of subjects; have different and elaborate luxuries of the table; and must even seek sensual indulgence, however unlawful the source, without fear of denial. These things having given rise in the one case to jealousy and offence, in the other to outburst of hatred and passionate resentment, the kingship became a tyranny: the first step in disintegration was taken; and plots began to be formed against the government, which did not now proceed from the worst men but from the noblest, most high-minded, and most courageous, because these are the men who can least submit to the tyrannical acts of their rulers.

But as soon as the people got leaders, they co-operated with them against the dynasty for the reasons I have mentioned; and then *kingship* and *despotism* were alike entirely abolished, and *aristocracy* once more began to revive and start afresh. For in their immediate gratitude to those who had deposed the despots, the people employed them as leaders, and entrusted their interests to them; who, looking upon this charge at first as a great privilege, made the public advantage their chief concern, and conducted all kinds of business, public or private, with diligence and caution. But when the sons of these men received the same position of authority from their fathers,—having had no experience of misfortunes, and none at all of civil equality and freedom of speech, but having been bred up from the first under the shadow of their fathers' authority and lofty position,—some of them gave themselves up with passion to avarice and unscrupulous love of money, others to drinking and the boundless debaucheries which accompanies it, and others to the violation of women or the forcible appropriation of boys; and so they turned an *aristocracy* into an *oligarchy*. But it was not long before they roused in the minds of the people the same feelings as before; and their fall therefore was very like the disaster which befell the tyrants.

For no sooner had the knowledge of the jealousy and hatred existing in the citizens against them emboldened some one to oppose the government by word or deed, than he was sure to find the whole people ready and prepared to take his side. Having then got rid of these rulers by assassination or exile, they do not venture to set up a king again, being still in terror of the injustice to which this led before; nor dare they intrust the common interests again to more than one, considering the recent example of their misconduct: and therefore, as the only sound hope left them is that which depends upon themselves, they are driven to take refuge in that; and so changed the constitution from an oligarchy to a *democracy*, and took upon themselves the superintendence and charge of the state. And as long as any survive who have had experience of oligarchical supremacy and domination, they regard their present constitution as a blessing, and hold equality and freedom as of the utmost value. But as soon as a new generation has arisen, and the democracy has descended to their children's children, long association weakens their value for equality and freedom, and some seek to become more powerful than the ordinary citizens; and the most liable to this temptation are the rich. So when they begin to be fond of office, and find themselves unable to obtain it by their own unassisted efforts and their own merits, they ruin their estates, while enticing and corrupting the common people in every possible way. By which means when, in their senseless mania for reputation, they have made the populace ready and greedy to receive bribes, the virtue of democracy is destroyed, and it is transformed into a government of violence and the strong hand. For the mob, habituated to feed at the expense of others, and to have its hopes of a livelihood in the property of its neighbours, as soon as it has got a leader sufficiently ambitious and daring, being excluded by poverty from the sweets of civil honours, produces a reign of mere violence. Then come tumultuous assemblies, massacres, banishments, redivisions of land; until, after losing all trace of civilisation, it has once more found a master and a despot.

This is the regular cycle of constitutional revolutions, and the natural order in which constitutions change, are transformed, and return again to their original stage. If a man have a clear grasp of these principles he may perhaps make a mistake as to the dates at which this or that will happen to a particular constitution; but he will rarely be entirely mistaken as to the stage of growth or decay at which it has arrived, or as to the point at which it will undergo some revolutionary change. However, it is in the case of the Roman constitution that this method of inquiry will most fully teach us its formation, its growth, and zenith, as well as the changes awaiting it in the future; for this, if any constitution ever did, owed, as I said just now, its original foundation and growth to natural causes, and to natural causes will owe its decay. My subsequent narrative will be the best illustration of what I say.

For the present I will make a brief reference to the legislation of Lycurgus: for such a discussion is not at all alien to my subject. That statesman was fully aware that all those changes which I have enumerated come about by an undeviating law of nature; and reflected that every form of government that was unmixed, and rested on one species of power, was unstable; because it was swiftly perverted into that particular form of evil peculiar to it and inherent in its nature. For just as rust is the natural dissolvent of iron, wood-worms and grubs to timber, by which they are destroyed without any external injury, but by that which is engendered in themselves; so in each constitution there is naturally engendered a particular vice inseparable from it: in kingship it is absolutism; in aristocracy it is oligarchy; in democracy lawless ferocity and violence; and to these vicious states all these forms of government are, as I have lately shown, inevitably transformed. Lycurgus, I say, saw all this, and accordingly combined together all the excellences and distinctive features of the best constitutions, that no part should become unduly predominant, and be perverted into its kindred vice; and that, each power being checked by the others, no one part should turn the scale or decisively out-balance the others; but that, by being accurately adjusted and in exact equilibrium, the whole might remain long steady like a ship sailing close to the wind. The royal power was prevented from growing insolent by fear of the people, which had also assigned to it an adequate share in the constitution. The people in their turn were restrained from a bold contempt of the kings by fear of the Gerusia: the members of which, being selected on grounds of merit, were certain to throw their influence on the side of justice in every question that arose; and thus the party placed at a disadvantage by its conservative tendency was always strengthened and supported by the weight and influence of the Gerusia. The result of this combination has been that the Lacedaemonians retained their freedom for the longest period of any people with which we are acquainted.

Lycurgus however established his constitution without the discipline of adversity, because he was able to foresee by the light of reason the course which events naturally take and the source from which they come. But though the Romans have arrived at the same result in framing their commonwealth, they have not done so by means of abstract reasoning, but through many struggles and difficulties, and by continually adopting reforms from knowledge gained in disaster. The result has been a constitution like that of Lycurgus, and the best of any existing in my time. . . .

I have given an account of the constitution of Lycurgus, I

will now endeavour to describe that of Rome at the period of their disastrous defeat at Cannae.

I am fully conscious that to those who actually live under this constitution I shall appear to give an inadequate account of it by the omission of certain details. Knowing accurately every portion of it from personal experience, and from having been bred up in its customs and laws from childhood, they will not be struck so much by the accuracy of the description, as annoyed by its omissions; nor will they believe that the historian has purposely omitted unimportant distinctions, but will attribute his silence upon the origin of existing institutions or other important facts to ignorance. What is told they depreciate as insignificant or beside the purpose; what is omitted they desiderate as vital to the question: their object being to appear to know more than the writers. But a good critic should not judge a writer by what he leaves unsaid, but from what he says: if he detects mis-statement in the latter, he may then feel certain that ignorance accounts for the former; but if what he says is accurate, his omissions ought to be attributed to deliberate judgment and not to ignorance. So much for those whose criticisms are prompted by personal ambition rather than by justice. . . .

Another requisite for obtaining a judicious approval for an historical disquisition, is that it should be germane to the matter in hand; if this is not observed, though its style may be excellent and its matter irreproachable, it will seem out of place, and disgust rather than please. . . .

As for the Roman constitution, it had three elements, each of them possessing sovereign powers: and their respective share of power in the whole state had been regulated with such a scrupulous regard to equality and equilibrium, that no one could say for certain, not even a native, whether the constitution as a whole were an aristocracy or democracy or despotism. And no wonder: for if we confine our observation to the power of the Consuls we should be inclined to regard it as despotic; if on that of the Senate, as aristocratic; and if finally one looks at the power possessed by the people it would seem a clear case of a democracy. What the exact powers of these several parts were, and still, with slight modifications, are, I will now state.

The Consuls, before leading out the legions, remain in Rome and are supreme masters of the administration. All other magistrates, except the Tribunes, are under them and take their orders. They introduce foreign ambassadors to the Senate; bring matters requiring deliberation before it; and see to the execution of its decrees. If, again, there are any matters of state which require the authorisation of the people, it is their business to see them, to summon the popular meetings, to bring the proposals before them, and to carry out the decrees of the majority. In the preparations for war also, and in a word in the entire administration of a campaign, they have all but absolute power. It is competent to them to impose on the allies such levies as they think good, to appoint the Military Tribunes, to make up the roll for soldiers and select those that are suitable. Besides they have absolute power of inflicting punishment on all who are under their command while on active service: and they have authority to expend as much of the public money as they choose, being accompanied by a quaestor who is entirely at their orders. A survey of these powers would in fact justify our describing the constitution as despotic,—a clear case of royal government. Nor will it affect the truth of my description, if any of the institutions I have described are changed in our time, or in that of our posterity: and the same remarks apply to what follows.

The Senate has first of all the control of the treasury, and regulates the receipts and disbursements alike. For the Quaestors cannot issue any public money for the various departments of the state without a decree of the Senate, except for the service of the Consuls. The Senate controls also what is by far the largest and most important expenditure, that, namely, which is made by the censors every *lustrum* for the repair or construction of public buildings; this money cannot be obtained by the censors except by the grant of the Senate. Similarly all crimes committed in Italy requiring a public investigation, such as treason, conspiracy, poisoning, or wilful murder, are in the hands of the Senate. Besides, if any individual or state among the Italian allies requires a controversy to be settled, a penalty to be assessed, help or protection to be afforded,—all this is the province of the Senate. Or again, outside Italy, if it is necessary to send an embassy to reconcile warring communities, or to remind them of their duty, or sometimes to impose requisitions upon them, or to receive their submission, or finally to proclaim war against them,—this too is the business of the Senate. In like manner the reception to be given to foreign ambassadors in Rome, and the answers to be returned to them, are decided by the Senate. With such business the people have nothing to do. Consequently, if one were staying at Rome when the Consuls were not in town, one would imagine the constitution to be a complete aristocracy: and this has been the idea entertained by many Greeks, and by many kings as well, from the fact that nearly all the business they had with Rome was settled by the Senate.

After this one would naturally be inclined to ask what part is left for the people in the constitution, when the Senate has these various functions, especially the control of the receipts and expenditure of the exchequer; and when the Consuls, again, have absolute power over the details of military preparation, and an absolute authority in the field? There is, however, a part left the people, and it is a most important one. For the people is the sole fountain of honour and of punishment; and it is by these two things and these alone that dynasties and constitutions and, in a word, human society are held together: for where the distinction between them is not sharply drawn both in theory and practice, there no undertaking can be properly administered,—as indeed we might expect when good and bad are held in exactly the same honour. The people then are the only court to decide matters of life and death; and even in cases where the penalty is money, if the sum to be assessed is sufficiently serious, and especially when the accused have held the higher magistracies. And in regard to this arrangement there is one point deserving especial commendation and record. Men who are on trial for their lives at Rome, while sentence is in process of being voted,—if even only one of the tribes whose votes are needed to ratify the sentence has not voted,—have the privilege at Rome of openly departing and condemning themselves to a voluntary exile. Such men are safe at Naples or Praeneste or at Tibur, and at other towns with which this arrangement has been duly ratified on oath.

Again, it is the people who bestow offices on the deserving, which are the most honourable rewards of virtue. It has also the absolute power of passing or repealing laws; and, most important of all, it is the people who deliberate on the question of peace or war. And when provisional terms are made for alliance, suspension of hostilities, or treaties, it is the people who ratify them or the reverse.

These considerations again would lead one to say that the chief power in the state was the people's, and that the constitution was a democracy.

Such, then, is the distribution of power between the several parts of the state. I must now show how each of these several parts can, when they choose, oppose or support each other.

The Consul, then, when he has started on an expedition with the powers I have described, is to all appearance absolute in the administration of the business in hand; still he has need of the support both of people and Senate, and, without them, is quite unable to bring the matter to a successful conclusion. For it is plain that he must have supplies sent to his legions from time to time; but without a decree of the Senate they can be supplied neither with corn, nor clothes, nor pay, so that all the plans of a commander must be futile, if the Senate is resolved either to shrink from danger or hamper his plans. And again, whether a Consul shall bring any undertaking to a conclusion or no depends entirely upon the Senate: for it has absolute authority at the end of a year to send another Consul to supersede him, or to continue the existing one in his command. Again, even to the successes of the generals the Senate has the power to add distinction and glory, and on the other hand to obscure their merits and lower their credit. For these high achievements are brought in tangible form before the eyes of the citizens by what are called "triumphs." But these triumphs the commanders cannot elaborate with proper pomp, or in some cases celebrate at all, unless the Senate concurs and grants the necessary money. As for the people, the Consuls are pre-eminently obliged to court their favour, however distant from home may be the field of their operations; for it is the people, as I have said before, that ratifies, or refuses to ratify, terms of peace and treaties; but most of all because when laying down their office they have to give an account of their administration before it. Therefore in no case is it safe for the Consuls to neglect either the Senate or the good-will of the people.

As for the Senate, which possesses the immense power I have described, in the first place it is obliged in public affairs to take the multitude into account, and respect the wishes of the people; and it cannot put into execution the penalty for offences against the republic, which are punishable with death, unless the people first ratify its decrees. Similarly even in matters which directly affect the senators,— for instance, in the case of a law diminishing the Senate's traditional authority, or depriving senators of certain dignities and offices, or even actually cutting down their property,—even in such cases the people have the sole power of passing or rejecting the law. But most important of all is the fact that, if the Tribunes interpose their veto, the Senate not only are unable to pass a decree, but cannot even hold a meeting at all, whether formal or informal. Now, the Tribunes are always bound to carry out the decree of the people, and above all things to have regard to their wishes: therefore, for all these reasons the Senate stands in awe of the multitude, and cannot neglect the feelings of the people.

In like manner the people on its part is far from being independent of the Senate, and is bound to take its wishes into account both collectively and individually. For contracts, too numerous to count, are given out by the censors in all parts of Italy for the repairs or construction of public buildings; there is also the collection of revenue from many rivers, harbours, gardens, mines, and land—everything, in a word, that comes under the control of the Roman government: and in all these the people at large are engaged; so that there is scarcely a man, so to speak, who is not interested either as a contractor or as being employed in the works. For some purchase the contracts from the censors for themselves; and others go partners with them; while others again go security for these contractors, or actually pledge their property to the treasury for them. Now over all these transactions the Senate has absolute control. It can grant an extension of time; and in case of unforeseen accident can relieve the contractors from a portion of their obligation, or release them from it altogether, if they are absolutely unable to fulfil it. And there are many details in which the Senate can inflict great hardships, or, on the other hand, grant great indulgences to the contractors: for in every case the appeal is to it. But the most important point of all is that the judges are taken from its members in the majority of trials, whether public or private, in which the charges are heavy. Consequently, all citizens are much at its mercy; and being alarmed at the uncertainty as to when they may need its aid, are cautious about resisting or actively opposing its will. And for a similiar reason men do not rashly resist the wishes of the Consuls, because one and all may become subject to their absolute authority on a campaign.

The result of this power of the several estates for mutual help or harm is a union sufficiently firm for all emergencies, and a constitution than which it is impossible to find a better. For when-

ever any danger from without compels them to unite and work
together, the strength which is developed by the State is so
extraordinary, that everything required is unfailingly carried out
by the eager rivalry shown by all classes to devote their whole
minds to the need of the hour, and to secure that any determina-
tion come to should not fail for want of promptitude; while each
individual works, privately and publicly alike, for the accomplishment of the business in hand. Accordingly, the peculiar constitution of the State makes it irresistible, and certain of obtaining
whatever it determines to attempt. Nay, even when these external
alarms are past, and the people are enjoying their good fortune
and the fruits of their victories, and, as usually happens, growing
corrupted by flattery and idleness, show a tendency to violence
and arrogance,—it is in these circumstances, more than ever, that
the constitution is seen to possess within itself the power of correcting abuses. For when any one of the three classes becomes
puffed up, and manifests an inclination to be contentious and
unduly encroaching, the mutual interdependency of all the three,
and the possibility of the pretensions of any one being checked
and thwarted by the others, must plainly check this tendency:
and so the proper equilibrium is maintained by the impulsiveness
of the one part being checked by its fear of the other. . . .

The Roman Republic Compared with Others]

Nearly all historians have recorded as constitutions of eminent
excellence those of Lacedaemonia, Crete, Mantinea, and Carthage.
Some have also mentioned those of Athens and Thebes. The
former I may allow to pass; but I am convinced that little need
be said of the Athenian and Theban constitutions: their growth
was abnormal, the period of their zenith brief, and the changes
they experienced unusually violent. Their glory was a sudden and
fortuitous flash, so to speak; and while they still thought themselves prosperous, and likely to remain so, they found themselves
involved in circumstances completely the reverse. The Thebans
got their reputation for valour among the Greeks, by taking advantage of the senseless policy of the Lacedaemonians, and the
hatred of the allies towards them, owing to the valour of one,
or at most two, men who were wise enough to appreciate the

situation. Since fortune quickly made it evident that it was not the peculiarity of their constitution, but the valour of their leaders, which gave the Thebans their success. For the great power of Thebes notoriously took its rise, attained its zenith, and fell to the ground with the lives of Epaminondas and Pelopidas. We must therefore conclude that it was not its constitution, but its men, that caused the high fortune which it then enjoyed.

A somewhat similar remark applies to the Athenian constitution also. For though it perhaps had more frequent interludes of excellence, yet its highest perfection was attained during the brilliant career of Themistocles; and having reached that point it quickly declined, owing to its essential instability. For the Athenian demus is always in the position of a ship without a commander. In such a ship, if fear of the enemy, or the occurrence of a storm induce the crew to be of one mind and to obey the helmsman, everything goes well; but if they recover from this fear, and begin to treat their officers with contempt, and to quarrel with each other because they are no longer all of one mind,—one party wishing to continue the voyage, and the other urging the steersman to bring the ship to anchor; some letting out the sheets, and others hauling them in, and ordering the sails to be furled,—their discord and quarrels make a sorry show to lookers on; and the position of affairs is full of risk to those on board engaged on the same voyage: and the result has often been that, after escaping the dangers of the widest seas, and the most violent storms, they wreck their ship in harbour and close to shore. And this is what has often happened to the Athenian constitution. For, after repelling, on various occasions, the greatest and most formidable dangers by the valour of its people and their leaders, there have been times when, in periods of secure tranquillity, it has gratuitously and recklessly encountered disaster. Therefore I need say no more about either it, or the Theban constitution: in both of which a mob manages everything on its own unfettered impulse—a mob in the one city distinguished for headlong outbursts of fiery temper, in the other trained in long habits of violence and ferocity.

Passing to the Cretan polity there are two points which deserve our consideration. The first is how such writers as Ephorus, Xenophon, Callisthenes and Plato—who are the most learned of the ancients—could assert that it was like that of Sparta; and secondly how they came to assert that it was at all admirable. I can agree with neither assertion; and I will explain why I say so. And first as to its dissimilarity with the Spartan constitution. The peculiar merit of the latter is said to be its land laws, by which no one possesses more than another, but all citizens have an equal share in the public land. The next distinctive feature regards the possession of money: for as it is utterly discredited among them, the jealous competition which arises from inequality of wealth is entirely removed from the city. A third peculiarity of the Lacedaemonian polity is that, of the officials by whose hands and with whose advice the whole government is conducted, the kings hold an hereditary office, while the members of the Gerusia are elected for life.

Among the Cretans the exact reverse of all these arrangements obtains. The laws allow them to possess as much land as they can get with no limitation whatever. Money is so highly valued among them, that its possession is not only thought to be necessary but in the highest degree creditable. And in fact greed and avarice are so native to the soil in Crete, that they are the only people in the world among whom no stigma attaches to any sort of gain whatever. Again all their offices are annual and on a democratical footing. I have therefore often felt at a loss to account for these writers speaking of the two constitutions, which are radically different, as though they were closely united and allied. But, besides overlooking these important differences, these writers have gone out of their way to comment at length on the legislation of Lycurgus: "He was the only legislator," they say, "who saw the important points. For there being two things on which the safety of a commonwealth depends,—courage in the face of the enemy and concord at home,—by abolishing covetousness, he with it removed all motive for civil broil and contest: whence it has been brought about that the Lacedaemonians are the best governed and most united people in Greece." Yet while giving utterance to these sentiments, and though they see that, in contrast to this, the Cretans by their ingrained avarice are engaged in countless public and private seditions, murders and civil wars, they yet regard these facts as not affecting their contention, but are bold enough to speak of the two constitutions as alike. Ephorus, indeed, putting aside names, employs expressions so precisely the same, when discoursing on the two constitutions, that, unless one noticed the proper names, there would be no means whatever of distinguishing which of the two he was describing.

In what the difference between them consists I have already stated. I will now address myself to showing that the Cretan constitution deserves neither praise nor imitation.

To my mind, then, there are two things fundamental to every state, in virtue of which its powers and constitution become desirable or objectionable. These are customs and laws. Of these the desirable are those which make men's private lives holy and pure, and the public character of the state civilised and just. The objectionable are those whose effect is the reverse. As, then, when we see good customs and good laws prevailing among certain people, we confidently assume that, in consequence of them, the men and their civil constitution will be good also, so when we see private life full of covetousness, and public policy of injustice, plainly we have reason for asserting their laws, particular customs, and general constitution to be bad. Now, with few exceptions, you could find no habits prevailing in private life more steeped in treachery than those in Crete, and no public policy more inequitable. Holding, then, the Cretan constitution to be neither like the Spartan, nor worthy of choice or imitation, I reject it from the comparison which I have instituted.

Nor again would it be fair to introduce the Republic of Plato, which is also spoken of in high terms by some philosophers. For just as we refuse admission to the athletic contests to those actors or athletes who have not acquired a recognised position or trained for them, so we ought not to admit this Platonic constitution to the contest for the prize of merit unless it can first point to some genuine and practical achievement. Up to this time the notion of bringing it into comparison with the constitutions of Sparta, Rome, and Carthage would be like putting up a statue to compare with living and breathing men. Even if such a statue were faultless in point of art, the comparison of the lifeless with the living would naturally leave an impression of imperfection and incongruity upon the minds of the spectators.

I shall therefore omit these, and proceed with my description of the Laconian constitution. Now it seems to me that for securing unity among the citizens, for safe-guarding the Laconian territory, and preserving the liberty of Sparta inviolate, the legislation and provisions of Lycurgus were so excellent, that I am forced to regard his wisdom as something superhuman. For the equality of landed possessions, the simplicity in their food, and the practice of taking it in common, which he established, were well calculated to secure morality in private life and to prevent civil broils in the State; as also their training in the endurance of labours and dangers to make men brave and noble minded: but when both these virtues, courage and high morality, are combined in one soul or in one state, vice will not readily spring from such a soil, nor will such men easily be overcome by their enemies. By constructing his constitution therefore in this spirit, and of these elements, he secured two blessings to the Spartans,— safety for their territory, and a lasting freedom for themselves long after he was gone. He appears however to have made no one provision whatever, particular or general, for the acquisition of the territory of their neighbours; or for the assertion of their supremacy; or, in a word, for any policy of aggrandisement at all. What he had still to do was to impose such a necessity, or create such a spirit among the citizens, that, as he had succeeded in making their individual lives independent and simple, the public character of the state should also become independent and moral. But the actual fact is, that, though he made them the most disinterested and sober-minded men in the world, as far as their own ways of life and their national institutions were concerned, he left them in regard to the rest of Greece ambitious, eager for supremacy, and encroaching in the highest degree.

For in the first place is it not notorious that they were nearly the first Greeks to cast a covetous eye upon the territory of their neighbours, and that accordingly they waged a war of subjugation on the Messenians? In the next place is it not related in all histories that in their dogged obstinacy they bound themselves with an oath never to desist from the siege of Messene until they had taken it? And lastly it is known to all that in their efforts for supremacy in Greece they submitted to do the bidding of those whom they had once conquered in war. For when the Persians invaded Greece, they conquered them, as champions of the liberty of the Greeks; yet when the invaders had retired and fled, they betrayed the cities of Greece into their hands by the peace of Antalcidas, for the sake of getting money to secure their supremacy over the Greeks. It was then that the defect in their constitution was rendered apparent. For as long as their ambition was confined to governing their immediate neighbours, or even the Peloponnesians only, they were content with the resources and supplies provided by Laconia itself, having all material of war ready to hand, and being able without much expenditure of time to return home or convey provisions with them. But directly they took in hand to despatch naval expeditions, or to go on campaigns by land outside the Peloponnese, it was evident that neither their iron currency, nor their use of crops for payment in kind, would be able to supply them with what they lacked if they abided by the legislation of Lycurgus; for such undertakings required money universally current, and goods from foreign countries. Thus they were compelled to wait humbly at Persian doors, impose tribute on the islanders, and exact contributions from all the Greeks: knowing that, if they abided by the laws of Lycurgus, it was impossible to advance any claims upon any outside power at all, much less upon the supremacy in Greece.

My object, then, in this digression is to make it manifest by actual facts that, for guarding their own country with absolute safety, and for preserving their own freedom, the legislation of Lycurgus was entirely sufficient; and for those who are content with these objects we must concede that there neither exists, nor ever has existed, a constitution and civil order preferable to that of Sparta. But if any one is seeking aggrandisement, and believes that to be a leader and ruler and despot of numerous subjects, and to have all looking and turning to him, is a finer thing than that,—in this point of view we must acknowledge that the Spartan constitution is deficient, and that of Rome superior and better constituted for obtaining power. And this has been proved by actual facts. For when the Lacedaemonians strove to possess themselves of the supremacy in Greece, it was not long before they brought their own freedom itself into danger. Whereas the Romans, after obtaining supreme power over the Italians themselves, soon brought the whole world under their rule,—in which achievement the abundance and availability of their supplies largely contributed to their success.

Now the Carthaginian constitution seems to me originally to have been well contrived in these most distinctively important particulars. For they had kings, and the Gerusia had the powers of an aristocracy, and the multitude were supreme in such things as affected them; and on the whole the adjustment of its several parts was very like that of Rome and Sparta. But about the period of its entering on the Hannibalian war the political state of Carthage was on the decline, that of Rome improving. For whereas there is in every body, or polity, or business a natural stage of growth, zenith, and decay; and whereas everything in them is at its best at the zenith; we may thereby judge of the difference between these two constitutions as they existed at that period. For exactly so far as the strength and prosperity of Carthage preceded that of Rome in point of time, by so much was Carthage then past its prime, while Rome was exactly at its zenith, as far as its political constitution was concerned. In Carthage therefore the influence of the people in the policy of the state had already risen to be supreme, while at Rome the Senate was at the height of its power: and so, as in the one measures were deliberated upon by the many, in the other by the best men, the policy of the Romans in all public undertakings proved the stronger; on which account, though they met with capital disasters, by force of prudent counsels they finally conquered the Carthaginians in the war.

If we look however at separate details, for instance at the provisions for carrying on a war, we shall find that whereas for a naval expedition the Carthaginians are the better trained and prepared,—as it is only natural with a people with whom it has been hereditary for many generations to practise this craft, and to follow the seaman's trade above all nations in the world,—yet, in regard to military service on land, the Romans train themselves to a much higher pitch than the Carthaginians. The former bestow their whole attention upon this department: whereas the Carthaginians wholly neglect their infantry, though they do take some slight interest in the cavalry. The reason of this is that they employ foreign mercenaries, the Romans native and citizen levies. It is in this point that the latter polity is preferable to the former. They have their hopes of freedom ever resting on the courage of mercenary troops: the Romans on the valour of their own citizens and the aid of their allies. The result is that even if the Romans have suffered a defeat at first, they renew the war with undiminished forces, which the Carthaginians cannot do. For, as the Romans are fighting for country and children, it is impossible for them to relax the fury of their struggle; but they persist with obstinate resolution until they have overcome their enemies. What has happened in regard to their navy is an instance in point. In skill the Romans are much behind the Carthaginians, as I have already said; yet the upshot of the whole naval war has been a decided triumph for the Romans, owing to the valour of their men. For although nautical science contributes largely to success in sea-fights, still it is the courage of the marines that turns the scale most decisively in favour of victory. The fact is that Italians as a nation are by nature superior to Phoenicians and Libyans both in physical strength and courage; but still their habits also do much to inspire the youth with enthusiasm for such exploits. One example will be sufficient of the pains taken by the Roman state to turn out men ready to endure anything to win a reputation in their country for valour.

Whenever one of their illustrious men dies, in the course of his funeral, the body with all its paraphernalia is carried into the forum to the Rostra, as a raised platform there is called, and sometimes is propped upright upon it so as to be conspicuous, or, more rarely, is laid upon it. Then with all the people standing round, his son, if he has left one of full age and he is there, or, failing him, one of his relations, mounts the Rostra and delivers a speech concerning the virtues of the deceased, and the successful exploits performed by him in his lifetime. By these means the people are reminded of what has been done, and made to see it with their own eyes,—not only such as were engaged in the actual transactions but those also who were not;—and their sympathies are so deeply moved, that the loss appears not to be confined to the actual mourners, but to be a public one affecting the whole people. After the burial and all the usual ceremonies have been performed, they place the likeness of the deceased in the most conspicuous spot in his house, surmounted by a wooden canopy or shrine. This likeness consists of a mask made to represent the deceased with extraordinary fidelity both in shape and colour. These likenesses they display at public sacrifices adorned with much care. And when any illustrious member of the family dies, they carry these masks to the funeral, putting them on men whom they thought as like the originals as possible in height and other personal pecularities. And these substitutes assume clothes according to the rank of the person represented: if he was a consul or praetor, a toga with purple stripes; if a censor, whole purple; if he had also celebrated a triumph or performed any exploit of that kind, a toga embroidered with gold. These representatives also ride themselves in chariots, while the fasces and axes, and all the other customary insignia of the particular offices, lead the

way, according to the dignity of the rank in the state enjoyed
by the deceased in his lifetime; and on arriving at the Rostra they
all take their seats on ivory chairs in their order. There could
not easily be a more inspiring spectacle than this for a young
man of noble ambitions and virtuous aspirations. For can we conceive any one to be unmoved at the sight of all the likenesses
collected together of the men who have earned glory, all as it
were living and breathing? Or what could be a more glorious
spectacle?

Besides the speaker over the body about to be buried, after
having finished the panegyric of this particular person, starts
upon the others whose representatives are present, beginning with
the most ancient, and recounts the successes and achievements
of each. By this means the glorious memory of brave men is
continually renewed; the fame of those who have performed
any noble deed is never allowed to die; and the renown of those
who have done good service to their country becomes a matter
of common knowledge to the multitude, and part of the heritage
of posterity. But the chief benefit of the ceremony is that it
inspires young men to shrink from no exertion for the general
welfare, in the hope of obtaining the glory which awaits the
brave. And what I say is confirmed by this fact. Many Romans
have volunteered to decide a whole battle by single combat; not
a few have deliberately accepted certain death, some in time of
war to secure the safety of the rest, some in time of peace to
preserve the safety of the commonwealth. There have also been
instances of men in office putting their own sons to death, in
defiance of every custom and law, because they rated the interests
of their country higher than those of natural ties even with their
nearest and dearest. There are many stories of this kind, related
of many men in Roman history; but one will be enough for our
present purpose; and I will give the name as an instance to prove
the truth of my words.

The story goes that Horatius Cocles, while fighting with two
enemies at the head of the bridge over the Tiber, which is the
entrance to the city on the north, seeing a large body of men
advancing to support his enemies, and fearing that they would
force their way into the city, turned round, and shouted to those
behind him to hasten back to the other side and break down the
bridge. They obeyed him: and whilst they were breaking the
bridge, he remained at his post receiving numerous wounds, and

checked the progress of the enemy: his opponents being panic stricken, not so much by his strength as by the audacity with which he held his ground. When the bridge had been broken down, the attack of the enemy was stopped; and Cocles then threw himself into the river with his armour on and deliberately sacrificed his life, because he valued the safety of his country and his own future reputation more highly than his present life, and the years of existence that remained to him. Such is the enthusiasm and emulation for noble deeds that are engendered among the Romans by their customs.

Again the Roman customs and principles regarding money transactions are better than those of the Carthaginians. In the view of the latter nothing is disgraceful that makes for gain; with the former nothing is more disgraceful than to receive bribes and to make profit by improper means. For they regard wealth obtained from unlawful transactions to be as much a subject of reproach, as a fair profit from the most unquestioned source is of commendation. A proof of the fact is this. The Carthaginians obtain office by open bribery, but among the Romans the penalty for it is death. With such a radical difference, therefore, between the rewards offered to virtue among the two peoples, it is natural that the ways adopted for obtaining them should be different also.

But the most important difference for the better which the Roman commonwealth appears to me to display is in their religious beliefs. For I conceive that what in other nations is looked upon as a reproach, I mean a scrupulous fear of the gods, is the very thing which keeps the Roman commonwealth together. To such an extraordinary height is this carried among them, both in private and public business, that nothing could exceed it. Many people might think this unaccountable; but in my opinion their object is to use it as a check upon the common people. If it were possible to form a state wholly of philosophers, such a custom would perhaps be unnecessary. But seeing that every multitude is fickle, and full of lawless desires, unreasoning anger, and violent passion, the only resource is to keep them in check by mysterious terrors and scenic effects of this sort. Wherefore, to my mind, the ancients were not acting without purpose or at random, when they brought in among the vulgar those opinions about the gods, and the belief in the punishments in Hades: much rather do I think that men nowadays are acting rashly and fool-

ishly in rejecting them. This is the reason why, apart from anything else, Greek statesmen, if entrusted with a single talent,
though protected by ten checking-clerks, as many seals, and
twice as many witnesses, yet cannot be induced to keep faith:
whereas among the Romans, in their magistracies and embassies,
men have the handling of a great amount of money, and yet from
pure respect to their oath keep their faith intact. And, again,
in other nations it is a rare thing to find a man who keeps his
hands out of the public purse, and is entirely pure in such matters:
but among the Romans it is a rare thing to detect a man in the
act of committing such a crime....

Recapitulation and Conclusion]

That to all things, then, which exist there is ordained decay
and change I think requires no further arguments to show: for
the inexorable course of nature is sufficient to convince us of it.
But in all polities we observe two sources of decay existing
from natural causes, the one external, the other internal and self-
produced. The external admits of no certain or fixed definition,
but the internal follows a definite order. What kind of polity,
then, comes naturally first, and what second, I have already stated
in such a way, that those who are capable of taking in the whole
drift of my argument can henceforth draw their own conclusions
as to the future of the Roman polity. For it is quite clear, in my
opinion. When a commonwealth, after warding off many great
dangers, has arrived at a high pitch of prosperity and undisputed
power, it is evident that, by the lengthened continuance of great
wealth within it, the manner of life of its citizens will become
more extravagant; and that the rivalry for office, and in other
spheres of activity, will become fiercer than it ought to be. And
as this state of things goes on more and more, the desire of office
and the shame of losing reputation, as well as the ostentation and
extravagance of living, will prove the beginning of a deteriora-
tion. And of this change the people will be credited with being
the authors, when they become convinced that they are being
cheated by some from avarice, and are puffed up with flattery
by others from love of office. For when that comes about, in
their passionate resentment and acting under the dictates of anger,

they will refuse to obey any longer, or to be content with having equal powers with their leaders, but will demand to have all or far the greatest themselves. And when that comes to pass the constitution will receive a new name, which sounds better than any other in the world, liberty or democracy; but, in fact, it will become that worst of all governments, mob-rule.

With this description of the formation, growth, zenith, and present state of the Roman polity, and having discussed also its difference, for better and worse, from other polities, I will now at length bring my essay on it to an end.